Thorsten Grötker
Ulrich Holtmann
Holger Keding
Markus Wloka

The Developer's Guide to Debugging

2nd Edition

Don't Panic

Thorsten Grötker
Ulrich Holtmann
Holger Keding
Markus Wloka

Internet: http://www.debugging-guide.com
Email: authors@debugging-guide.com

ISBN-13: 978-1470185527
ISBN-10: 1470185520

Foreword

Of all activities in software development, debugging is probably the one that is hated most. It is *guilt-ridden* because a technical failure suggests personal failure; because it points the finger at us showing us that we have been wrong. It is *time-consuming* because we have to rethink every single assumption, every single step from requirements to implementation. Its worst feature though may be that it is *unpredictable*: You never know how much time it will take you to fix a bug - and whether you'll be able to fix it at all.

Ask a developer for the worst moments in life, and many of them will be related to debugging. It may be 11pm, you're still working on it, you are just stepping through the program, and that's when your spouse calls you and asks you when you'll finally, *finally* get home, and you try to end the call as soon as possible as you're losing grip on the carefully memorized observations and deductions. In such moments, you may eventually be choosing between restarting your debugging task or restarting your relationship. My personal estimate is that debugging is the number one cause for programmer's divorces.

And yet, debugging can be a joy, as much thrill as solving puzzles, riddles, or murder mysteries – if you proceed in a systematic way and if you are equipped with the right tools for the job. This is where *The Developer's Guide to Debugging* comes into play. Thorsten Grötker, Ulrich Holtmann, Holger Keding, and Markus Wloka speak directly to the entrenched developer, give straight-forward advice on solving debugging problems and come up with solutions *real fast*. Whether it is solving memory problems, debugging parallel programs, or dealing with problems induced by your very tool chain - this book offers first aid that is tried and proven.

I would have loved to have such a book at the beginning of my debugging career – I would have gazed at it in amazement of what these debugging tools can do for me, and by following its advice, I could have saved countless hours of manual debugging – time I could have spent on other activities. For instance, I could have made my code more reliable such that in the end, I would not have had to do any debugging at all.

This, of course, is the long-term goal of professional programming: To come up with code that is right from the start, where all errors are prevented (or at least detected) by some verification or validation method. Today already, assertions and unit tests help a lot in increasing confidence into our programs. In the future, we may even have full-fledged verification of industrial-size systems. We're not there yet; it may take years to get there; and even if we get there, whatever method we come up with certainly will not be applicable to programming languages as we know them. When dealing with today's programs, especially those written in C and C++, we'll still spend some time on debugging – and that's where *The Developer's Guide to Debugging* provides truly priceless advice.

Saarland University, Spring 2008 *Andreas Zeller*

Preface

At the time of writing this book, we – the authors – are all working for a technology company that produces software, and more. Not on the same project or product, though. Yet we have all been called to support customers and colleagues when it came to debugging C and C++ programs – as part of our software engineering work, because we produce tools that let users write optimized simulation programs, or simply because we happen to develop debugging tools. And we kept repeating the same fundamental techniques, time and again, as there was no good textbook on debugging we could refer to.

Until now.

Preface to 2nd Edition

For the 2nd edition, we decided to self-publish our book as a paperback and E-book, to reach a wider audience. We also incorporated a number of corrections and bug fixes.

The Book's Website

We have created the website http://www.debugging-guide.com to augment the book, by listing up-to-date references on the topic of software debugging: access to tools, books, journals, research papers, conferences, tutorials, and web links. The examples used in this book can be downloaded from this website. The website also has an up-to-date list of errata.

Acknowledgments

This book would not have come to exist without the help of numerous people.

To begin with, we owe Mark de Jongh from Springer for encouraging us to write this book, for his support, and for his endless patience, which we stress-tested so many times.

We are also grateful to a large number of people, among them our colleagues at Synopsys, for coming up with a steady stream of challenges in the area of software debugging, and for teaching us tricks how to crack tough nuts. This has been the seedbed for this book. Any attempt at presenting a complete list of names here is bound to fail.

We would like to mention Andrea Kroll, as she was the first person asking us to write down a structured approach to debugging a simulation program, and Roland Verreet, for his encouragement and insights on marketing. We also thank Joachim Kunkel and Debashis Chowdhury for their support.

Software has bugs, and so have books, especially early drafts. The help of brave people led to considerable improvements of this book's quality and readability. We would like to thank, in alphabetical order, the following people for their contributions to this process: Ralf Beckers, Joe Buck, Ric Hilderink, Gernot Koch, Rainer Leupers, Olaf Scheufen, Matthias Wloka, and Christian Zunker.

We are grateful to Scott Meyers for his input on how to organize chapters and for his suggestions on how to present key material.

We also want to express thanks to Andrea Hölter for her insightful comments written up during repeated front-to-back reviews.

Mike Appleby, Simon North, and Ian Stephens deserve credit for helping us turn disjoint bursts of information into something – hopefully – much more intelligible, and also for covering up the many crimes against the English language we had committed. Any remaining errors and shortcomings are our own.

Finally, it must be mentioned that this book would not have been possible without the enduring support from our families.

Thank you!

About the Authors

Thorsten Grötker was born in 1965 in Mönchengladbach, Germany. He received a diploma and doctorate degree in Electrical Engineering from Aachen University of Technology. Thorsten joined Synopsys in 1997, working in various functions in the areas of system level design and hardware verification. Thorsten enjoys travel and photography.

Ulli Holtmann was born in 1964 in Hildesheim, Germany. He studied Computer Science at the Technical University of Braunschweig and received his doctorate in 1995. He joined Synopsys in 1995 as an R&D engineer. From 1995–2000, he worked at the U.S. headquarters in Mountain View, and since then in Herzogenrath, Germany. He is married and has two children.

Holger Keding was born in 1970 in Kempen, Germany. He studied Electrical Engineering and Information Technology at Aachen University of Technology, where he received his doctorate in 2002. He joined Synopsys in 2001 as Corporate Application Engineer, focusing on system level design and simulation methodology. In his spare time he enjoys sailing, music, skiing, and spending time with his family and friends. Holger is married and has two children.

Markus Wloka was born in Heidelberg in 1962, and grew up in Kiel, Germany. He received his Ph.D. in Computer Science from Brown University, USA, in 1991. From 1991–1996 he worked for Motorola SPS (now Freescale) in Tempe, USA, on projects that applied parallel processing to low power optimization of ASIC chips. In 1996 he joined Synopsys in Germany, where he currently holds the position of Director R&D. He is married to Anke Brenner, and has 3 children: Sarah, Thomas, and Kristin. His hobbies include reading, sailing, traveling, and buying the latest-and-greatest technological gadgets.

Aachen,
February 2012

Thorsten Grötker
Ulrich Holtmann
Holger Keding
Markus Wloka

Contents

Chapter 1
You Write Software; You have Bugs
(*Why You Need This Book*)

This is a book about analyzing and improving C and C++ programs, written by software developers for software developers.

In the course of our software development work we have often been called upon to support customers and coach colleagues on how to find bugs. They were aware of the topics they had been taught in school: object-orientation, code reviews, and black-box vs. white-box testing, but most had only superficial knowledge of debugging tools, and rather fuzzy ideas about when to use a particular approach and what to do if the debugging tools gave confusing or even wrong results.

So, time and time again we found ourselves having to teach people how to track down bugs. It surprised us that it simply had not occurrred to a lot of programmers that debugging could be turned into a systematic approach. While a lot of steps in software development can be captured in a process, when it came to debugging, the accepted belief was that you not only needed deep insight into the code – you also needed a sudden burst of brilliance when it came to tracking down a bug. Unfortunately, Richard Feynman's method of *"write down the problem; think very hard; write down the answer"* is not the most efficient and successful approach to fixing software problems.

Once we realized that we were continually writing down the same step-by-step rules, and explaining the operation and limitations of the same tools for every bug report, the idea was born to gather all of our practical experience, collect all of this advice, and turn it into the book you are now holding. We can now point to the book when someone is faced with yet another bug-finding task. We also believe that a book such as this on systematic debugging patterns will be an interesting addition to a programming class, or a class on problem solving in software. In the end, the reason is simple ...

Software has bugs. Period.

Unfortunately, it is true. Even the good old `"hello, world"` program, known to virtually every C and C++ programmer in the world, can be considered to be buggy.[1] Developing software means having to deal with defects; old ones, new ones, the ones you created yourself, and those that others have put in the code.

Software developers debug programs for a living.

Hence, good debugging skills are a must-have. That said, it is regrettable that debugging is hardly taught in engineering schools.

The Developer's Guide to Debugging is a book for both professional software developers seeking to broaden their skills and students that want to learn the tricks of the trade from the ground up. With small examples and exercises it is well suited to accompany a computer science course or lecture. At the same time it can be used as a reference guide to address problems as the need arises.

This book goes beyond the level of simple source code debugging scenarios. In addition, it covers the most frequent real-world problems from the areas of program linking, memory access, parallel processing, and performance analysis. The picture is completed by chapters covering static checkers and techniques to write code that leans well towards debugging.

This book is not a replacement for a debugger manual, though. Nor is it a book focused on Microsoft's Visual Studio or GNU's GDB either, although we mention these debugging tools quite frequently. In fact, we describe basic and advanced debugging independent of operating system and compiler/debugger combinations where possible. Of course, we point out any such dependencies where required.

We use the GCC compiler and the GDB debugger in most of our examples. The reason is simple: These tools are free and widely available on many systems, including UNIX, Linux, Windows, and a number of embedded platforms. Most examples can be "translated" using Table A in the appendix on page 193, which presents equivalent Visual Studio commands. We try to give more details whenever this straightforward conversion is not feasible.

OK, so how to best read this book? Well, it depends ...

You can read the book cover-to-cover, which isn't a bad approach if you want to learn debugging from the ground up. Chapter 2 (*A Systematic Approach to Debugging*) presents an overview of various opportunities to gather information and analyze problems. Then in Chapter 3 (*Getting to the Root – Source Code Debuggers*) you'll take a closer look at key techniques such as running a program in a debugger, analyzing data, and controlling the flow of execution. Next, you will learn in Chapter 4 (*Fixing Memory Problems*) how to deal with programs that fail for mysterious reasons, due to memory bugs. The following two chapters focus on optimizations in their broadest sense: Chapter 5 (*Profiling Memory Use*) addresses memory consumption and Chapter 6 (*Solving Performance Problems*) explains how to analyze execution speed. Chapter 7 (*Debugging Parallel Programs*) covers difficulties related to multi-threaded programs and asynchronous events. Chapter 8 (*Finding*

---

[1] Incomplete output may be generated if the program receives an asynchronous signal during the `printf()` call, if there is no code to check its return value.

Environment and Compiler Problems) comes next. This is then followed by Chapter 9 (*Dealing with Linking Problems*) that tells you what to do if your program won't even link to begin with. It also helps you cope with other issues you may encounter when linking programs. Now you are ready for challenges such as analyzing initialization time problems or debugging code compiled without debug information, which are described in Chapter 10 (*Advanced Debugging*). This chapter also covers techniques such as conditional breakpoints, watchpoints and capturing asynchronous events. Finally, Chapter 11 (*Writing Debuggable Code*) and Chapter 12 (*How Static Checking Can Help*) will put you in a good position when it comes to writing your own source code.

Alternatively, if you are sweating over some actual debugging problem, you can easily find the section of this book that addresses your needs. Taking a look at Chapter 4 (*Fixing Memory Problems*) is almost always a good idea, especially if the problem you are facing appears to defeat the rules of logic.

Chapter 2
A Systematic Approach to Debugging

2.1 Why Follow a Structured Process?

Richard Feynman was a fascinating figure. Reading about his adventures can be quite interesting at times. His well-known approach was appropriate for a number of problems he solved.

> *"Write down the problem; think very hard; write down the answer."*
> According to Murray Gell-Mann, NY Times

This scheme is not without appeal. It is universal, simple, and does not require much more than paper and pencil, and a well-oiled brain.

When you apply it to debugging software, you need to know next to nothing about systematic debugging processes or tools. You have to know a whole lot about your problem, though.

This is not practical if your problem – your software – is too big, or was written by other people. It is not economical either: you can't carry your knowledge over to the next project – unfortunately, it is "back to square one" then.

If you want to make a living as a software developer, then an investment into a systematic approach to debugging will pay off. In fact, you will experience that the return on investment is quite substantial.

2.2 Making the Most of Your Opportunities

This chapter brings structure to the process of bug finding at a more general level. The specifics of addressing different kinds of challenges are dealt with in subsequent chapters.

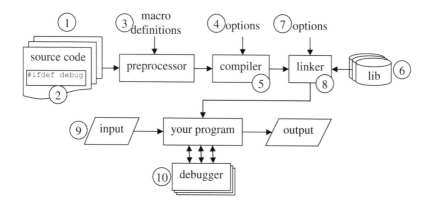

Fig. 2.1 Simplified build and test flow

First, let us identify opportunities for debugging in the simplified flow depicted in Figure 2.1.

The source code – and this includes header files – can be written in a more or less debuggable way (1). One can also write additional code – often referred to as "instrumentation" – to increase the observability and controllability of the software (2). Typically, this is enabled by macro definitions (3) given to the preprocessor that processes the source code and includes the header files. Compiler flags (4) can be used to generate code and information needed for source code debugging and profiling tools.

In addition to paying attention to compiler warnings, one can alternatively run static checker tools (5). At link time one can select libraries with more or less debugging information (6). Linker options can be used, for instance, to force linking additional test routines into the resulting executable (7). One can also use tools that automatically instrument the executable by adding or modifying object code for the purpose of analyzing performance or memory accesses (8).

Once we have an executable we can choose how we stimulate it (9). Selecting a good test case can have a big impact on the time it takes to analyze a problem. Various debugging tools can be used at runtime (10), including source code debuggers, profilers, memory checkers, and programs that produce a trace of OS calls. Some can even be applied "post mortem", that is, after the executable has run (or crashed).

Now, please take a bit of time to put the following three aspects into perspective. This will assist you in making best use of this book.

1. The *build and test flow* with its *debugging opportunities*, as depicted in Figure 2.1. The specific flow you are using to build and test your software may vary a little, but the basic elements should be present.

2. There are *13 golden rules* that are generally applicable at any stage of this flow. These are described in Section 2.3.
3. The subsequent chapters deal with *specific challenges* you may encounter along the way. For instance, Chapter 3 addresses source code debugging while Chapter 9 deals with linker problems.

Please note that the book is organized in a solution-oriented way, ranging from basic skills to more advanced topics. The sequence of chapters does not follow the flow as shown in Figure 2.1. The following will help you establish a correspondence.

Opportunities how to find Bugs

1. Debuggable source code: Chapter 11
2. Instrumentation: Chapters 5, 6, 7, and 11
3. Macro definitions: Chapter 11
4. Compiler flags: Chapters 3, 6, 8, 9, and 12
5. Static checkers: Chapter 12
6. Selected libraries: Chapters 4, 5, 6, and 11
7. Linker options: Chapters 9 and 11
8. Code instrumentation tools: Chapters 4, 5, and 6
9. Test case / input data: Chapter 2
10. Debuggers

   a. Source code: Chapters 3 and 10
   b. Profiling: Chapters 5 and 6
   c. Memory access: Chapters 4 and 5
   d. OS call tracers such as `truss` or `strace`: Chapter 8

Of course which opportunities one can take advantage of depends on the problem at hand. To that end there are natural limits to defining a one-size-fits-all, step-by-step debugging process.

Now that you know *where* to go bug hunting we need to address the *how*. We will do this in two steps, as described above. First, we present a set of "golden rules" in the next section. These are guidelines that – if taken with a grain of salt – you should find helpful in all types of debugging situations. The later chapters of this book then deal with specific challenges in a solution-oriented way.

2.3 13 Golden Rules

Experience tells us that there are a number of generally applicable hints which should not be neglected. The *"13 Golden Rules of Debugging"* can be seen as an extension of *"The Nine Indispensable Rules for Finding Even the Most Elusive Software and Hardware Problems"* formulated by D.J. Agans in [Agans02].

The 13 Golden Rules of Debugging

1. Understand the requirements
2. Make it fail
3. Simplify the test case
4. Read the right error message
5. Check the plug
6. Separate facts from interpretation
7. Divide and conquer
8. Match the tool to the bug
9. One change at a time
10. Keep an audit trail
11. Get a fresh view
12. If you didn't fix it, it ain't fixed
13. Cover your bugfix with a regression test

2.3.1 Understand the Requirements

Make sure you understand the requirements before you begin to debug and fix anything. Is there a standards document or a specification to look at? Or other documentation? Maybe the software is not malfunctioning after all. It could be a misinterpretation instead of a bug.

2.3.2 Make it Fail

You need a test case. Make your program fail. See it with your own eyes. A test case is a must-have for three reasons:

1. How else would you know that you have eventually fixed the problem if not by seeing that it finally works?
2. You will need a test case to obey rule 13 (*"Cover Your Bugfix with a Regression Test"*).
3. You have to understand all factors that contribute to making your software fail. You need to separate facts from assumptions. An environment variable may be a factor, or the operating system, or the window manager being used.

Bug reports share a similarity with eyewitness reports of a car accident or crime: more often than not, facts and interpretation are blended, and key pieces of information may be missing although the witnesses have the best intentions and are convinced that they describe the complete and unabridged truth.

2.3.3 Simplify the Test Case

The next step is to simplify the test case. You do this in order to

- rule out factors that do not play a role,
- reduce the runtime of the test case and, most importantly,
- make the test case easier to debug. Who wants to deal with data containers filled with hundreds or thousands of items?

2.3.4 Read the Right Error Message

Something went wrong and you face a screen full of error messages.

Which ones do you focus on?

It is surprising how many people don't give the correct answer.

The ones that come out first![1]

And that is not necessarily the first one you see; scroll back if need be. Everything that happened after the first thing went wrong should be eyed with suspicion. The first problem may have left the program in a corrupt state.

So, first things first – fix the problems in the order of appearance, or have a very good reason for breaking this rule.

2.3.5 Check the Plug

Next, check the seemingly obvious. Were all parts of the software up and running when the problem occurred? Permissions OK? Enough disk quota? Is there enough space on all relevant file systems (including the likes of `C:\WINDOWS`, `/tmp`, and `/var`)? Does the system have enough memory?

Think of ten common mistakes, and ensure nobody made them.

---

[1] Of course, there's no rule without exception. But more often than not this simple rule holds.

2.3.6 Separate Facts from Interpretation

Don't jump to conclusions. Maintain a list of things you know for a fact, and why. Ask yourself: "Can you prove it?" Is the behavior reproducible?

Is what you consider a fact really a fact? *"It fails when I select a blue item but it always works for red items"* a bug report may state. So misbehavior depends on the color? Maybe not. It could be that the user selected the blue item with a mouse click and everything else via the keyboard, by specifying its name.

2.3.7 Divide and Conquer

The National Institute of Standards and Technology defines *divide and conquer* as an algorithmic technique to *"solve a problem, either directly because solving that instance is easy [...] or by dividing it into two or more smaller instances."* And further *"the solutions are combined to produce a solution for the original instance."*

This strategy can be successfully applied to debugging in order to deal with complex situations when multiple factors can play a role. In larger software projects problems often arise from interference of concurrent development activities, especially when many developers work on the same source code base. The program still runs fine, by and large, but a particular feature is dead. For example, it used to work last Wednesday but now it flatlines. And it is far from obvious which change has caused the failure. What do you do? In the following text we describe one possible divide-and-conquer approach.

Divide and Conquer Debugging 101

- Assemble a list of potential problems and how to debug them
- Separate changes of the environment and source code changes

  - Track down changes of the environment
  - Isolate source code changes via back-out builds

- Zoom in and conquer

  - Memory debugger
  - Conventional source code debugging
  - Side-by-side debugging

2.3.7.1 Assemble a List of Potential Problems and How to Debug Them

Obviously, the first step is to understand how to slice and dice the problem. Begin by assembling a list of possible problems and how to debug them. Changes to the source-code base are one, but not the only possible reason for a bug that suddenly appears. Was the compiler modified? Were third-party libraries changed? Perhaps the program invokes other programs outside of the source-code control system and one of them changed? When the feature worked last Wednesday, was it run on the same host as today? Were operating system libraries modified? Did environment variables change? And so on. There is almost no end to this list of environment-related questions. In the end debugging boils down to trial-and-error. Try to understand the likelihood of certain changes causing the failure and the cost of undoing them for testing purposes.

2.3.7.2 Separate Changes of the Environment vs. Source Code Changes

There is a practical way to find out if one of the source code changes is related to the bug. Get access to a revision of the program that reflects the source-code base as of last Wednesday. We will refer to it as the "good" revision. Now, from within the exact same environment (same host, set setting of environment variables, same shell if possible) run both the "good" and the current version with the same test case. If both fail, then a difference in the environment is the likely cause of the bug. Here is what you need to check next:

- Do you know which factors are likely to cause the failure? Look at Chapter 8 for some examples of environment-related bugs.
- Can you determine what has changed? Often changes of the environment are not reflected in changing the contents of a revision control system. Did you change your computer account settings? Did your IT team perform any upgrade?
- Can you restore the original environment? Build a virtual copy of your machine and environment in VMware, (see Appendix B.3.2), and store a checkpoint before each change to the OS, tools, and installed software. You can then easily return to previous states of your machine.

If, however, the old source code revision works but the current breaks, then a difference in the source code base is the likely cause. If source code changes are the problem, then you can try to narrow down the search space and isolate the problematic changes using *back-out builds*. The basic idea is simple: use your revision control system to determine the last version of the source code that did not misbehave, by checking out complete configurations with different time tags and building them. Similarly, determine the first version that exhibits the problem. Then analyze the source code changes between these two versions – your bug is hiding there.

2.3.7.3 Zoom in and Conquer

It may still not be obvious what is causing the problem. Running a memory debugger (see Chapter 4) and normal source code debugging (see Chapter 3) may not solve the puzzle for you. You may have to bite the bullet and face the tedious task of *side-by-side debugging* comparing data, log files and the flow of control in both versions, concurrently, side-by-side.

2.3.8 Match the Tool to the Bug

Leave your comfort zone. Debug where the problem is and not where you find it convenient to debug.

Some debugging tools are easier to use than others in a given situation. But not all are equally helpful. It is natural to focus on the tools and processes you feel most comfortable with. Show discipline. Focus on those aspects that are most promising – even though this may entail tedious work or a trip into uncharted territory.

For instance, it is not uncommon for software developers to try to work around the use of memory debuggers. *"They produce lots of strange, cryptic output"* is one of the frequently heard excuses, even in situations that clearly suggest memory problems, such as intermittent failures and inexplicable random behavior.

2.3.9 One Change at a Time

Do not change more than one thing at a time if possible. Then check if it makes sense and, if not, revert back before trying out the next idea. (No rule without exception: when discussing *"Bugs Hiding Behind Bugs"* in Section 2.5.4 we will suggest you break this rule – at the price of even more bookkeeping.)

It is good practice to add comments to source code changed during debugging sessions, indicating type and reason of change. Mind that any code change may introduce new problems. Restrict yourself to solving one problem at a time while debugging.

2.3.10 Keep an Audit Trail

Often you will have to deal with a problem involving multiple parameters. You need to try out a number of combinations. It is all too easy to loose track of your changes.

Keep an audit trail!

This is especially important in the case of spurious failures. For manual testing, write down what you did, in what order, and what happened. Instruct the program to create log files and print status messages. Once the bug hits, your notes and the logs may be the only information left to correlate the bug to the environment. Spurious failures usually do not hit randomly per se. They are triggered by well-defined but perhaps obscure events, which are not yet known to you.

2.3.11 Get a Fresh View

When you are stuck, go and find somebody to talk to. Make sure to draw a clear line between the facts – and why they are facts – and your theories. Chances are good that your theories may be less than perfect.

The process of explaining the situation to somebody else may help you to separate truth from myths. And you may get a fresh view. Needless to mention: it is advisable to talk to an expert. However, non-experts can be quite helpful too, because you have to explain more.

2.3.12 If You Didn't Fix it, it Ain't Fixed

Occasionally, a bug will just disappear after you modified some statements. Unless you have a good explanation why your fix is effective, you are better off to assume that the bug still exists and will hit again in the future. Your source code change may merely change the environment and thus change the probability for the bug to re-occur.

Even if you have a good explanation, verify that the fix is effective: take your fix out again and check that the bug comes back. Building your program from scratch after putting the change back in may be a good idea too. The dependencies in your build process may not be perfect and, as a result, the object code may not entirely correspond to the sources.

2.3.13 Cover your Bugfix with a Regression Test

So the problem is fixed ... today. What about tomorrow?

To make the bug fix last, you should turn your simplified test case (rule number 3) into a regression test. Think of it as a safety bolt. It prevents others with access to the source code base from accidentally breaking a feature you have put quite some work into. Your customers will like it too – few things are as annoying as bugs that keep coming back.

Check out Section 2.4.2.1 if you have never heard about regression tests before. There is no excuse for ignoring automated testing. Granted, effort has to be spent making software testable and maintaining a regression test system. But this is an integral part of professional software development.

Developing software: more than writing code

Developing software takes more than the ability to write source code. Software architecture, profiling, debugging, ...; the list is long. One thing that is easily overlooked is planning for the future, including going that extra mile to develop testable software and regression tests.

In some ways software is like wine. It takes time to age and becomes valuable. Software that is tied to millions of dollars in revenue does not get created over night – it takes several years.

Got regression tests?

That's it! These were *the 13 golden rules*. Allow us to present one last set of general recommendations before we begin presenting solutions to specific debugging and optimization problems.

2.4 Build a Good Toolkit

You won't be surprised to read that you should install and test drive the complete range of debugging tools before the big crash. It is so much easier without your customer on the phone and without your boss standing next to you asking all sorts of not-so-helpful questions.

Good software developers have some traits of master craftsmen and artists. You need a workshop, stocked with usable and easy to find tools, and you need to be practiced at using these tools.

Keep your workshop in order

- Have the following installed and tested with the software you are developing (a 10-line test program does not count):

  - A source code debugger (see Chapter 3)
  - A memory debugger (see Chapter 4)
  - A profiler (see Chapters 5 and 6)

- Ensure that your debuggers are compatible with your compiler
- Run and maintain unit and system tests
- Automate frequent tasks

2.4.1 Your Workshop

You may think *"I don't need a memory debugger."* Think again! Chapter 4 will shed some light on why software developers need it. Bear in mind that it is typically too late to think of buying life-saving equipment by the time you really need it.

You don't need a profiler either? Same story. There are usable freeware solutions available on most platforms. Consider these if nothing else works for you.

It is part of your due diligence to check that your entire suite of debugging tools still works when you change compiler versions. Ensure that they work with the software you are developing. Getting them to run on a 10-line test program does not count. It's got to be your software, in all its "glory."

It may not be required that every individual software developer in a large organization tests the full range of debugging tools time and time again. But before you declare this task to be "somebody else's problem," consider that "somebody else" does not fix your bugs, and does not get the phone calls when they are not fixed. In fact, "somebody" may not even be around when the going gets tough. Check your tools from time to time, especially whenever the environment changes.

2.4.2 Running Tests Every Day Keeps the Bugs at Bay

This is not a book about software testing. It is an important topic though. In this section we can only scratch its surface and point out a few aspects related to debugging in the broadest sense. More in-depth information can be found for instance in [Meyers04].

2.4.2.1 Regression Tests

If you did't test it, then it does not work (anymore).

There's a lot of truth to this. Granted, it sounds a bit strange at first. Why do I have to test something in order to keep it working?

Well, think about it. How do you convince yourself that a new piece of code does what it is supposed to do? You test it.

And how do you ensure it still runs throughout the year? You keep testing it, frequently. The term *regression test* means something along the lines of *"check whether yesterday's functionality is still working well today."*

These tests should be automated in order to allow for frequent and efficient execution. And the tests should be self-checking. That is, there should be a *regression test system* – typically a collection of scripts – that executes a steadily growing set of tests. The outcome is one list of tests that passed and one that shows a set of failing tests. Tests are added for each new feature and whenever a bug is fixed.

2.4.2.2 Unit Tests and System Tests

It makes sense to distinguish two types of regression tests: *unit tests* and *system tests*. A system test uses your software as a whole. These tests are necessary; they emulate normal operation and ensure end-user functionality.

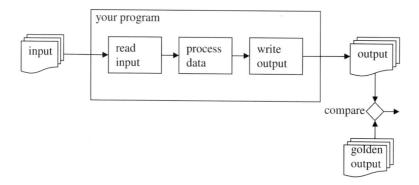

Fig. 2.2 Simple test system

Figure 2.2 shows a simplified example where we assume that your program consists of only three software modules: something that reads input data, something that processes data and something that generates output files. A simple regression test will run the software with a given set of input files and then compare the output with a set of "golden reference files."

Unit tests on the other hand focus on individual building blocks of your software in isolation. Typically, they require extra effort in the form of additional test executables or test interfaces. But it pays off:

- Unit tests can be developed before the complete system is operational.
- Unit test interfaces can increase the observability and controllability of the software.
- And, last but not least, they ease the task of debugging.

Imagine if the system test depicted in Figure 2.2 failed. Wouldn't it be nice to be able to narrow down the search space right from the start? Unit tests for the components of your program can help you. With the right infrastructure in place you can figure out quickly whether data input, data processing, or data output caused the failure.

Figure 2.3 depicts one possible approach. Here, unit test support has been built into the program so that the output of each unit can be stored. Additionally, one can bypass the regular flow of data by directly feeding into units that would otherwise be

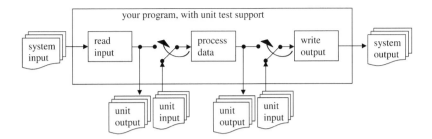

Fig. 2.3 Simple test system with unit test support

hard to reach or control. Alternatively, one could create separate unit test executables for the three functional units shown in Figure 2.3.

One can distinguish between *white box* and *black box* unit tests.   Black box tests are focusing on verifying the intended functionality of a component, ignoring its actual implementation. The advantage of black box tests is their portability – even if the implementation changes, these tests will still work correctly. White box tests on the other hand are focused at testing corner cases of the implementation and your "insanely clever hacks." They make really good watchdogs.

2.5 Know Your Enemy – Meet the Bug Family

"Forgive your enemies, but never forget their names."
John F. Kennedy

One can distinguish between different types of bugs requiring specific measures to be taken. The following sections attempt to classify; a classification that is best taken with a grain of salt.

2.5.1 The Common Bug

The common bug dwells in source code. It is a nuisance but behaves rather predictably. Ambiguous specifications and holes in your test plan often lead to its proliferation. The common bug has a couple of nasty cousins, which we will describe in the following sections.

2.5.2 Sporadic Bugs

While the common bug strikes predictably, given the right test case, this is not the case for the sporadic bug. It cannot be lured out of its cover easily. It hits when you are not prepared. The key to success is:

- Leave a trap in place: add watchdog code to your executable, which will alert you when it is around. It goes without saying that you need to preserve and check log files, or else your watchdog may howl in vain.
- Find the right bait. Show stamina. Keep notes. Mind that subtle changes can make or break it.

If your regression tests are affected by this type of pest, then consider keeping[2] core files and analyzing them post-mortem using a source code debugger.

2.5.3 Heisenbugs

A Heisenbug can drive you mad. Its name stems from Werner Heisenberg's uncertainty principle on quantum physics.

"The more precise the position is determined, the less precisely the momentum (mass times velocity) is known in this instant and vice versa."

There is an analogy in software debugging: the harder you try to debug the better certain bugs are hiding.[3]

- *"The bug was gone when I turned on debugging information in the compiler."*
- *"I added a printf() statement and it worked. I removed the printf() and it failed. But I can't ship a program generating debug output to my customer."*
- *"After I linked my test code into the executable I could not spot the bug anymore. I didn't even call one of the routines. It's a mystery."*

You need to understand the Heisenbug traits in order to successfully hunt this elusive creature. Typically, it is either a race-ist, a memory outlaw, or an idealist.

2.5.3.1 The Race-ist

So-called *race conditions* are often the reason for Heisenbugs. This refers to situations where the program behavior depends on the order of execution of certain

---

[2] You can also force the generation of a core dump if necessary.

[3] Mind the subtle but important difference between sporadic bugs and Heisenbugs. Sporadic bugs may be difficult to spot. Yet, once a test case is found they are reproducible. This is not the case for Heisenbugs though.

pieces of code, and this order is not well defined. Parallel, multi-threaded programs with inappropriate inter-task communication mechanisms or missing means of synchronization often show such problems (see Chapter 7). But even single-threaded programs can be affected; order-of-initialization problems are just one example (see Chapter 10).

All cases have in common that the execution order is – at least to some degree – undefined. Hence, any small change such as adding a `printf()` statement or generating "slower" code with debug information can change the behavior and result in the Heisenbug-style behavior.

2.5.3.2 The Memory Outlaw

Memory access violations such as reading uninitialized variables, dangling pointers, or array bound violations can also result in Heisenbugs. Seemingly unrelated changes such as adding a local variable or moving code around can result in slightly different memory layout of heap or stack. The good news is that memory debuggers are very helpful when it comes to solving these type of problems (see Chapter 4).

2.5.3.3 The Idealist

This type of bug dwells in optimizations of abstract data types and algorithms, and strikes when the corresponding code takes some sort of illegal shortcut.

Of course you are thinking of compiler optimizations right now. Granted, at times compiler optimizations are buggy. But it is not unlikely that it is an optimization sitting in your program that is the culprit. Either way, small changes may either change the effect or disable the optimization altogether.

A first-level analysis is not too difficult in these situations. If you suspect an optimization is part of the problem, then switch it off.

2.5.4 Bugs Hiding Behind Bugs

Always consider the possibility of multiple bugs. In some cases, more than one problem needs to be fixed before you notice a change in your program's behavior.

If you suspect that you are dealing with multiple bugs that play such games with you, then consider violating rule 9 (*"One Change at a Time"*) at the price of doubling your bookkeeping efforts (rule 10).

2.5.5 Secret Bugs – Debugging and Confidentiality

Another nasty cousin of the common bug is the "secret bug". It strikes when your customer is using your software. The next thing you know is that your customer tells you that you can't have the test case, either because it is confidential or because the customer is simply not in the position to extract, package, and ship all relevant pieces of information. Neither can you ship a debuggable version of your software including source code. Result ... Catch 22.

You should consider the following three alternatives: try to reproduce the problem in-house, debug on-site at the customer, or use a secure connection for remote debugging.

2.5.5.1 Reproduce Bugs In-house

Always ask for the test case or a stripped-down test case. If that is not possible due to confidentiality or time constraints, then try to reproduce the same bug in house.

First, try to get a good, clear error description from the customer. Ask for log files. Make use of memory checkers (see Chapter 4) and tracers like `truss` or `strace` (see Chapter 8.2.4) to get more details. Analyze the error description and log files and form a theory what might have gone wrong. Then build a test case that results in an error matching the customer's description and log files. The next steps are obvious: debug the failure, fix it, ship a new release to the customer, and cross your fingers that the problem is gone.

2.5.5.2 On-site Debugging

A different approach is to debug on-site. Compile your software with debug information. Send it to your customer but leave out all source-code files.[4] The symbolic debug information has some value in an attempt to reverse-engineer a program, but certainly less than the source code. Now visit your customer and bring your laptop containing relevant portions of the source code, preferably encrypted. Because your program has symbolic information, the debugger running the program on your customer's computer will work fine: you can set breakpoints in functions, step through lines, get stack traces, get or set variables. It can't display source code, though. Instead it will tell you about file name and line number, and you will have to look at the source code using your laptop.

Bring your cell phone – being able to call a colleague can save the day.

---

[4] On Solaris you also need to send the object code files as they, not the executable, contain most of the debugging information.

This style of debugging is expensive and time consuming (travel), and stressful too, due to time pressure and customers looking over your shoulder. But it may be your last and only option.

2.5.5.3 Using Secure Connections

You can optimize this approach by using a reasonably secure remote desktop access mechanism such as WebEx (see Appendix B.9.7) or VNC (Appendix B.9.6) over SSH. The situation is mostly the same: your customer's computer is running a debuggable version of your software, and the source code is still on your computer. You can still see what's going on with your software, and maybe even interact with software and debugger yourself. But no travel is involved, and you have retained full access to your company's computer network.

2.5.6 Further Reading

For a highly entertaining introduction to debugging, not just of software, you should read David J. Agans book *Debugging: The Nine Indispensable Rules for Finding Even the Most Elusive Software and Hardware Problems* [Agans02].

We used Andreas Zeller's book *Why Programs Fail: A Guide to Systematic Debugging* [Zeller09] as the reference for bug-finding technology and scientific progress in the field of automatic debugging. You can find examples and course material on the associated website http://www.whyprogramsfail.com.

If you are working on embedded systems, our favorite introduction is *Programming Embedded Systems*, by M. Barr, and A. Massa [Barr06]. There is a section on debugging, covering downloading the binary image, remote debuggers, and emulation. Also recommended is *Debugging Embedded Microprocessor Systems* by S. Ball [Ball98].

Further reading material on various debugging topics can be found in [Brown88], [Ford02], [Kaspersky05], [Lencevicius00], [Metzger03], [Pappas00], [Stitt92], [Telles01], and [Rosenberg96]. For current research topics, refer to [Zeller09] and [Fritzson93].

We recommend that you become familiar with the documentation of your debugging tools. The GDB debugger manual is available as a book [Stallmann02]. See Appendix B.2.3 for finding GDB documentation on the web. For Visual Studio, the documentation is called the *MSDN Library for Visual Studio*, and is available as part of the software installation. More information can be found in Appendix B.1.1.

Chapter 3
Getting to the Root – Source Code Debuggers

3.1 Visualizing Program Behavior

The quickest and most efficient tool to visualize a program's behavior is a debugger, a program to test and debug other programs. A debugger is called a *source code debugger* or *symbolic debugger* if it can show the current point of execution, or the location of a program error, inside the program's source code.

With a source code debugger, (from here on simply referred to as "debugger"), you can step through your code line by line, see what path is taken through the program's conditional and loop statements, show what functions are called, and where in the function call stack you are. You can inspect the values of variables. You can set breakpoints on individual lines of code, and then let the program run until it reaches this line; this is convenient for navigating through complicated programs.

A debugger will show you what the program does, which is a prerequisite to fixing any bug. In case you wrote the code, the debugger will let you match expected behavior, i.e. what you thought the code would be doing, to real behavior. In case somebody else wrote the code, the debugger will present to you a dynamic view into the code's execution, to augment a static code inspection.

In this chapter, we describe the basic source code debugger features and show how to apply them to find bugs in C and C++ programs. We will keep the description of the debugger features independent of a particular computer platform or tool. We will use two very common debuggers in the examples: GDB and Visual Studio. We will list the commands of GDB and Visual Studio to access each discussed feature. To save valuable space in the book, we will only show the abridged output of GDB. We will give short descriptions of how Visual Studio will output results, but we will not show screen shots.

The GNU debugger GDB represents debuggers run from a *command shell* with a *command line interface*. GDB is used together with the GCC compiler, and has been ported to many operating systems, including Windows, Solaris, UNIX, Linux, and operating systems for embedded systems. See Appendix B.2.3 for download information and documentation of GDB.

Microsoft Visual Studio is a debugger for Microsoft Windows systems, and works together with the Visual C++ compiler. Visual Studio is a GUI (graphical user interface) program, and is part of an IDE *Integrated Development Environment*. See Appendix B.1.1 for more information on Visual Studio.

Most source code debuggers share a common feature set, with similar commands. Table A in the appendix on page 193 gives a translation table of debugger commands for the two common debuggers GDB and Visual Studio. dbx is a command-line debugger for Sun Solaris. TotalView (see Appendix B.2.5) is a GUI-based debugger for Linux and MacOS, with support for debugging parallel programs based on threads, OpenMP, and MPI. ARM Development Studio 5 and Lauterbach TRACE32 are debuggers for systems that have an ARM CPU.

We recommend getting familiar with any new debugger, and its basic features, by using the debugger on a simple predictable example. We will show how to build a small test program, and run the program together with the debugger. The essential features of doing a stack trace on a program crash, breakpoints, stepping through the code, and inspecting variables will be demonstrated on the example.

In Chapter 10 will we show advanced features, for example modifying the state of a running program, and calling functions from the debugger.

3.2 Prepare a Simple Predictable Example

As an example in this chapter, we will compute the factorial function $n!$ for any non-negative integer n, where $0! = 1$ and $n! = n * (n - 1)!$ for $n > 0$.

Figure 3.1 shows the source code of the program `factorial` to compute the factorial function. We chose to implement the function `factorial(int n)` as a recursive call to itself. Note that the code is quite unsafe, since there is no guard against negative values of n, and no guard against incorrect results due to 32-bit integer overflow for $n > 12$. The example intends to highlight the basic debugger features for finding these bugs.

3.3 Get the Debugger to Run with Your Program

In order to get started, you need to get your program running with the debugger. The compiler has to be instructed to put debug information into the object code of the program. This debug information, also called *debug symbols* or *symbolic information*, contains the names of functions and variables, and the relationship between CPU instructions, source files, and line numbers. Note that most compilers do not have debug enabled in their default or optimized modes, since the debug information in the object code makes the program larger. Also, most compiler optimizations are disabled in debug mode, so the program runs slower.

```
 1   /* factorial.c */
 2   #include <stdio.h>
 3   #include <stdlib.h>
 4
 5   int factorial(int n) {
 6       int result = 1;
 7       if(n == 0)
 8           return result;
 9       result = factorial(n-1) * n;
10       return result;
11   }
12
13   int main(int argc, char **argv) {
14       int n, result;
15       if(argc != 2) {
16           fprintf(stderr, "usage: factorial n, n >=0\n");
17           return 1;
18       }
19       n = atoi(argv[1]);
20       result = factorial(n);
21       printf("factorial %d = %d\n", n, result);
22       return 0;
23   }
```

Fig. 3.1 factorial.c: recursive function calculating n!

For the GNU compiler GCC, and most other compilers, the compiler flag for debugging is −g. Here is how we compile the factorial program with GCC.

```
>  gcc -g -o factorial factorial.c
```

For the Visual Studio debugger, the most convenient way to build and debug the program is to create a project. Please refer to *How to build and run a program in Visual Studio 2008* on page 26 for instructions for creating a project, building the program, entering the command arguments for a console program, and running the program.

The next step is to load the program in the debugger and run it. A debugger will always have a mode to run the program until you interrupt it, the program crashes, or the program exits by itself.

For the GDB debugger, you type the command gdb and enter the program name as the first argument. GDB will start up with a command shell, where you can type in commands to control the debugger. The command to run the program is run, followed by the command line arguments that you want to pass to your program. Here is how to run GDB with our example:

```
>  gdb factorial
<lots of copyright stuff..>
(gdb) run 1
<messages about Loaded symbols..>
factorial 1 = 1
Program exited normally
```

How to build and run a program in Visual Studio 2008

Create a project:

- Put the file `factorial.c` into a new directory.
- Start Microsoft Visual Studio
- Create a new Project by clicking on the menu item **File/New/Project From Existing Code...**
- Select **Visual C++** as project type, and click on **Next**. Enter the path to the source code file **factorial.c** under **Project file location**, and enter `factorial` under **Project name**.
- The next dialog in project creation is **Specify Project Settings**. Under the item **Use Visual Studio, Project type**, select **Console application project**. Do *not* select **Add support for ATL** or any other package.
- Click on **Finish** to let the Wizard create the factorial project.
- Check that you see a project `factorial` in the **Solution Explorer** tree view.

Build the program:

- Compile the program by hitting F7 or clicking on the menu item **Build/Build Solution**. You will get a debug build by default. The configuration for the debug build will contain all the correct debug flags and libraries.
- Check that the program compiles without errors.

Add command line arguments:

- Select the project `factorial` by right-clicking on it, and go to the menu item **Project/Properties**. The **Property Page** for the `factorial` project will appear. Go to **Configuration Properties/Debugging**, and look for the item **Command Arguments** in the table of properties. Enter the desired value for the `factorial` command line arguments, and close the dialog with **OK**.

Run the program:

- Hit the F5 function key, or select the menu item **Debug/Start Debugging** to run the program.

Attaching to an already running program:

- Click on menu item **Debug/Attach to Process...**, and then click on the program process that you want to debug.

One annoying aspect of debugging console applications in Visual Studio is the handling of the command line console. For our example, a console window is created, pops up, the program runs and prints to `stdout`, and then the console vanishes without a trace. A good workaround is to right-click on the last line of the program, line 22, and select **Breakpoint/Insert Breakpoint**.

We will have more information on breakpoints later, but for now, this workaround is good enough to let us look at the program's output:

```
factorial 1 = 1
```

At this point, we can already do some useful testing with the debugger. We run our program with the argument $n = -1$, which will cause the recursion to not end:

```
(gdb) run -1
Program received signal SIGSEGV, Segmentation fault.
factorial (n=-103583) at factorial.c:6
6           int result = 1;
```

This GDB output tells us that the program hit a memory error in line 6 of the function factorial, as it was trying to make yet another call to itself. GDB shows the actual source tode line where the error occurred.

In Visual Studio, change the program argument to -1, and run the program again by hitting F5. You will get a new window with the Message:

```
Unhandled exception at <..> in factorial.exe: Stack overflow
```

To find the location of the crash in Visual Studio, click on **Break** in this window. The debugger will show you the source code window containing the file factorial.c, and a yellow arrow representing the location of the current position of the program pointing at line 5, the beginning of the factorial function.

3.4 Learn to do a Stack Trace on a Program Crash

Visual Studio already told us what caused the crash: a stack overflow. The *stack* of a C/C++ program is a segment of memory assigned to storing one *stack frame* for each active functions call. A stack frame consists of the return address, and the function's arguments and local variables. A *stack trace* is the actual chain of stack frames from the topmost function where the debugger is currently stopped or paused, down to the function main(). A *stack overflow* occurs when the chain of nested function calls gets so long that the stack does not have enough memory to store the current stack frame.

In addition to showing the location of a program crash in the source code, a debugger will also show the stack frame and stack trace of the crash. A stack trace is useful information for debugging a crash, since it tells you the chain of functions calls that led to the crash.

The GDB debugger refers to the stack frames by numbers, where the current frame has stack frame number 0, and the frame of the main() function has the highest number. This number is also the size of the call stack. The GDB command for a stack trace is bt, backtrace, or where. For the crash in the example above, the stack trace confirms that we created an overflow of the program stack, by making many recursive calls to the factorial() function:

```
(gdb) backtrace
#0 <..> in factorial (n=-105582) at factorial.c:9
<lots of frames..>
#103581 <..> in factorial (n=-2) at factorial.c:9
#103582 <..> in factorial (n=-1) at factorial.c:9
```

27

```
#103583 <..> in main (argc=2, argv=0x761ce8) at factorial.c:20
```

You can navigate up and down the call stack, and inspect the values of function arguments and local variables. In GDB, you can use the commands `up` or `down` to move through the stack.

In Visual Studio, you will see a window named **Call Stack**. This window only shows the first 1000 frames. Click on the line items in the **Call Stack** Window to navigate in the call stack.

3.5 Learn to Use Breakpoints

Interactive debugging requires the ability to suspend the execution of a program before it terminates, and to navigate through the program code in a controlled manner. This is done with breakpoints. A debugger provides a range of breakpoint commands, as described in the following list:

- Line breakpoint – will pause the program when it reaches a specific line in the source code.
- Function breakpoint – will pause the program when it reaches the first line of a specific function.
- Conditional breakpoint – will pause the program if a certain condition holds true.
- Event breakpoint – puts the program in pause mode if a certain event occurs. Supported events include `signals` from the operating system, and *C++ exceptions*.

A complete list of debugger commands can be found in the appendix on page 193. Chapter 10 discusses event breakpoints in more detail: Section 10.4 on *conditional breakpoints*, Section 10.6 on *watchpoints*, Section 10.7 on *catching signals* and Section 10.8 on *catching exceptions*.

3.6 Learn to Navigate Through the Program

We have seen above that a debugger has commands to run and pause the program.

- run – The *run* command will start the program. There is a way to control and alter the environment that the program runs in, such as command line arguments and environment variables.
- start – The *start* command will run the program until the first line of `main()`, and stop execution of the program. This saves the work of searching for the file containing the `main()` function, and putting an explicit breakpoint in the first line.
- pause – The *pause* command will interrupt a running program. In some debuggers, typing Ctrl-C or clicking the `Pause` key will have the same effect.

- continue – The debugger command *continue* will cause the paused program to resume execution.

To understand the behavior of a complicated piece of code, we need to go through the source code line by line. A debugger provides the feature of line-by-line *stepping*. There are three separate stepping modes, *step-into*, *step-over*, and *step-out* that differ by how they deal with functions calls. We will describe in the following how these modes work. We recommend that you try out these modes on the `factorial` example, to become familiar with navigating through the program by stepping.

- Step-into – The debugger command *step-into*, or `step` in GDB, will go to the next executable line of code. In case the current line is a function call, the debugger will step into the function, and stop at the first line of the function's body. A *step-into* can lead you to initially puzzling code locations. For example, the function call and the function itself may be in separate files. See Chapter 10, Section 10.3 for details on step-into in C++ implicit function calls.
- Step-over – The debugger command *step-over*, or `next` in GDB, will go to the next executable line of code in the same call-stack level. If the current line is a function call, the debugger will stop at the next statement after the function call. The debugger will not go into the function's body. If the current line was the last line in a function, *step-over* will go down one level in the stack, and stop in the next line of the calling function.
- Step-out – The debugger command *step-out*, or `finish` in GDB, will go down one level in the stack, and stop in the next line of the calling function.

Again, please refer to Table A on page 193 for the most common commands in GDB and Visual Studio.

3.7 Learn to Inspect Data: Variables and Expressions

Here is how you show the value of a variable: Put a breakpoint in line 7 of the `factorial` example in Figure 3.1, and start the program. When the program pauses in line 7, type `print n` in GDB.

- print – The *print* command will print the current value of a variable, or an expression.
- display expression – continuous display of an expression value. The value gets updated whenever the program execution is paused.

In Visual Studio, you can put the cursor on the function argument n, to have a small **DataTip** window pop up and display the variable name and value. You can also use the menu item **Debug/Windows/Locals** to create a window that displays the local variables of the current function or method. To display global variables in Visual Studio, go to the menu item **Debug/Windows/Watch**, open a **Watch** window, and enter in the **Name** column the names of the global variables you want to watch.

In many cases, it is convenient to print the value of an expression. A debugger will evaluate an expression using variable values from the current stack frame, and will show the result in an output area or as console output. The expressions can consist of variable names, or can be composed from operators, variables, type casts, and function calls. The format for printing the result of an evaluated expression will depend on the data type of the expression: an expression of type `float` is printed with a decimal point, whereas, an expression of type `int` is printed as an integer. You can chose different output formats for the `print` command. For example, a variable containing status bits can be displayed in binary or hexadecimal format.

If the same expression has to be analyzed and printed repeatedly, you can use the *display* feature to evaluate and print the result of an expression automatically every time that the debugger is paused. The *display* feature will let you efficiently monitor variables of interest, while navigating through the program in the debugger. In GDB, this command is `display`. In Visual Studio, you can open a **Watch** window for displaying variables and expressions.

The debugger maintains a list of display expressions, similar to the list of breakpoints. You can disable, enable, add, or remove expressions in the display list. Please refer to your debugger's documentation on how to do this. You should not overuse displays, because too many data expressions shown by the debugger will hide the relevant information. The most common print and display commands in GDB and Visual Studio are listed in the appendix on page 193.

3.8 A Debug Session on a Simple Example

Let us recapitulate the debugger commands and features described in the previous sections. We take the `factorial` example from Figure 3.1, and apply the debugger to find out why the program returns an incorrect value for $n >= 13$. Our program returns the value 1932053504 for 13!, whereas the correct value is $13! = 6227020800$.

The first task is to start the program with the argument 13, pause in the first line of `main()`, and then step over each line until we reach line 20, where the `factorial()` function is called. The purpose is to check that the command line argument is parsed correctly, and that an integer value of 13 is passed to the `factorial()` function. We then step into the function `factorial()`. We use GDB for this example.

```
> gdb factorial
...
(gdb) start 13
(gdb  next
...
(gdb) next
20        result = factorial(n);
(gdb) print n
$1 = 13
```

```
(gdb) step
factorial (n=13) at factorial.c:6
6      int result = 1;
```

We need to check that the recursion works, so we place a breakpoint in line 8, to check that for $n = 0$, the function does not call itself again. We also place a breakpoint in line 10, so we can look at the return value of each call to factorial. Rather than stepping, we then let the program continue to the first breakpoint.

```
(gdb  break 8
Breakpoint 2 at <..>: file factorial.c, line 8
(gdb) break 10
Breakpoint 3 at <..>: file factorial.c, line 10
(gdb) continue
Continuing.
Breakpoint 2, factorial (n=0) at factorial.c:8
```

We print the variables n and result, to check that the function works properly. We can also use the display command on the variable result, so we do not have to repeat typing the print command.

```
(gdb) print n
$1 = 0
(gdb) print result
$2 = 1
(gdb) display result
1: result = 1
```

As we keep repeating the continue command, we get a printout of the variable result at line 10 in the program, for $n = 0, 1, .., 13$. We pause when n is 13.

```
(gdb) continue
Breakpoint 3, factorial (n=1) at factorial.c:10
1: result = 1
(gdb) continue
...
Breakpoint 3, factorial (n=12) at factorial.c:10
1: result = 479001600
(gdb) continue
Breakpoint 3, factorial (n=13) at factorial.c:10
1: result = 193053504
(gdb) print 13 * 479001600
$5 = 193053504
```

Note that the result for $n = 12$ is still correct, but that the multiplication with the value 13 calculates an incorrect result. We repeat the calculation done in line 9, by printing the expression $13 * 479001600$, and note that it reproduces the calculation error. The reason for this is that the value for 13! is too large to be stored in a 32-bit variable of type int, so the multiplication causes an incorrect result due to an integer overflow.

Lessons learned:

- Use a source code debugger to visualize a program's behavior.
- Prepare a simple example to familiarize yourself with the features of the debugger.
- Get the debugger to run with your program.
- Learn to analyze the stack trace of a program crash.
- Learn to use breakpoints.
- Learn to navigate through the program.
- Learn to inspect variables and expressions.
- Do a debug session on a simple example.

Change "There is three common reasons" to "There are three common reasons"

Chapter 4
Fixing Memory Problems

This chapter is about finding bugs in C/C++ programs with the help of a *memory debugger*. A memory debugger is a runtime tool designed to trace and detect bugs in C/C++ memory management and access. It does not replace a general debugger. In the following sections, we will describe the memory access bugs that typically occur in C/C++ programs, introduce memory debuggers, and show with two examples how these tools find bugs. We will then show how to run memory and source code debuggers together, how to deal with unwanted error messages by writing a suppression file, and what restrictions need to be considered.

4.1 Memory Management in C/C++ – Powerful but Dangerous

The C/C++ language is able to manage memory resources, and can access memory directly through pointers. Efficient memory handling and "programming close to the hardware" are reasons why C/C++ replaced assembly language in the implementation of large software projects such as operating systems, where performance and low overhead play a major role. The allocation of dynamic memory (also known as *heap memory*) in C/C++ is under the control of the programmer. New memory is allocated with functions such as `malloc()` and various forms of the operator `new`. Unused memory is returned with `free()` or `delete`.

The memory handling in C/C++ gives a large degree of freedom, control, and performance, but comes at a high price: the memory access is a frequent source of bugs. The most frequent sources of memory access bugs are *memory leaks*, *incorrect use of memory management*, *buffer overruns*, and *reading uninitialized memory*.

4.1.1 Memory Leaks

Memory leaks are data structures that are allocated at runtime, but not deallocated once they are no longer needed in the program. If the leaks are frequent or large, eventually all available main memory in your computer will be consumed. The program will first slow down, as the computer starts swapping pages to virtual memory, and then fail with an *out-of-memory* error. Finding leaks with a general debugger is difficult because there is no obvious faulty statement. The bug is that a statement is *missing* or not called.

4.1.2 Incorrect Use of Memory Management

A whole class of bugs is associated with incorrect calls to memory management: freeing a block of memory more than once, accessing memory after freeing it, or freeing a block that was never allocated. Also belonging to this class is using `delete` instead of `delete[]` for C++ array deallocation, as well as using `malloc()` together with `delete`, and using `new` together with `free()`.

4.1.3 Buffer Overruns

Buffer overruns are bugs where memory outside of the allocated boundaries is overwritten, or *corrupted*. Buffer overruns can occur for global variables, local variables on the stack, and dynamic variables that were allocated on the heap with memory management.

One nasty artifact of memory corruption is that the bug may not become visible at the statement where the memory is overwritten. Only later, another statement in the program will access this memory location. Because the memory location has an illegal value, the program can behave incorrectly in a number of ways: the program may compute a wrong result, or, if the illegal value is in a pointer, the program will try to access protected memory and crash. If a function pointer variable is overwritten, the program will do a jump and try to execute data as program code. The key point is that there may be no strict relation between the statement causing the memory corruption and the statement triggering the visible bug.

4.1.4 Uninitialized Memory Bugs

Reading uninitialized memory can occur because C/C++ allows creation of variables without an initial value. The programmer is fully responsible to initialize all global and local variables, either through assignment statements or through the various C++ constructors. The memory allocation function `malloc()` and operator `new` also do not initialize or zero out the allocated memory blocks. Uninitialized variables will contain unpredictable values.

4.2 Memory Debuggers to the Rescue

The above categories of memory access bugs created a need for adequate debugging tools. Finding bugs related to leaked, corrupted, or uninitialized memory with a conventional debugger such as GDB turned out to be unproductive. To deal with memory leaks in large software projects, many programmers came up with the same idea. They created memory management functions/operators with special instrumentation to track where a memory block was allocated, and if each block was properly deallocated at the end of the program.

Since everybody had the same memory bugs in their C/C++ programs, and since everybody improvised with custom instrumentation to track down at least some of these bugs, a market for a tool called *memory debugger* was created. The most well-known tool is Purify, released in 1991 by Pure Software. Purify's name has since become synonymous with memory debugging. There is also Insure++, Valgrind, and BoundsChecker, among others. See the tools Appendix B.4 starting on page 198 for references and the survey in [Luecke06] for a comparison of features.

Memory debuggers do detailed bookkeeping of all allocated/deallocated dynamic memory. They also intercept and check access to dynamic memory. Some memory debuggers can check access to local variables on the stack and statically allocated memory. Purify and BoundsChecker do this by *object code instrumentation* at program link time, Insure++ uses *source code instrumentation*, and Valgrind executes the program on a virtual machine and monitors all memory transactions. The code instrumentation allows the tools to pinpoint the source code statement where a memory bug occurred.

The following bugs are detectable by a memory debugger:

- Memory leaks
- Accessing memory that was already freed
- Freeing the same memory location more than once
- Freeing memory that was never allocated
- Mixing C `malloc()`/`free()` with C++ `new`/`delete`
- Using `delete` instead of `delete[]` for arrays
- Array out-of-bound errors
- Accessing memory that was never allocated
- Uninitialized memory read
- Null pointer read or write

We will show in the next section how to attach a memory debugger to your program, and how the tool finds and reports bugs.

4.3 Example 1: Detecting Memory Access Errors

Our first example is a program that allocates an array in dynamic memory, accesses an element outside the final array element, reads an uninitialized array element, and finally forgets to deallocate the array. We use the public domain tool Valgrind on Linux as the memory debugger, and demonstrate how the tool automatically detects these bugs. This is the code of our program main1.c:

```
1   /* main1.c */
2   #include <stdio.h>
3   int main(int argc, char* argv[]) {
4     const int size=100;
5     int n, sum=0;
6     int* A = (int*)malloc( sizeof(int)*size );
7
8     for (n=size; n>0; n--)   /* walk through A[100]...A[1] */
9         A[n] = n;            /* error: A[100] invalid write*/
10    for (n=0;n<size; n++)    /* walk through A[0]...A[99]  */
11        sum += A[n];         /* error: A[0] not initialized*/
12    printf ("sum=%d\n", sum);
13    return 0;                /* mem leak: A[]              */
14  }
```

We compile the program with debug information and then run under Valgrind:

```
> gcc -g main1.c
> valgrind --tool=memcheck --leak-check=yes ./a.out
```

In the following sections we go through the error list reported by Valgrind.

4.3.1 Detecting an Invalid Write Access

The first – and perhaps most severe – error is a buffer overrun: the accidental write access to array element A[100]. Because the array has only 100 elements, the highest valid index is 99. A[100] points to unallocated memory that is located just after the memory allocated for array A. Valgrind thus reports an "invalid write" error:

```
==11323== Invalid write of size 4
==11323==    at 0x8048518: main (main1.c:9)
==11323==  Address 0x1BB261B8 is 0 bytes after a block
==11323==    of size 400 alloc'd
==11323==    at 0x1B903F40: malloc
==11323==    (in /usr/lib/valgrind/vgpreload_memcheck.so)
==11323==    by 0x80484F2: main (main1.c:6)
```

The string "==11323==" refers to the process ID and is useful when Valgrind is checking multiple processes [1]. The important piece of information is that an invalid

---

[1] Valgrind will, per default, check only the first (parent) process that has been invoked. Use option --trace-children=yes to check all child processes as well.

write occurs in line 9 of `main1.c`. There is also additional information revealing the address of the closest allocated memory block and how it was allocated. The memory debugger guesses that the invalid write in line 9 is related to this memory block. The guess is correct because both belong to the same array `A`.

Note that Valgrind is able to catch an out-of-array-bounds errors only when the array is allocated as dynamic memory with `malloc()` or `new`. This is the case in the example with the statement in line 6:

```
6    int* A = (int*)malloc( sizeof(int)*size );
```

If the example were instead written as `int A[size]` in line 6, then `A` would be a *local* variable located on the stack and not on the heap. It turns out that Valgrind does not detect such an error but Purify is able to catch it. This shows that not all memory debuggers will report exactly the same errors.

4.3.2 Detecting Uninitialized Memory Reads

The next error in `main1.c` is an uninitialized memory read. Due to the incorrect index computation in line 8, element `A[0]` was never written with an initial value. This element is later read by statement `sum += A[n]` in line 11, which means that variable `sum` gets "infected" as well.

It is important to point out *when* Valgrind reports this uninitialized memory error. The infection of `sum` happens in line 11. However, the error is not reported at that point, but later, when the variable `sum` is observed by printing its value in line 12:

```
==11323== Use of uninitialised value of size 4
==11323==    at 0x1BA429B7: (within /lib/tls/libc.so.6)
==11323==    by 0x1BA46A35: _IO_vfprintf (in .../libc.so.6)
==11323==    by 0x1BA4BDAF: _IO_printf (in .../libc.so.6)
==11323==    by 0x804855C: main (main1.c:12)
==11323==
==11323== Conditional jump or move depends on
==11323== uninitialised value(s)
==11323==    at 0x1BA429BF: (within .../libc.so.6)
==11323==    by 0x1BA46A35: _IO_vfprintf (in .../libc.so.6)
==11323==    by 0x1BA4BDAF: _IO_printf (in .../libc.so.6)
==11323==    by 0x804855C: main (main1.c:12)
```

Valgrind, unfortunately, does not give a detailed explanation where the variable `sum` was infected, so you have to find out yourself. Analyzing the source code is one way. A temporary workaround is to add a dummy statement after line 11, inside the for-loop: `if (sum>0) do_nothing()`. This makes Valgrind observe the value of `sum` earlier.

4.3.3 Detecting Memory Leaks

The final bug is a memory leak. Memory for array A has been allocated with the statement malloc(sizeof(int)*size) in line 6 but it has never been deleted with a corresponding free(A) statement. The memory debugger reports this leak when the program ends:

```
==11323== 400 bytes in 1 blocks are definitely lost
==11323==    in loss record 1 of 1
==11323==    at 0x1B903F40: malloc
==11323==    (in /usr/lib/valgrind/vgpreload_memcheck.so)
==11323==    by 0x80484F2: main (main1.c:6)
```

4.4 Example 2: Broken Calls to Memory Allocation/Deallocation

The second example, main2.c, demonstrates how to find memory allocation bugs in a program that uses C strings of type char*:

```
1   /* main2.c */
2   #include <stdio.h>
3   #include <stdlib.h>
4   #include <string.h>
5   int main(int argc, char* argv[]) {
6       char* mystr1=strdup("test");
7       char* mystr2=strdup("TEST");
8       mystr1=mystr2;
9
10      printf ("mystr1=%s\n", mystr1);
11      free(mystr1);
12
13      printf ("mystr2=%s\n", mystr2);
14      free(mystr2);
15      return 0;
16  }
```

Function strdup() returns a copy of its string argument. It allocates the necessary memory on the heap. It is the responsibility of the calling function to deallocate the memory later. We compile the program and run it:

```
> gcc -g main2.c
> valgrind --tool=memcheck --leak-check=yes ./a.out
```

The actual error happens at the statement mystr1=mystr2 in line 8. The coding style suggests that mystr1 and mystr2 both have their individually allocated memory. This is true until line 8 is reached. Afterwards both variables point to the same memory location. However, the programmer did not consider that and so several errors occur subsequently.

The first problem occurs in line 13 when `mystr2` is printed. Since the memory was already deallocated in line 11, `mystr2` is now a pointer to freed memory. Accessing it in the `printf()` statement constitutes an invalid read access:

```
==11787== Invalid read of size 4
==11787==    at 0x1BA71903: strlen (in .../libc.so.6)
==11787==    by 0x1BA4BDAF: _IO_printf (in .../libc.so.6)
==11787==    by 0x8048554: main (main2.c:13)
==11787== Address 0x1BB26060 is 0 bytes inside a block
==11787== of size 5 free'd
==11787==    at 0x1B9040B1: free (in ...memcheck.so)
==11787==    by 0x8048541: main (main2.c:11)
```

Note that the memory debugger provides the location of the faulty statement (line 13) as well as the statement where the invalid memory location was previously deallocated (line 11).

The next bug in line 14 deallocates the memory to which `mystr2` points. This is illegal because this memory was already deallocated in line 11:

```
==11787== Invalid free() / delete / delete[]
==11787==    at 0x1B9040B1: free (in ...memcheck.so)
==11787==    by 0x8048562: main (main2.c:14)
==11787== Address 0x1BB26060 is 0 bytes inside a block
==11787== of size 5 free'd
==11787==    at 0x1B9040B1: free (in ...memcheck.so)
==11787==    by 0x8048541: main (main2.c:11)
```

Finally, there is a memory leak. Before the variable `mystr1` was altered in line 8, it used to point to its own memory allocated in line 6. This memory is never deallocated. Since there is no longer any pointer referring to the memory allocated in line 6, it becomes a leak:

```
==11787== 5 bytes in 1 blocks are definitely lost in
==11787== loss record 1 of 1
==11787==    at 0x1B903B7C: malloc (in ...memcheck.so)
==11787==    by 0x1BA7163F: strdup (in .../libc.so.6)
==11787==    by 0x8048504: main (main2.c:6)
```

Lessons learned:

- Memory debuggers take little effort to use.
- A memory debugger is the most efficient tool to detect memory leaks.
- A memory debugger can detect memory access errors: buffer overruns, incorrect array indexing, null pointer access.
- Memory debuggers can find uninitialized memory read errors before they cause unpredictable program behaviour.
- Use a memory debugger to detect incorrect use of memory management routines.
- Use a memory debugger if you use C-style strings and functions from `<string.h>`: `strdup()`, `strcpy()`.

4.5 Combining Memory and Source Code Debuggers

When the memory debugger reports an error, it gives context information, such as the call-chain (up to a certain length). This information may not be sufficient to understand why the bug occurs. Memory debuggers therefore provide hooks to source code debuggers such as GDB for a more in-depth analysis.

Let us try this in our example. The first error reported by Valgrind was an invalid write in line 9 of `main1.c`, `A[n] = n`. This statement is embedded into a for-loop, so the value of variable `n` is not immediately obvious and it would be helpful to query the value of `n` with a source code debugger.

In case of Valgrind, we can use option `--db-attach=yes` to attach a source code debugger. The option makes Valgrind stop the program execution at each reported error and each time asks the user whether to attach the source code debugger:

```
> valgrind --tool=memcheck --leak-check=yes \
  --db-attach=yes ./a.out
```

Once Valgrind stops and asks whether to attach the debugger, we confirm this and the debugger comes up. We then query the value of `n`, which turns out to be 100. The default debugger is GDB. The option `--db-command=<command>` lets you specify another debugger.

Purify has a similar concept by calling function `purify_stop_here()` immediately after an error has been reported. Start the source code debugger, set a breakpoint in `purify_stop_here()`, and run the program. The source code debugger will stop directly in the function that causes the memory error.

Insure++ has the same concept by calling the function `_Insure_trap_error()`.

Combining memory and source code debuggers

- If source code location and stack trace alone do not give enough hints, combine using a source code debugger along with a memory debugger.
- All good memory debuggers have APIs to attach a source code debugger when needed. Read the user guide to find out how.
- Use the source code debugger to inspect variable values and call debug functions.

4.6 Cutting Down the Noise – Suppressing Errors

Your memory debugger will have a mechanism to suppress error messages, by filtering them out of the generated report. This mechanism lets you write precise suppression rules. The rules follow a grammar, and can be generated either in an interactive tool, or entered as text in a *suppression file*. In most tools, you can filter by:

- Error type – Example: suppress all uninitialized-memory accesses
- Function call chain – Example: suppress all array-bound-write errors only if they occur in the call chain ...->A()->B()->C()
- Object or source file name

For example, in Purify, the suppression rules are stored in a .purify file in your home directory, or in the program's directory. The rules look as follows:

```
suppress UMR                # uninitialized memory reads, all
suppress ABW ...;A;B;C       # array bounds write, on call chain
suppress MLK "myleak.c"      # memory leaks, in file
```

Now, in theory it is a good idea to demand that your application and all its components are "Purify clean," or whatever equivalent term is used for your memory debugger. The best approach is to analyze each memory error, fix it, and repeat the process until there are no more errors.

In practice, this is often infeasible. Your application will contain operating system libraries, third-party libraries where no source code is available, or libraries where the developer is unwilling or unable to fix the reported memory errors. Such a library can generate an avalanche of thousands of error messages when run in a memory debugger. Sorting through a large number of error messages, to find the messages relevant to your code, is impractical. Also, if your error report always contains a few thousand messages, you will not be able to quickly detect if a new memory bug is introduced: the message will get lost in the noise. Therefore, most software projects create a suppression file for those error messages that are accepted as either harmless or unfixable.

However, do not automatically suppress all errors related to a third party library. There are good reasons to be alert. You may be using a library function in the wrong way. For example, you may be giving the wrong function arguments, or not adhering to the proper calling sequence. For some functions, you may have to allocate a buffer before the functions calls, for others, the function will allocate memory, but you may be responsible to deallocate the return argument, or to call a cleanup function. So, double-check each group of error messages before you filter them out.

Also, when using a suppression file, there is always the risk that you are filtering out legitimate error messages. At regular intervals, when you update libraries in your program, or when you switch to a new compiler or memory debugger version, rebuild your suppression file from scratch.

4.7 When to Use a Memory Debugger

Using memory debuggers throughout the software development process improves the software quality; many bugs will be caught before the software reaches the customer. At the same time, using memory debuggers takes little effort, as we have demonstrated. We recommend using memory debuggers on following occasions:

- When porting your software to a new operating system.
- When your program crashes.
- When beginning to debug a "strange" bug: When things have even a slight tendency to look like *"this is just not possible,"* *"what a weird stack trace,"* or *"we never had problems with this function."*
- As an integral part of your regression tests.

4.8 Restrictions

4.8.1 Prepare Test Cases with Good Code Coverage

A memory debugger is a tool for finding runtime bugs. You need to have very good *code coverage* in your test cases, since the tool can only detect a bug when the program executes the statement containing the bug.

4.8.2 Provide Additional Computer Resources

The use of a memory debugger is resource-intensive. The amount of dynamic memory used by the program increases significantly, due to book-keeping information added to each data structure. An increase by a factor of 2–4 is typical here. The book-keeping to check all memory access also increases the run time of the program, often by an order of magnitude. And finally, if the memory debugger is based on object code instrumentation, a large amount of disk space will be needed to cache system and program runtime libraries.

4.8.3 Multi-Threading May Not be Supported

Multi-threaded programs *may* confuse the memory debugger. A popular thread packages such as POSIX Threads will probably be supported, but less frequently used packages may cause problems.

4.8.4 Support for Non-standard Memory Handlers

Your program may contain its own low-level memory handler that defines functions such as `malloc()` and `free()`. Internally, this memory handler will probably make system calls to `sbrk()` or `mmap()` to receive blocks of memory from the OS.

There are three common reasons for a custom memory handler: better performance, and less space required, for a particular application domain. The third reason is that a module of the program is so broken or un-maintainable that memory cannot be safely deallocated with `free` or `delete`. Instead, once the module is done, the complete internal contents of the memory manager are deallocated in one step, without regard to any data structure that was allocated with the memory manager.

A memory debugger cannot detect that a non-standard memory handler is used, and will not reliably report memory leaks or access violations for data structures allocated with the new memory handler. However, the memory debugger usually has an API to register calls to the custom memory handler, to enable detection of memory leaks, buffer overruns, and uninitialized memory reads. Please refer to the documentation of Purify, Insure++, and Valgrind for more details.

Lessons learned:

- Use a suppression file to reduce the number of error messages from harmless or unfixable memory bugs.
- Memory debuggers are runtime tools: A bug can only be detected if the statement containing the bug is executed. You need test cases with good code coverage.
- Memory debuggers will significantly slow down program execution and increase memory usage.
- Some thread packages are incompatible to memory debuggers.
- Non-standard memory handlers can be integrated by using an API.

Chapter 5
Profiling Memory Use

This chapter is about memory profiling, i.e. debugging programs that consume too much memory. Excessive memory consumption can be due to either inefficient data structures, missing memory deallocation, or simply because of an incorrect estimate on how much memory the program will need. Excessive memory use can also increase the runtime of a program, by forcing the program to access main memory instead of the faster cache, and by overflowing the available main memory (*paging*), so this chapter augments Chapter 6 on how to find performance bugs.

5.1 Basic Strategy – The First Steps

We present a 4-step approach to memory profiling.

Step-by-step approach to memory profiling

- Step 1. Check that there are no major leaks.
- Step 2. Estimate the expected memory use.
- Step 3. Measure memory consumption over time, with multiple inputs.
- Step 4. Find the data structures that consume memory.

The first step is to check that there are no memory leaks as well as no memory corruption. It is unwise to do a systematic search of when and where in your program memory is consumed, if you can do a straightforward search with a memory leak checker instead. Use a tool such as Purify or Valgrind, as described in Chapter 4, and deallocate unneeded data structures at the earliest possible point in the program.

The second step, after checking for leaks, is to prepare a rough "back-of-the-envelope" estimate for the memory use of a program. The estimates will serve as a sanity check for later measurements.

In step three, find out when the memory is consumed and roughly where in the program flow this does happen. Measure how the overall memory consumption grows over time and how it correlates with the input data. Make sure to use meaningful input data for these measurements.

Finally, in step four, identify the statements and data structures that use the memory.

As part of this step-by-step approach to memory profiling, we discuss available tools, how to prepare the program with instrumentation code, and how to interpret the results. The chapter finishes with an example demonstrating the step-by-step approach.

5.2 Example 1: Allocating Arrays

As a first, and very simple example, we will use the program `testmalloc.c`. This program executes a loop, allocates a large array in dynamic memory, and then deallocates the array. The full source code is shown in Appendix C.1 and contains `#ifdef USE_NEW` statements to utilize either C++ `new`/`delete` or C `malloc()`/`free()` statements. We will use C++ `new`/`delete` statements throughout the chapter, by compiling the code with the flag −DUSE_NEW. These are the important statements after removing the `#ifdef` statements:

```
42   for(i=0; i<iterations; i++) {
43       wait_for_input("before malloc: ",...);
45       myarray = new int*[n];
49       for(j=0; j<n; j++)
51           myarray[j] = new int[blocksize];
56       wait_for_input("after malloc:  ",...);
57       for(j=0; j<n; j++)
59           delete [] myarray[j];
66       delete [] myarray;
70   }
```

The program has three arguments: when the first argument is set to `i`, then the program will wait before each memory allocation and deallocation step. The second argument, n, tells the program how many integer blocks of `blocksize=1024` should be allocated, and the third argument tells the program how many loop iterations should be done. All arrays are deallocated at the end of the iteration and are allocated again when the next iteration begins.

5.3 Step 1: Look for Leaks

The first step in the analysis of a program that is suspected using too much memory is to run a memory checker such as Purify, or Valgrind, as described in Chapter 4. If you find one or more memory leaks this way, you should fix the problem, or at least make an estimate to determine the amount of memory that is leaked. For most cases where a fix is not possible, such as a leak in a system library, the memory leak may be just a few bytes, and can safely be ignored. We ran program `testmalloc` through Valgrind and verified that there are no memory leaks.

5.4 Step 2: Set Your Expectations

We recommend preparing a rough "back-of-the-envelope" estimate for the memory use of a program as the next step. This should be done before instrumenting the software or using debugging tools to do actual measurements. Doing an estimate is a reality check, in case the later measurements show any surprise: it is possible that the measurement tools are working incorrectly, the instrumentation code is in the wrong place, or the program is consuming memory in an unexpected place. If the measured memory usage is significantly above the estimate, then there may be a bug in the way how the data is stored, or some redundant data is stored.

We realize that estimating memory usage may be hard to do in many cases: the program may be large, old, non-modular, or confusing. You can only estimate well if you have some knowledge what the program is doing, how it works internally, and which data structures are used. However, this knowledge is needed to do decent memory profiling. Usually, the estimate is obtained through an iterative process: an initial guess is made, by reviewing the problem specification, implementation specification, and the source code. This is followed by a set of measurements, to find the data structures that use up most of the memory.

What is the estimate for the `testmalloc` example? The memory usage depends almost completely on the second argument, n, that tells the program how many integer blocks of size `1024` to allocate. Each block allocates $1024 * 4$ bytes, so a value of $n = 100000$, for example, will allocate $100000 * 1024 * 4 = 409,600,000$ bytes or approximately 390.6 M bytes, where 1 M byte $= 1024 * 1024$ bytes.

There are other data structures in the example that need memory as well, namely the stack and the array `myarray` holding the pointers of the allocated blocks. However, they are small compared to the blocks themselves so we can ignore them.

5.5 Step 3: Measure Memory Consumption

In this section we will show how to measure the actual memory consumption of a program using the `testmalloc` program as an example. We will also show how memory consumption varies with the input values.

We are not only interested in the maximum amount of memory used by the program. During its execution, the program will go through multiple time intervals or phases. We are looking to correlate the program phases to memory allocation and deallocation, by making measurements at the phase boundaries. The measurements can be refined with a classical divide-and-conquer strategy, by looking for the phases with the most relevant increases or decreases in memory. Insert more measurement points in these phases to get close to the program location where the interesting memory allocation/deallocation behavior is.

5.5.1 Use Multiple Inputs

Before you can measure the memory use of a program, make sure that the program runs with relevant input data. There must have been some reason why it was deemed necessary to perform memory profiling in the first place, for example because the program *"runs OK for small input files but really bad for large files."* Make sure to use input data that stimulates the "really bad" behavior, otherwise all further activities will measure irrelevant data and you will focus on irrelevant parts of the program.

There will be some correlation between input data and memory consumption. We will explain the differences between logarithmic, linear, quadratic, or exponential growth in more detail on page 69 of Chapter 6. At the very least, make sure to use no less than three data samples. If you take just two samples, then you will not be able to distinguish linear from, for example, quadratic growth.

Once you have a reasonable understanding what the correlation between input data and memory consumption is, compare it to the estimates from step two. If there are major differences – for example quadratic or exponential growth rather than linear growth – then this knowledge will help to find the guilty program locations.

Further, you should keep notes about the memory measurements and check these against the initial estimates. The notes are important for multiple reasons: checking for measurement errors, having some evidence during a problem review, and, very important, to check later if a bug fix or software re-architecture actually improves memory use.

5.5.2 Stopping the Program at Regular Intervals

Finding the relevant (most memory consuming) location in the program flow is done by inserting stop points and measuring memory usage. How can one insert stop points?

The two easiest ways to observe the program at predetermined intervals are either to use breakpoints in the source level debugger, or to insert the following code fragment:

```
if(getenv("MEM_DEBUG")) {
  char c;
  printf("stage xxx\n");
  printf("hit return to continue\n");
```

```
    fflush(stdout);
    c = getchar();
}
```

If the environment variable MEM_DEBUG is set, then the program will stop and wait until you press the RETURN key. If the environment variable is not set, then the program runs as usual without the stop. To set the environment variable on UNIX, use the command setenv MEM_DEBUG 1 for csh, or MEM_DEBUG=1; export MEM_DEBUG for sh, bash. In Windows use **Control Panel / System / Advanced / Environment Variables** to set the environment variable.

It is of course up to you to select the program locations where the stop points can be inserted. Putting stop points at the begin of each major module is a good starting point. Next, use a divide-and-conquer strategy to locate the program sections that show the largest increase in memory use and add more stop points in those sections.

5.5.3 Measuring Memory Consumption with Simple Tools

We recommend initially measuring the overall memory usage with simple tools such as the UNIX utility top or the Windows Task Manager. There are more sophisticated tools such as memory profilers, as explained in Section 5.5.8 below, but they should not be used right away. The amount of data that they produce might be overwhelming at first and the data might also be misinterpreted. With a simple tool, you get one number, the overall amount of memory allocated by your program.

5.5.4 Use top

The simplest mechanism to display memory usage on a Linux or UNIX machines is to use the utility top. On a Windows machine either use the Task Manager (see below) or use the top command that is part of the Cygwin environment, well-hidden as a command in the package system/procps. To keep program outputs separate, you should run top in a shell that is separate from the program being observed. The relevant column is RSS, the size of the physical memory of a task, composed of code and data.

For the testmalloc example, we set the second argument to 100000. We already estimated that this results in the allocation of $100000 * 1024 * 4 = 409,600,000$ bytes or approx. 390.6 M bytes. Here is the output of the top command on our program testmalloc i 100000 8, before memory is being allocated:

```
> top
...
PID USER  PRI SIZE RSS SHARE STAT %CPU %MEM TIME CPU COMMAND
475 wloka 21  312  312   268 S     0.0  0.0 0:00   0 testmalloc
```

Here is the output after `malloc()` allocated $100000 * 1024 * 4$ bytes. The value in column RSS increases as estimated from 312 bytes to 391 M bytes:

```
PID USER  PRI SIZE RSS SHARE STAT %CPU %MEM TIME CPU COMMAND
475 wloka 16  391M 391M  300 S    4.0 15.6 0:00   1 testmalloc
```

Here is the output after `free()` released the dynamic memory:

```
PID USER  PRI SIZE RSS SHARE STAT %CPU %MEM TIME CPU COMMAND
475 wloka 16  488  488   300 S    0.0  0.0 0:00   1 testmalloc
```

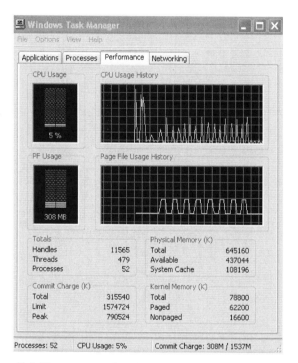

Fig. 5.1 Windows Task Manager output for `./testmalloc i 100000 8`

5.5.5 Use the Windows Task Manager

On Windows, an even simpler way than using `top` is to start the Task Manager program with Ctrl-Alt-Delete, click on the **Processes** tab, sort the processes alphabetically by clicking on **Image Name**, and then look at the column named **Mem Usage**. The memory usage will be given in K (kilobytes). To visualize the memory use over time, click on the **Performance** tab in Task Manager, and look at the

Page File Usage History graph. Figure 5.1 shows the output of running `./testmalloc i 100000 8` and hitting the return key every 5 seconds to advance the program. Note that the graph shows the memory consumed by *all* tasks on the computer, not only for `testmalloc` alone. The effect of `testmalloc` can only be seen clearly if the memory usage of all other tasks remains stable.

5.5.6 Select Relevant Input Values for `testmalloc`

The measurement is repeated with different input values. By reducing the number of blocks by factor of 10 to $n = 10000$ the memory consumption shrinks as expected to just 39 *M* bytes. On the other hand, increasing or decreasing the number of iterations has no effect on the peak memory usage. This is in line with the estimation.

We will from now on use input value $n = 100000$ and 8 iterations and can now be sure to trigger a "normal" behavior of the program. Virtually all of the allocated 391 *M* bytes have been allocated because of this value of *n*.

5.5.7 Determine how Memory is Deallocated on Your Machine

Before proceeding to discuss tools for measuring memory use, we need to point out that on some machines the deallocation of dynamic memory inside a program will not cause the program's process actually giving back the memory to the OS. This is dependent on the OS, compiler, and C/C++ runtime libraries that are installed on your machine. Table 5.5.7 lists how deallocation behaves on some typical development systems. The previous example was measured on machines that do release memory to the OS.

Table 5.1 Behavior of `free()` and `delete` on different OS platforms

Platform	Effect of free() / delete()
SunOS 5.8, GCC 3.3.2	memory not released to OS
Linux Red Hat Enterprise 3.0, GCC 3.3.2	memory released to OS
Linux Red Hat 7.2, GCC 3.3.2	memory released to OS
Suse 10.0, GCC 4.0	memory released to OS
Windows XP, VC++ 8.0 SP1 (.Net 2005)	memory released to OS
Windows XP, Cygwin 1.5.25, GCC 3.4.4	memory not released to OS

On some platforms you will observe that the memory used by the program stays constant at about 391 *M* after the first allocation of memory. The call to `free()`, and all subsequent calls to `malloc` and `free()` have no observable effect in `top`, you will continue to see the same result:

```
PID USER  PRI SIZE RSS SHARE STAT %CPU %MEM TIME CPU COMMAND
```

```
475 wloka 16   391M 391M  300 S     4.0 15.6 0:00   1 testmalloc
```

This behavior is not a bug, but a difference in how dynamic memory is implemented on each combination of operating system and compiler. When `malloc()` is called to allocate a memory element, the C or C++ runtime library will request a large block of memory from the operating system, the memory element is placed somewhere inside the memory block, and some book keeping is done to keep track of how much memory is allocated, and where the memory elements are. All subsequent calls to `malloc/free()` happen inside this large pre-allocated block of memory. If no more space inside this block is available, another system call to the OS is made to either extend the memory block, or to allocate another memory block.

The observed difference in the behavior of dynamic memory is due to the following choice of how to implement memory deallocation. Let us look at what happens after a call to `free()` creates a completely empty memory block, as the `testmalloc.c` example does:

One possibility is to give the memory block back to the operating system, so that it is available to other programs and users. This makes more efficient use of memory, but the system call to give back the memory block costs time. In the worst case scenario, repeated calls to `malloc/free()` right at the boundary of a memory block could cause a lot of system calls. Therefore, the alternative choice for handling the large memory blocks is to *not* give them back to the OS. This has the effect that the observed memory consumption of a program can only increase over the runtime of the program. For most programs, there is little practical difference on how dynamic memory deallocation is handled by the C runtime library. However, for a program that needs a lot of memory during startup, and then runs for a long time with very little memory, the overhead caused by the missing deallocation can be significant.

We recommend compiling and running the `testmalloc.c` program as a quick test on how memory deallocation is handled on your OS and compiler platform, so you will not draw false conclusions from the results of `top` and Task Manager.

Lessons learned:

- On some operating system/compiler combinations, releasing memory with `free()`/`delete` may not have an immediately visible effect. The memory reported by `top` does not shrink.
- If in doubt, use the program `testmalloc.c` to find out how memory is released on your operating system/compiler combination.

5.5.8 Use a Memory Profiler

The approach of using `top` for measuring memory consumption has the advantage of being simple to implement, and works if other tools are unavailable. However, adding the instrumentation code (for example code to make the program wait for a key stroke) and keeping manual notes is work intensive, especially if many different modules in the program use dynamic memory. It is convenient to reduce this manual work by using a tool for memory profiling.

Memory profilers are tools that do detailed book keeping of memory usage. Because most of these tool only watch dynamic memory allocated on the heap with `malloc()`/`new`, they are also called *heap profilers*. A memory profiler keeps records when a piece of dynamic memory is allocated, by whom (call stack) it was allocated, its size and when and by whom it was deallocated. After the program ends, the memory profiler outputs graphs and log files which reveal details about the memory usage and make it easy to locate the largest memory users.

A variety of tools is available and briefly described in Appendix B. On Windows, one can use the *AQtime* (Appendix B.5.4) performance and memory debugger. AQtime can be used standalone, or integrated into Visual Studio. On Linux, we recommend *Massif* (Appendix B.4.2), which is part of the Valgrind debugging and profiling tool suite. *mpatrol* (Appendix B.5.5) is available on both Windows and UNIX/Linux, is Open Source but has fewer capabilities.

We will use Massif for the rest of this chapter because its capabilities are representative of other memory profilers, it is Open Source, and has a simple use model. Usage of Massif is straightforward. No special compiler flags, recompiling, or re-linking of the program is required. The command is simply added on the command shell in front of the program to be executed. If you compile the program with the debug information flag `-g`, Massif will enable line references in the statistics output.

```
> valgrind --tool=massif ./testmalloc n 100000 8
```

The graph in Figure 5.2 shows the memory allocation and deallocation behavior of `testmalloc`. The graph is directly generated by Massif as a Postscript file. The program executes 8 loop iterations. In each iteration, a large number (100000) of integer arrays are allocated and then deallocated again, so the iterations are visible as 8 sharp spikes on the graph. Since the memory allocation is not done as one call to `malloc`, but rather as a sequence of 100000 calls, the spike has a distinctive slope. If the memory allocation were to be done in one call, the graph would look more like a square wave.

The text output of Massif provides you with information on how much memory was allocated. For each allocation Massif lists the call chain in form of function name and, if compiled with debug information, source file name and line number. We will discuss later in Section 5.7 how to use this Massif feature to measure memory consumption over data structures.

Here is the text output of Massif for the `testmalloc` program:

```
Command: testmalloc n 100000 8
```

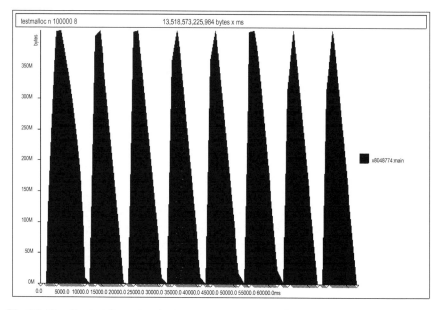

Fig. 5.2 Massif output for `valgrind --tool=massif ./testmalloc n 100000 8`

```
Heap allocation functions accounted for 88.8% of measured
spacetime

Called from:
  84.9% : 0x8048773: main (testmalloc.c:53)
   3.9% : 0x8048746: main (testmalloc.c:47)
...
```

The output of Massif shows that most memory (around 85%) is allocated from line 53, where the call to `malloc()` for the integer block of size 1024 is made. A smaller fraction of the memory is consumed in line 47, where the array of pointers to the memory blocks is allocated.

5.6 Step 4: Identifying Greedy Data Structures

The goal of step four is to find those data structures and code locations in the program that are most relevant to the overall memory consumption. There are at least two methods how to do a detailed analysis: instrumenting data structures, or using the memory profiler's output.

A memory profiler is convenient to use because no source code modifications are needed and it gives precise detailed feedback. However, it may give too much detailed data, by doing a dump of all memory allocation statements.

5.6.1 *Instrumenting Data Structures*

The other method to measure which statements allocate how much memory is to instrument the source code, specifically data structures. Add helper functions that keep track how often a data structure is used, how much memory it approximately needs, and, if possible, which statements are allocating the data structures. For example, you can add a method to a C++ class that gives an approximate value for the memory usage (including memory usage of members) of the class object. Another example is to count the number of active class objects, which can be accomplished by defining all new and delete operators of the class and incrementing/decrementing a static counter.

The testmalloc program is too simple to show any meaningful instrumentation code, so we will now explain the concept of data structure instrumentation on a more complex example, the genindex program.

5.7 **Putting it Together – The** genindex **Example**

The source code of the program can be found in the C++ file genindex.cc listed in Appendix C.2. The initial requirement of genindex was to read a text file, and to print out an index of words in the file. The index is a sorted list of unique words, where each word is followed by a comma-separated list of line numbers where the word occurs.

Just as in real life, genindex had a requirements specification that had features added during the development process. genindex started out as a simple UNIX filter program, which would open a text file, use a suspiciously simple state machine tokenizer to break the text into words, and store each word along with the current line number in the index data structure.

Over time, several requirements were added: first, to process multiple files at any one time, and second, after some problems debugging the tokenizer, a function was added to cross-check the generated index for correctness. Also, after some concerns about problems with dynamic memory leaks, plus well-founded distrust of do-it-yourself list and hash table data structures, the program was rewritten to use containers from the C++ Standard Library in order to implement the index data structure.

The program was then tested on a regression test database of sample input files, was checked for leaks and memory corruption with Purify as described in Chapter 4, and run through both gcc -Wall and the static analysis program Coverity, as described in Chapter 12. The program passed all tests. Still, something was wrong: the program ran quite slow, especially on large files, and also when many files were given as input. Initially, the problems were blamed on user impatience and old computer hardware, but then it was decided to do a quick analysis of the program.

We first iterate through the first 3 steps of our analysis strategy: making sure it is not a (big) leak, calculate expected usage, measure over time, and with multiple inputs. Then we focus in step 4 on the actual reason why we introduced this example, by instrumenting the code, and measuring which data structures and code locations are consuming the memory.

In the next 4 sections we will go through each step.

5.7.1 Check that There are No Major Leaks

The first step is to run the Purify tests again, which pass. This is not surprising, since the program uses data structures from the C++ Standard Library, has not a single `malloc()` or `new` inside, and thus does not show any obvious opportunity to create a memory leak.

5.7.2 Estimate the Expected Memory Use

The second step is to estimate memory usage. This is now not as easy as with the first example. The program needs to store an item in the index table for each unique word in the file. An item consists of the string for the word itself and a list of integers (the references to the location in the input file). Assuming a doubly-linked list, it needs $2 * size(pointer) + size(int) = 12$ bytes per list entry[1]. When the next word from the input file is processed, then there are two choices: if the word is already known, then just a new list entry is added to an existing item in the index table. That will cost 12 bytes. If the word is not yet known, then we need a new item to store the word itself and also a first list entry. That will cost also 12 bytes plus the string size of the word. The second choice needs more memory, so the worst case is when all words are unique.

Assuming that all words were to be 4 characters long and also unique, how much data is needed for an input file with n bytes? We need to store the text itself (n characters) plus the $n/4$ list entries (12 bytes each), altogether $n + 12 * (n/4) = 4 * n$ bytes. In addition to that, there is memory needed to store the words in a searchable way but the overhead for this single search table should be far less than the items themselves. Altogether, we estimate the amount of memory needed to a few times that of the input file.

The second important estimation is that the memory should not grow with the number of input files. The reason is that no data needs to be stored between processing of two files. The index is printed at the end of each file and all memory allocated so far should be released at that point. Only the names of the files will be stored throughout the entire runtime, however, that should be very small overhead compared to the memory needed to process a file.

---

[1] Our example assumes 32-bit pointers. 20 bytes are needed for 64-bit pointers.

5.7.3 Measure Memory Consumption

The next step is to measure the memory consumption over time and with different input files. We insert and call the wait_for_input() code to pause the program after each file was processed. The code is enabled by compiling with the PAUSE_INDEX option.

```
> g++ -g -DPAUSE_INDEX -o genindex genindex.cc
> ./genindex input1.txt input1.txt input1.txt input1.txt
```

The output of top (not shown) is 4.6 M bytes after reading the first file, followed by an increase of 2.3 M bytes for each additional file input1.txt of size 20 K bytes read, for a final total of 11.4 M bytes. The measured memory usage per file, 2.3 M bytes, is above the estimated value of 80 K for an input file of 20 K bytes. Furthermore, the measured memory usage grows with the number of files while the estimation says that it should stay flat. Both discrepancies indicate that something is wrong.

5.7.4 Find the Data Structures that Consume Memory

Next, we take a detailed look which data structures are using how much memory, first with Massif, then with instrumentation code. First, invoke Massif running genindex with four input files:

```
> g++ -g -o genindex genindex.cc
> valgrind --tool=massif \
  ./genindex input1.txt input1.txt input1.txt input1.txt >log
```

The graphical output is shown in Figure 5.3. Massif confirms that the program's memory use increases very quickly, and total memory use is more than 11 M bytes. The text output of Massif shows that most memory is used by the string data type:

```
Called from:
   93.0% : 0x3AA1F460: std::string::_Rep::_S_create(unsigned,
           unsigned, std::allocator<char> const&)
           (in /usr/lib/libstdc++.so.6.0.6)
```

In order to analyze which data structure is using the memory, we add instrumentation code to the program to estimate memory usage. To keep things simple, a method print_memory_stats() traverses the main data structure wordindex after each file is read. We use some very rough approximations to get a lower bound on memory usage: the size of an additional element to the index map is assumed to be just the payload, a pair consisting of a string, and a list of integers. The approximation ignores that inside the map usually a red-black tree data structure is created to enable fast searches for the key element. For the doubly-linked list container, we assume as before that each list element has an integer as payload plus two pointers.

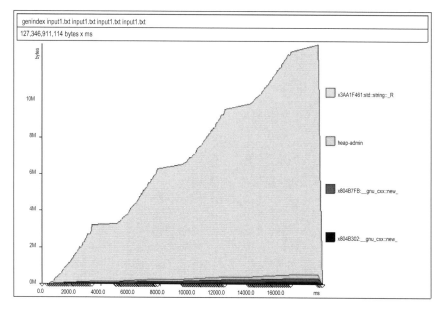

Fig. 5.3 Massif output for genindex: memory use increases very quickly, 2.3 *M* bytes per 20 *K* byte input file

The program produces the following debugging output:

```
-- memory size for index of 'input1.txt' file size=20016:
--      filename=14 wordindex=47211 lines=2340979 total=2388204
...
-- memory size for all data structures: 9552816 bytes
```

Most memory is consumed by the `lines` member variable that stores the lines of text in a file. This variable was added during development of the verification code to allow cross-checking of the index by the member function `verify_index()`. For a file of 20016 characters, 2.3 million bytes are needed for storage, which is unreasonable.

A code inspection reveals the following problem: The only code that actually writes to the `lines` data structure is in line 126, in `scan_file()`:

```
126                  lines.push_back(buffer);
```

Variable `buffer` is used to store the current input line, so it grows with each character that is read from the input file:

```
105  int FileIndexType::scan_file(char *fname) {
         ...
112      string buffer;
         ...
119      while(1) {
120          c = getc(fp);
```

```
121
122              if(c == EOF || c == '\n') {
123                    add_to_index(newword, current_line);
124                    newword = "";
125                    current_line++;
126                    lines.push_back(buffer);
                       ...
133              else if(c == ' ' || c == '\t' || c == '\r') {
                       ...
137                    buffer = buffer + (char) c;
138              }
139              else {
                       ...
141                    buffer = buffer + (char) c;
142              }
143              filesize++;
144        }
```

The reset of the `buffer` variable at the end of an input text line was forgotten, so it contains not only the current line but all previous lines as well. Worse, the memory size of the `lines` array will grow quadratically because each new element will contain all previous lines

Note how the error checking in `verify_index()` is not affected by the bug: for each word in the index, and each line number where the word is supposed to occur, the verification function still determines that the word is present in the line of text. The string search just may take a very long time to run.

The next step in debugging the memory consumption of `genindex` is to fix the bug, by resetting the buffer at the end of the line:

```
119        while(1) {
120             c = getc(fp);
121
122             if(c == EOF || c == '\n') {
123                    add_to_index(newword, current_line);
124                    newword = "";
125                    current_line++;
126                    lines.push_back(buffer);
                       ...
128                    buffer = "";   // <---- this is the bug fix
```

The bug fix is already prepared in the code listed in Appendix C.2 and we activate it by compiling with the `-DFIX_LINES` flag. Next, we re-analyze the instrumentation code with Massif. The output of Massif after the bug fix is shown in Figure 5.4.

```
> g++ -g -o genindex -DFIX_LINES genindex.cc
> ./genindex input1.txt input1.txt input1.txt input1.txt >log
-- memory size for index of 'input1.txt' file size=20016:
--      filename=14 wordindex=47211 lines=19318 total=66543
...
-- memory size for all data structures: 266172 bytes
```

We can see that memory use per file is now reasonable, about 200 *K* per file according to Massif, and about 68 *K* bytes according to our instrumentation function.

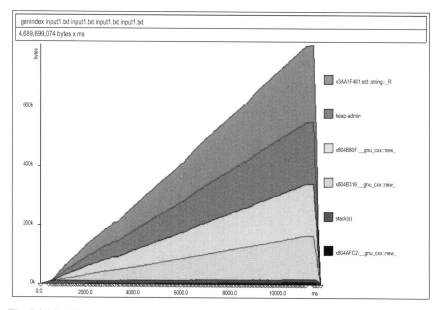

Fig. 5.4 Massif output for `genindex` compiled with `-DFIX_LINES`: memory use per file reduced to 200 *K*, but total memory use is still increasing

Note that we probably underestimated the overhead of the `map` data structure by a factor of three. Still, looking at the Massif graph in Figure 5.4, it is obvious that the program does not scale well: the memory increases for each file that is processed. A further code inspection shows the reason: the C++ object that is created for each file is kept around for the duration of the program's run time.

As a further modification, we rearrange the program's flow so that for each file, the index is created, verified, and output immediately. Then, the containers are cleared to free up the memory. The rearranged code is enabled by compiling with the `-DCLEAR_INDEX` flag.

```
> g++ -g -o genindex -DFIX_LINES -DCLEAR_INDEX genindex.cc
> ./genindex input1.txt input1.txt input1.txt input1.txt >log
-- memory size for index of '' file size=0:
--      filename=4 wordindex=0 lines=0 total=4
...
-- memory size for all data structures: 16 bytes
```

The output of Massif is shown in Figure 5.5. Note that we still keep adding elements to the index container, so we see a slight increase of memory usage over time in Massif. Since our instrumentation code measures just the payload, which got cleared, it is not accurate enough to measure this small increase. A further revision of the code would remove the array of `FileIndexType`, and keep reusing one variable of type `FileIndexType` as a storage unit.

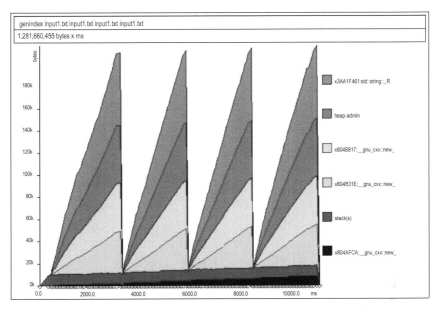

Fig. 5.5 Massif output for `genindex...` compiled with `-DFIX_LINES -DCLEAR_INDEX`: total memory use and memory use per file have been reduced.

Lessons learned:

- We used a 4-step approach to locate the memory bug:
  1. We first confirmed that there were no memory leaks (step 1).
  2. We estimated that we need roughly 80 K bytes memory for a sequence of input files with 20 K bytes each (step 2).
  3. The real memory usage (step 3) was way above the estimate, and also grew with the number of input files.
  4. The Massif memory profiler (step 4) pinpointed that variable `lines` used most memory. Code instrumentation confirmed this. A code review then revealed the real bug, which was a missing statement to reset a line buffer. After fixing the bug, real and estimated memory usage were close enough to be acceptable.

- A second round of measurements and code changes yielded further improvements.

Chapter 6
Solving Performance Problems

In this chapter, we discuss how to find bugs related to the runtime performance of a program. The most common case is that there is a program that simply runs too long, and we want to find out how to make the program run faster. In other cases, a program runs unexpectedly fast because there is a bug. For example, certain functions of a program may not be called, so the program runs really fast, but does not do what it is supposed to do.

We start by showing how to analyze a performance problem. We will discuss some general techniques that are independent of any debugging tool other than a simple clock on the wall, and the `time` command. Next, we describe tools for performance analysis, also called *profilers*, and apply them to an example. The chapter concludes with a section dealing with debugging I/O performance problems. Throughout the chapter, important lessons that can be applied to many other performance problems will be highlighted and discussed in detail.

6.1 Finding Performance Bugs – A Step-by-Step Approach

Some very sophisticated tools are available to a software developer for visualizing and analyzing the runtime behavior of a program. We will discuss some of these tools in the next sections. However, we have learned from experience that it is important to do some basic analysis up front, rather than solely rely on a particular tool.

> ### *Before starting a profiling tool, do an upfront analysis*
>
> - Step 1. Create a set of meaningful test cases of varying size. Make sure the program runs correctly: no crashes, correct output values are produced.
> - Step 2. Measure with a simple tool such as `/usr/bin/time` how runtime correlates to test case size. Make sure the program uses the correct algorithm.
> - Step 3. Select a test case that exposes the major runtime bottleneck. Proceed with a profiling tool to identify the cause of the bottleneck.

6.1.1 Do an Upfront Analysis

Doing an upfront analysis answers the following questions:

1. Do you have a test case to reproduce the performance problem?
2. Does the program compute the correct result?
3. Can you modify the test case to observe the effect of problem size, input data and environment?
4. Is the performance problem really caused by the program itself and not a side effect of something else, for example slow network, slow license server, or low memory (paging/swapping)?
5. Is the correct algorithm being used, appropriate to problem size and input data?

The advantages of doing an upfront analysis and having answers to questions 1–5 is that you will be reasonably certain that a bug exists and can be reproduced reliably with a test case. One possible reason for the bug is usage of the wrong algorithm. This may be revealed by analyzing how the run time increases with the input size. Another reason for the performance bug are implementation issues which are best found by using one of the performance measurement tools described in the following sections.

In order to complete the upfront analysis, the necessary tools are a piece of paper or a file to note down results, a simple method to measure time, and an environment to run the program, many times if necessary.

6.1.2 Use a Simple Method of Measuring Time

The most basic time measurement tool is a clock capable of displaying seconds. There are situations where some of the sophisticated tools described later either will not work, or need to be crosschecked in case of inaccuracies.

Convenient for use on a UNIX, Linux, or Windows computer with the Cygwin package installed is the `time` command. The command is usually located in `/bin` or `/usr/bin`, or built into the command shell. The `time` command is used by placing it in front of the program name:

```
> time <program> [<program_args...>]
```

The `time` command will run the program, and produces the following output:

```
9.179u 1.363s 0:10.89 96.6%
```

The first value `u` is the program's user CPU time, the second value `s` is the time spent in system calls, and the third value is the elapsed real time between program start and end. Please note that the exact output depends on the operating system and also which variant of the `time` command is used: the built-in `time` shell command of `sh`, `csh` and `/usr/bin/time` all use different formatting and ordering of the results. The option `-p` forces most but not all variants to use the same format.

For the measurement tables in this chapter, we will use the CPU time, since it measures the quantity of most interest: the time spend by the program in calculations. The effect of system calls does not play a role for this example. The real time value contains time spent on interruptions by other programs or when the program was waiting for something, for example user input, completion of a network transaction, memory to be paged back in, etc.

The example for the lessons discussed in this chapter is the `isort.c` program shown in Appendix C.3. The program contains two algorithms for sorting floating-point numbers, *insertion sort* and *Quicksort*.

6.1.3 Create a Test Case

Finding a problem is much easier if a test case is available that can be run repeatedly, on which experiments can be performed and which can be demonstrated to another person on a different machine and environment. If a test case is not available, then you risk spending a lot of effort on improving a code section that has no significant influence on the overall runtime. It may also happen that a reasonable-looking code change actually makes the program run slower.

In the `isort.c` example, there is a command line argument for selecting one of the two algorithms, an argument for defining how many numbers are to be sorted, and another argument to run the sorting algorithm for many iterations. There is also code for generating an array of random numbers that are to be sorted.

6.1.4 Make the Test Case Reproducible

In order to make the time measurements reproducible over all runs of the example, the random numbers always start from the same seed value, and the `isort.c` program thus always has the same input values. Without that, different runs will have different starting conditions (input values) and need different run times because sorting would be randomly more or less difficult. This would introduce some "noise" in the measurements. Measuring the effect of optimizations that cause a runtime improvement below this noise level requires averaging over a large number of test runs.

6.1.5 Check the Program for Correctness

A very common occurrence during development is that the program has a bug, and is computing the wrong data. For example, in the isort.c program assume that the condition at the top of the isort() function is written incorrectly:

```
if(n >= 1) return;
```

so that the program will run in constant time for all array sizes. The symptom in this case would obviously be that the numbers in the result array are not sorted. For this example, the solution is to invest the extra development time to write a separate function to verify that the numbers in the array result are sorted. You should proceed with performance analysis and optimization only when there is reasonable certainty that the program is running correctly.

6.1.6 Make the Test Case Scalable

A common mistake is to do a performance problem analysis, followed by code changes to speed up the program, all based on a single test case. The test setup should allow for multiple measurements. It is often possible to vary the parameters of a program, by changing the problem size, the input data, or the environment. Your test setup should support making these changes in a repeatable and reproducible way.

Having a scalable test case allows you to test at the correct operating point. In practice, you may have to choose completely different algorithms depending on problem size. For the example given, you should vary the size of the input array, to observe the effect of problem size on the sorting algorithm. We know from the literature on sorting algorithms that for small problem size $n \approx 10$, insertion sort is actually more efficient than Quicksort. Furthermore, Quicksort's performance, as implemented in our example, deteriorates when given partially sorted input arrays, so a mechanism to randomize the selection of the pivot element is usually added.

At the other end of the scale, it could be that n is so large that the array will not fit in the cache or main memory of the computer. In this case, you will see a massive decrease in runtime performance as parts of the array are swapped from main memory to virtual memory on a hard disk. One solution would be to change algorithms, so that the array is partitioned into pieces that do fit into main memory, sorting the pieces, and then merging the sorted pieces back into one sorted array.

6.1.7 Isolate the Test Case from Side Effects

Once you have created a set of reproducible test cases, we recommend to try out small, controlled changes, and to observe the influence on program runtime. It is important that you are able to reproduce experiments reliably so that you can be sure that the results depend only on the program itself and are not the side effect of something else. Here are examples how runtime measurements may be affected:

- Runtime is too short: make sure that the program runs for at least 5 seconds of user+system time, preferably a few minutes. If the program runs too short, then the inaccuracy of `time` command may dominate the measurement. We recommend to keep the runtime below 10 minutes. Run times longer than an hour make it very difficult to work with the test case.
- File I/O: In many cases, the program does some file I/O, for example printing some debug message to `stdout` or to a log file. Make sure to turn off as many print statements as possible. In the worst case, executing the print statements takes more time than the core functionality of the program. If so, then you will measure the speed of your disk or the drawing performance of your graphical user interface, and not the CPU time of your algorithm.
- System calls: if possible, avoid calling routines of the operating system during runtime measurements. This can be anything from calls to `getenv()` up to spawning other processes with `system()`, `exec()`, `fork()`, and so on. How long such an OS call will take is hard to predict and thus adds some uncertainty into the measurement.
- Not enough main memory: make sure that the machine where the program is run has plenty of free memory. If memory is low, then the operating system may temporarily move parts of the program's memory onto disk and later back (*paging, swapping*). This can indirectly affect the measured CPU time and certainly increases real runtime.
- Varying CPU clock speed: one example for a large effect that can completely confuse performance measurements is the ability of modern CPUs to automatically run at a lower clock speed, to reduce their heat output. You need to disable this feature, or at least run some monitor software, to ensure that the CPU speed was constant during the experiments. There may be other factors influencing performance that were not foreseen during program development.
- Other processes: Make sure that there are as few other users as possible (preferably none) on your computer when you measure runtime. As the load on the computer goes up, the reported real time will certainly increase. To make matters worse, the user and system runtime may also increase due to cache misses and memory swaps.

6.1.8 Measurement with `time` *can have Errors and Variations*

The time measurement on a computer can also have errors and variations. On modern operating systems, many programs are running at the same time on the same CPU, in a time-sliced way. Other user's programs, device drivers, services and (our favorite!) screen savers are all competing for time on the same CPU.

The `time` command will remove most of the effects of other programs by reporting time spent on the CPU, but it is important to note that this is not accurate: As the load on the computer goes up, cache misses and memory swaps will increase the runtime reported by `time`.

As a minimum safeguard, repeat each measurement at least 3 times, note the results, and check for variation. You can rule out system load as the cause for large measurement variations by removing users or tasks from the computer, or by running the measurements on a different system. In case you suspect network load to influence the measurements, you can remove the computer from the network or run experiments when there is less network traffic.

Lessons learned:

- Measuring runtime with `/usr/bin/time` or similar tools may have errors.
- The environment may have a significant effect on the program and can make measuring real runtime (wall-clock time) useless. Watch out for file I/O, system calls, low memory (swapping/paging), varying CPU clock speed or other processes that interfere.
- Do each measurement at least 3 times and check for variations.
- Select the test case such that the program runs for at least 5 seconds but less than 10 minutes.

6.1.9 Select a Test Case that Exposes the Runtime Bottleneck

Once you have good, scalable test cases and reliable data, measure how runtime and input/problem size correlate. Figure 6.1 shows a few typical cases. For many simple programs, the runtime is a linear function $O(n)$ of the size of the input data or problem size n, shown by curve A. Curve B shows a rapid increase of runtime, for example quadratic $O(n^2)$ or exponential growth $O(2^n)$, which is typical for some optimization problems. Curve **C** shows logarithmic growth, $O(log(n))$, typical for search algorithms. We expect each curve to have some constant offset, since the runtime will never completely go down to 0 even for the smallest test cases.

In the real world with real-life programs, the relation of runtime to input size can be more complicated. Measuring the correlation between input size and runtime may be difficult, and collecting each data point may require serious work. Even so, it is

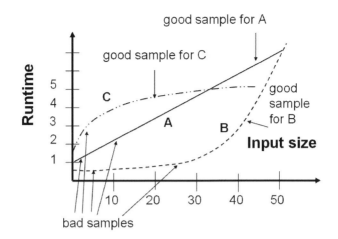

Fig. 6.1 Select a test case that exposes the runtime bottleneck well

worth the effort. If the program has even a slight tendency to look like the quadratic-growth curve B in Figure 6.1, then collecting more measurements with increasingly larger input sizes will reveal this. The point where the runtime starts increasing significantly is also the point where the program becomes being impractical. This is where the performance bug hits and is worth analyzing. A good test case (input data sample) for curve B is a test case where the runtime starts getting out of control but is still small enough to be handled by a profiling tool.

A tendency for the program's performance to behave like logarithmic curve C will also become evident with increasingly larger input sizes. If so, then a good test case (data sample) for profiling is where the curve starts looking more or less flat.

In case of linear growth (curve A), choose the test case for profiling such that the overall runtime is at least one order of magnitude above the constant amount of time that is needed to run the smallest test case.

If you do not know what kind of curve you are facing, then make sure always using at least three or more data samples. For the `isort.c` example, and for many other problems related to performance measurement, the following polemic generalizations hold:

- All programs run in constant time, if only one measurement is made.
- All programs show linear increase in runtime as a function of problem size (curve A), if one or two measurements are made.

Just imagine two arbitrary samples on curve B and then draw a straight line like curve A through them. If you have just these two samples, then there is no way to distinguish A, B, and C. The difference between both will become evident only if you have at least one more sample.

6.1.10 The Difference Between Algorithm and Implementation

Any reader familiar with the introductory chapters of a basic algorithm book, such as [Cormen01] and [Sedgewick01], will of course have detected why insertion sort was selected as an example to demonstrate the need for an up-front analysis of a performance problem: it is the wrong algorithm for reasonable problem sizes, that is, for sorting more than 10 numbers. However, a performance measurement tool will not tell you this. Rather, such a tool, plus step-by-step refinement, will suggest the following:

- Optimizing the `insert()` function to leave the for-loop early will give a 50% improvement.
- Inlining the `less()` and `swap()` functions will give an improvement.
- Inlining the `insert()` function and removing the recursion from `isort()`, by writing the algorithm as one function with two for-loops will show an improvement.
- Coding the `insert_sort()` function in assembly code or micro code will show an improvement.

The trick is that none of the improvements listed above will you give a satisfactory result. In order to see what is wrong with the insertion sort algorithm, you need to run some experiments with varying problem sizes.

Table 6.1 Runtime samples for insertion sort, runtime chosen too small

Program	command line arguments			user runtime
	algorithm	array size	#iterations	[s]
isort	i	100	1	0
isort	i	800	1	0

First, the program is run so that the input array of size 100 is sorted once. Table 6.1.10 shows the results. We can make two observations: the program completes too quickly for any reasonable time measurement, and it is possible that the test code loading random numbers into the input array influences the measurement. Therefore, the iterations argument, which is the number of times that the sorting will be repeated, is set to a "reasonable" size. In our example, a value of 10000 is selected, so that much more sorting than generating input numbers is done, and so that the program runs for at least some seconds on the PC. The value of 10000 is not a function of the example alone, but an outcome of the combination of example and computer used.

The results in Table 6.1.10 tell us that something is terribly wrong with the insertion sort algorithm: whenever the problem size increases by a factor of two, the runtime increases by a factor of four. By doing a calculation of the runtime complexity of insertion sort, or by referring to one of the above algorithm books, this is

Table 6.2 Runtime samples for insertion sort, runtime chosen correct

Program	command line arguments			user runtime
	algorithm	array size	#iterations	[s]
isort	i	100	10000	1.9
isort	i	200	10000	6.8
isort	i	400	10000	25.7
isort	i	800	10000	102

actually no surprise: the algorithmic complexity is $O(n^2)$, where n is the size of the array to be sorted.

No amount of tuning of this algorithm will help with the problem. The runtime will become prohibitively long for large arrays. The same algorithm books will show that the Quicksort algorithm has a much better complexity: $O(n \log(n))$, meaning that as the input array grows in size, sort times growing slightly worse than linear can be expected.

Using the q argument switches the isort.c program to use Quicksort. We increase the number of iterations by a factor of 10, to make the program run for at least a few seconds. The results are shown in Table 6.1.10.

Table 6.3 Runtime samples for Quicksort

Program	command line arguments			user runtime
	algorithm	array size	#iterations	[s]
isort	q	100	100000	3
isort	q	200	100000	6.2
isort	q	400	100000	15
isort	q	800	100000	33

Please note that the quicksort() implementation given in the example is by no means optimal. For the sake of simplicity and readability the following improvements were *not* done:

- Inlining the partition() function
- Inlining the swap() function
- Choosing the pivot element in partition() at random, to make sure the array to be sorted is partitioned into two parts of about equal size. In the given implementation, we use the last element of the array. This works fine for sorting random numbers, but results in $O(n^2)$ runtime performance for partially sorted arrays.

6.2 Using Profiling Tools

A profiler is a tool that will show you where a program spends its time during execution. Other common features of a profiler include listing the number of calls to each function in the program, and generating the distribution of calls and time to called functions and callers of each function. The resolution of measurement in a profiler ranges from functions (supported by all tools), to program blocks, lines, expressions down to individual machine instructions.

As we will show in the following sections, the feature set as well as the resolution and accuracy of a profiler varies, due to implementation decisions done by the developer of the profiling tool. We will give short introductions to `gprof`, Callgrind, and Quantify to let you "get up and running" on a small example. Furthermore, we give references to documentation in case you need more detail. We will focus on how to use a profiling tool in a systematic approach to finding performance bugs. We pay special attention to describing where each tool is accurate, and, more interestingly, where it is not accurate.

6.2.1 Do Not Write Your Own Profiler

One temptation for programmers is to ignore the sophisticated profiling tools described in the following sections, and to create their own profiler by manually inserting time measurement code in their application. Our general advice is *"don't do this"* unless there is commercial incentive to replicate most of the technology present in a typical profiler.

Homegrown approaches often use the system calls `time()` or `ctime()` to measure time. The problem with these system calls is that the cost of calling them is very high, and that their accuracy is low. As a good rule of thumb, do not use these system calls when you measure functions, program blocks, or time between events that take less than 0.1s to run.

The next problem with homegrown approaches is that a large amount of data is collected during profiling. Unless some effort goes into the design of the data structures that store the profiling data, the computational effort of storing the data and the memory traffic during storage, could be much larger than the computation and memory traffic of the program being profiled. The potential overhead and measurement inaccuracy rule out most practical uses for a homegrown profiler.

Get familiar with runtime profiling tools

- Do not write your own runtime profiler.
- Use a commercial or public domain profiler; there are plenty of them available. It takes some effort to understand their output formats, but this effort is well spent.

6.2.2 How Profilers Work

The goal of a profiling tool is to give a concise overview where the program spent its runtime and at the same time provide accurate and detailed data about specific functions or even individual statements. There are two core areas for the profiler: collecting data and presenting it.

6.2.2.1 Collecting Data

Profilers use different techniques to figure out where the runtime is spent. The main techniques are sampling and instrumentation.

Sampling has a straightforward approach: interrupt the program at regular time intervals (the *sampling interval*), look at the call stack and keep track of how often each function shows up at the top of the call stack. The more runtime a specific function needs, the more frequently will it show up at the top of the call stack. The benefits of sampling are a relatively small program slow-down and that it can work without the need to modify the program. The main penalty is an inherent inaccuracy. Because the samples are taken at certain wall-clock times, small variations in the program speed, for example due to cache misses, mean that the samples are taken at different program locations each time that you run the program again. The reported results may thus have a variance, especially for functions that need only a small fraction of the overall runtime and therefore show up in only few samples. If you want to profile a certain part of the program by sampling, then make sure that the total runtime of that part is at least two orders of magnitude above the sampling interval of the profiler.

The second technique used by profilers is *instrumentation*. Extra statements are inserted into the program that keep track how often a function is called and by whom. Instrumentation can be added during compilation (gprof, gcc flag -pg), during linking (Purify, VTune), or during emulation of the executable (Callgrind). The inside of the function may also be instrumented, for example to account for each basic block. A basic block is a sequence of statements without any conditional or jump statement in them. The execution time for a basic block never varies and can be computed statically (if we disregard cache effects). The overall execution time of the program can be found by multiplying the number of clock cycles for each basic block with the corresponding number of executions. The main benefit of instrumentation is accuracy up to the level of CPU cycles. The main penalty is a higher slow-down compared to sampling.

6.2.2.2 Presenting Data

A profiler will collect a large amount of data and finally needs to present it in a form that is both suitable to get an overview as well as to get detailed feedback about specific functions. Different profilers are more or less successful to present the data in an intuitive form.

One aspect that is always presented is the *flat profile*, which shows how much runtime each function used for itself. Another aspect is the *call graph*, which shows how functions call each other and how often did this happen. The key is to combine both. For example, the flat profile may reveal that 75% of the runtime is spend in function `strcmp()` and the call graph that 95,000 out of 100,000 calls to `strcmp()` come from `func1()`. That makes it clear that it will be worth looking into `func1()`. We will explain the flat profile and call graph in more detail based on `gprof` in the next section.

6.2.3 Familiarize Yourself with `gprof`

The GNU profiler `gprof` is a tool that measures how much time is spent in each function of a program and how many times a function is called from other functions. In addition, it is possible to see the time spent in each basic block of a program, if the program is compiled with the debug information (`gcc` option `-g`). The use of `gprof` requires three separate steps:

1. Compile and link the program with the `-pg` flag
2. Run the program; the profile data will be written into a file called `gmon.out`
3. Generate a profile report, by running the command
   `gprof <program> gmon.out`

As a first step, we compile the source files of a program with the `-pg` compiler flag. This will insert special instructions into the generated object code of each function. Whenever the function is called, a record is generated with a pair of data items: the function and its caller.

In the second step (running the program), a mechanism inserted at program startup will record at regular time intervals in which function the program counter currently is.

During the third step, the collected profiling data is ordered, and statistics are computed, as we will show in the following paragraphs. Further details on options to the `gprof` program are available in the `gprof` documentation. There are options to change the format and type of the data that is reported.

Some details of `gprof`'s implementation are helpful in order to understand the advantages as well as the shortcomings and inaccuracies of the tool. A description of the implementation of `gprof` can be found in the `gprof` documentation, under the *Details of Profiling/Implementation* section. Please check Appendix B.5.1 on where to find `gprof`-related information on the web.

Among the advantages of `gprof` are that it is easy to implement on new machine architectures and therefore is available on most platforms that you are likely to encounter. It is easy to restrict the scope of the profiling, by only using the `-pg` compile flag on those files you are interested in.

A drawback is that `gprof` does not profile time spend inside calls to the operating system and may be unable to handle shared libraries (`lib*.so`). Yet another drawback, shared by all profiling tools, is that the inserted profiling code introduces a significant slowdown. For the `isort.c` example running on a 2 GHz CPU under Linux and GCC 3.X, we observed a slowdown by a factor of four. While significant, other tools such as Quantify or Valgrind may cause even more slowdown.

In addition, the sampling approach is not fully accurate: `gprof` does not measure the exact time spent in a function, but rather records in which function the program counter is at regular intervals. These time intervals are much larger than the duration of a single CPU instruction in order to reduce the time spent on measuring and to reduce the amount of collected data. Furthermore, `gprof` has to guess the distribution of a function's time to its callers. This is a significant limitation.

6.2.3.1 Be Aware of `gprof`'s Measurement Errors

As general advice, we recommend that you make sure that the profiling data is generated during a representative and meaningful test run. This includes preparing a proper set of input data, and giving the program correct arguments. Since `gprof` is using a sampling-based approach, the measurement error depends on the total time spent in a particular function, not on the time it takes to execute a function once. This is very important, since functions with a small runtime can be analyzed with a high precision if they are executed sufficiently often. Conversely, functions with larger run times can have a large error if they are executed infrequently. In practice, you should set up the test case so that the minimum runtime is at least 5 seconds.

In some cases, it is necessary to increase the runtime of the `gprof`-instrumented program, so that the runtime of each relevant part of the software is at least two orders of magnitude above the sampling interval of the profiler. In the `isort.c` example, the sorting algorithm is repeated for many thousands of times on the same input data.

6.2.3.2 Flat Profile

As an example, here is how `gprof` is used to profile the `isort.c` program:

```
> gcc -o isort -pg isort.c
> ./isort i 100 100000
> gprof isort gmon.out >report.txt
```

The first important data in the `gprof` report is the flat profile at the top of the report file, shown in Figure 6.2. Keep in mind that the main program will run the insertion sort function 100000 times, on an array containing 100 samples. Also note that `gprof` does not count the recursive calls of the `isort()` functions to itself.

The total runtime of 33.64 seconds is four orders of magnitude above the sampling interval of 0.00195312 seconds, so our recommendation to have at least two orders of magnitude is well fulfilled.

```
Each sample counts as 0.00195312 seconds.
%   cumulative   self              self     total
time   seconds  seconds     calls ns/call   ns/call name
66.79    22.47    22.47 495000000   45.40     45.40 less
25.56    31.07     8.60   9900000  868.45   3356.02 insert_value
 6.41    33.22     2.16 219300000    9.83      9.83 swap
 1.03    33.57     0.35    100000 3476.56 335722.66 isort
 0.21    33.64     0.07                              main
```

Fig. 6.2 gprof flat profile of `isort.c`

The functions in Figure 6.2 are sorted by the third column (`self seconds`), the time spent in the function itself. The fourth column (`calls`) gives the number of calls to the function. The sixth column (`total ns/call`) gives the average time spent per call in this function and all of its descendants; it is the only field in this table where the call graph data is used. All other columns are less useful, and contain no new information, just different ways of presenting the same data.

Note the first line of Figure 6.2 where the time between samples is given. It is important to remember that all reported measurements in column 3 that are of similar magnitude or smaller than the sampling time are inherently unreliable.

Figure 6.3 shows the flat profile table after modifying the `insert_value()` function to take advantage of the fact that the elements from 1 to $n-1$ are already sorted. The function exits after finding the first pair of elements $i, i-1$ that does not have to be swapped. As the report shows, the runtime is reduced since there are fewer calls to the `less()` function in the for-loop of `insert_value()`.

```
Each sample counts as 0.00195312 seconds.
%   cumulative   self              self     total
time   seconds  seconds     calls ns/call   ns/call name
62.07    10.27    10.27 229000000   44.86     44.86 less
22.96    14.07     3.80   9900000  383.92   1626.03 insert_value
12.23    16.10     2.02 219300000    9.23      9.23 swap
 1.94    16.42     0.32    100000 3203.12 164179.69 isort
 0.80    16.55     0.13                              main
```

Fig. 6.3 gprof flat profile of `isort.c`, after speeding up `insert_value()`

6.2.3.3 Call Graph

The second table of interest in the report generated by gprof is the call graph. Figure 6.4 shows the call graph for the unmodified function `insert_value()`. The output format may at first feel a bit cryptic to read and needs some practice getting used to. Alternative tools with a graphical front-end such as Quantify tend to present that data in a form that is easier to read, however they all present the same

```
granularity:
each sample hit covers 4 byte(s) for 0.01% of 33.64 seconds

index %time  self children    called       name
                                               <spontaneous>
[1] 100.0   0.07 33.57                       main                    [1]
            0.35 33.22 100000/100000            isort               [2]
-----------------------------------------------
                       9900000                 isort               [2]
            0.35 33.22 100000/100000            main                [1]
[2]  99.8   0.35 33.22 100000+9900000     isort                    [2]
            8.60 24.63 9900000/9900000         insert_value        [3]
                       9900000                 isort               [2]
-----------------------------------------------
            8.60 24.63 9900000/9900000         isort               [2]
[3]  98.8   8.60 24.63 9900000            insert_value             [3]
           22.47  0.00 495000000/495000000  less                  [4]
            2.16  0.00 219300000/219300000  swap                  [5]
-----------------------------------------------
           22.47  0.00 495000000/495000000  insert_value         [3]
[4]  66.8  22.47  0.00 495000000            less                  [4]
-----------------------------------------------
            2.16  0.00 219300000/219300000  insert_value         [3]
[5]   6.4   2.16  0.00 219300000            swap                  [5]
```

Fig. 6.4 gprof call graph of isort.c

data: which function called which other function, how often did that happen, and how much time was spent for the calls.

The gprof call graph is organized in blocks separated by dashed lines. Each block deals with one function and reveals who called the function and how often the function was called. The block will also reveal the amount of time spent in the function itself (*self time*), which sub-functions were called and how much time was spent within these sub-function calls (*descendant time*). Blocks are sorted by accumulated (*self+descendant*) time. Functions that need most runtime for themselves or their descendants show up first. Function main is usually at the top.

Let us explain the format by looking at the second block dealing with function isort. The line starting with a square bracket and index number on the far left ([2]...isort [2]) is the function itself. Lines above the square bracket are functions that made a call to isort, which in this example are main and isort. The call graph also contains information how often function calls occurred. We can see that the main function called isort 100000 times and that isort called itself recursively for another 9900000 times. Lines below [2]...isort [2] are descendants called by isort. We can see that isort calls itself recursively and also calls insert_value.

The function call counts are given as a pair of numbers in the format <num of calls from this function/total number of calls>. In the example, 9900000/9900000 for isort calling insert_value means that there were 9900000 calls altogether. From those, 9900000, or all of them, came from `isort`.

The graph data contains the number of function calls and how much time was needed for all calls together. Looking into the forth block dealing with `less`, we can see that the function needed 22.47 seconds or 66.8% of the overall runtime. It was exclusively called by `insert_value` and (at average) each call to `insert_value` resulted in approximately 50 calls to `less`.

Keep in mind that `gprof` guesses the distribution of a function's total time to its callers. The distribution of *calls* is accurate but the distribution of *runtime* is just a guess by assuming that all calls need the same amount of runtime. If this assumption is not true, then the data presented in `total ns/call` will be incorrect and, worse, the call graph may be misleading as to where runtime is spend.

Lessons learned:

- The *flat profile* shows for each function how often it was called and how much CPU time it used altogether.
- The *call graph* explains how functions call each other and how often it happened.
- The key is to combine both: look into the flat profile to find where all the time was spend and analyze the call graph to understand why that happened.

6.2.3.4 What if Some Libraries are Not Compiled with `-pg`?

If possible, compile *all* source files with compiler flag `-pg`. However, this is not always possible, for example, when third-party libraries are available only as object files. `gprof` is able to handle this situation to some extend. The good news is that the flat profile remains available, with two caveats:

- The fields `calls`, `self ns/call`, and `total ns/call` remain empty for all functions that were compiled without `-pg` flag. The total number of calls is not known. The `self seconds` field will contain useful information.
- Functions compiled without `-pg` do not incur any runtime overhead caused by `gprof`. Because `gprof` is not able to remove that overhead when reporting results, functions compiled without `-pg` appear to run faster than functions compiled with `-pg` even if they really have identical run times.

The bad news is that the call graph is becoming more incomplete and less trustworthy with each function that is compiled without `-pg`. Book keeping about which-function-called-whom is no longer fully possible. Callers of functions compiled without `-pg` are reported as `<spontaneous>`. Child functions compiled without `-pg` disappear in the list of children altogether with no hint that they even exist. As a result, it is very difficult if not impossible to get a conclusive insight where the run time is really being spent.

Lessons learned:

- When using `gprof`, make sure to compile *all* source files with compiler flag −pg.
- Check the flat profile if significant fractions of runtime was spent in functions compiled without compiler flag −pg. If so, be cautious when interpreting the call graph because it can be misleading.

6.2.4 Familiarize Yourself with Quantify

Quantify is a very powerful commercial profiling tool sold by IBM as part of their IBM Rational family of software quality tools. Please check Appendix B.5.2 for more information on documentation and how to obtain the software.

Quantify's biggest advantages over `gprof` are an easy-to-use graphical user interface that gives you multiple ways of looking at the measured profiling data, and a time measurement and recording method that offers higher accuracy. Quantify works by inserting measurement instructions into the object code, to count instructions and the number of cycles each instruction takes. This gives us more precise and reproducible data than the `gprof` method of sampling the program counter at regular intervals. Another advantage is that Quantify records for each function call the time spent in the function together with what the calling function actually was. In practice, this is perhaps the most significant difference to `gprof`: the ability to show accurately the distribution of time in a function to both callers and called functions.

One drawback of Quantify is that the real execution time is considerably increased due to the inserted code. In the example that we will use below, the runtime was increased by a factor of 50. Because no sampling at random time is involved, the results of Quantify do not depend on long measurement periods. We can reduce the overall program runtime to achieve the same accuracy, and thus compensate for some of the runtime overhead of Quantify.

To use Quantify, you need to do the following steps:

1. Add `quantify` to the link command of the program.
2. Run the program. A graphical user interface will pop up and reveal collected data once the program has ended.

The `isort.c` example is used again:

```
> quantify cc -o isort isort.c
> ./isort i 100 10000
```

Quantify will insert profiling code into all object files and libraries that make up the program, including all OS and C++ runtime libraries. It is not necessary to have source code files available. Thus, Quantify is convenient when it is necessary to do a performance analysis on programs where source code is not readily available for all libraries. We recommend the following settings when using the Quantify GUI:

- Ignore the **Call Graph** display.
- In the **Function List** window, set the **Display data** option to **Function+descendants**. Also, set the **View/Scale Factors** to **seconds**.

The **Function List** will show how much time is spent in each function. Here is the Quantify **Function List** data for the example program:

```
0.59    main
0.59    isort
0.58    insert_value
0.20    less
0.13    swap
```

Click on the insert_value() item in function list, the **Function Detail** window will pop up. The contents of the **Function Detail** window are shown in Figure 6.5. Data will be displayed to show how many times insert_value() was called, and how much time was spent in the function. Furthermore, very conveniently, it is shown how many times insert_value() calls each of the descendant functions swap() and less(), and the callers of insert_value() and the frequency of calls to this function are shown. In this example there is only one caller to insert_value(), the isort() function.

```
Function name:                  insert_value
Called:                         990000 times
Function time:                  0.25 secs (41.84% of .root.)
Function+descendants time:      0.58 secs (98.60% of .root.)

Distribution to callers:
990000 times   isort

Contributions from descendants:
49500000 times (35.09%)   less
22870000 times (22.48%)   swap
```

Fig. 6.5 Quantify Function Detail of isort.c

Quantify will save the profiling data in a file with .qv extension. You can display the profiling data at a later time without having to rerun the program, by running

```
> quantify -view <file>.qv
```

6.2.5 *Familiarize Yourself with Callgrind*

Callgrind (see Appendix B.4.2) is part of the Valgrind debugging and profiling tool suite and can collect precise runtime data and callgraph information. To use Callgrind, you need to do the following steps:

1. Run the program with Callgrind. The profile data will be written into a file called `callgrind.out.<id>`.
2. Generate a profile report, by running the command `callgrind_annotate callgrind.out.<id>` or view the results with the graphical front-end KCachegrind (see Appendix B.4.3).

Note that it is not necessary to compile the program with specific flags or tools. Callgrind works with the existing executable, which is a very convenient use model.

The `isort.c` program is used again as an example. Note that the output from callgrind_annotate has been slightly modified, all lines and strings with little relevance have been removed. The results are reported in clock cycles:

```
> gcc -o isort -O isort.c
> valgrind --tool=callgrind ./isort i 100 10000
> callgrind_annotate callgrind.out.31612
  919,788,380  PROGRAM TOTALS
  545,100,000  insert_value
  198,000,000  less
  153,510,000  swap
   16,770,000  isort'2
```

Measurement results are reproducible because they are computed based on the Valgrind engine emulating the processor. No sampling at random time is involved. Just like Quantify, this allows us to reduce the measurement period to achieve the same accuracy and compensate the runtime overhead. The slowdown introduced by Callgrind is a factor of 40 for this example, a considerable drawback, and much higher than the slowdown introduced by `gprof`, which was only four.

Option `--tree=both` will also show the callgraph by listing for each function the callers and callees. Option `--auto=yes` prints annotated source files for files that were compiled with debug information.

Callgrind has some useful APIs, to get basic data, and to enable the profiling only in areas of special interest. This reduces the slowdown in areas that are of no interest. While one can read the callgraph in its textual form, it is usually much easier to view it with the graphical front-end, KCachegrind:

```
> kcachegrind callgrind.out.31612
```

Figure 6.6 shows the snapshot of KCachegrind. The two windows on the right-hand side can be configured to show the list of callers, list of callees, the call graph or a graphical distribution of CPU time across functions.

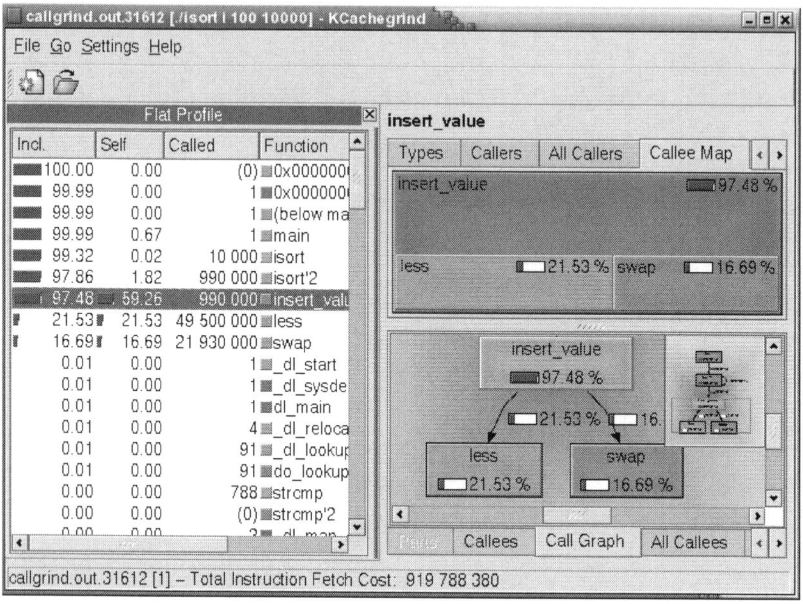

Fig. 6.6 Callgrind profile data of isort, displayed with KCachegrind front-end

6.2.6 Familiarize Yourself with VTune

Intel VTune (see Appendix B.5.3) is a commercial profiler for x86 and x64 CPUs, and is available on Windows and Linux. VTune has two modes: sampling, which is similar to gprof, and call graph, which is similar to Quantify. To use VTune on Windows, you need to do the following:

1. Start VTune.
2. In the **Easy Start** wizard, select **New Project**. then select **Sampling Wizard** or **Call Graph Wizard**.
3. Select **Windows...profiling**.
4. Enter the name of the application in **Application to Launch:**, and enter the command line arguments in the **Command Line Arguments** field.
5. Keep all other profiling options at default. Check the documentation, there are a large number of measurement options.
6. Vtune will automatically run your program after the wizard completes.

We pick the **Sampling Wizard** first. The isort.c program is used again as an example. We will run with command line options i 100 100000. Build isort in debug mode, and run it with VTune as described above. Once the program is done, VTune will show you a window with all processes active at runtime. Select Process isort.exe, and then click on the button **Drill Down to new Window**. The button is hard to find, and there is unfortunately no menu item. Keep on selecting **isort.exe** process, and click the **Drill down...** button until you see the functions inside `isort.exe` displayed. Vtune in sampling mode give us statistics for *CPU samples* and *percentage spent in each function*:

```
Name           CPU%
less           52.29%
swap           31.57%
insert_value   11.99%
isort           1.09%
main            0.35%
```

Note that VTune in sampling mode does not record the number of function calls, or the time that one function spends in calling another function. To measure this, we need to use the call graph mode.

Repeat the exercise, this time with the **Call Graph Wizard**. Note that to use the call graph feature, `isort.exe` needs to be build with debugging enabled, and the linker needs an option to generate relocatable code. Here are the command line options; they can also be entered into the Visual Studio project configuration.

```
> export LINK=/fixed:no
> cl -o isort isort.c /Zi
```

Figure 6.7 shows VTune after the program is done. The top window on the right shows the runtime statistics for each function The lower window on the right shows the call graph. Both windows were adjusted to show just the functions inside `main` and descendants. VTune in call graph mode gives us statistics for *number of calls*, *self time in function*, and *total time in function*.

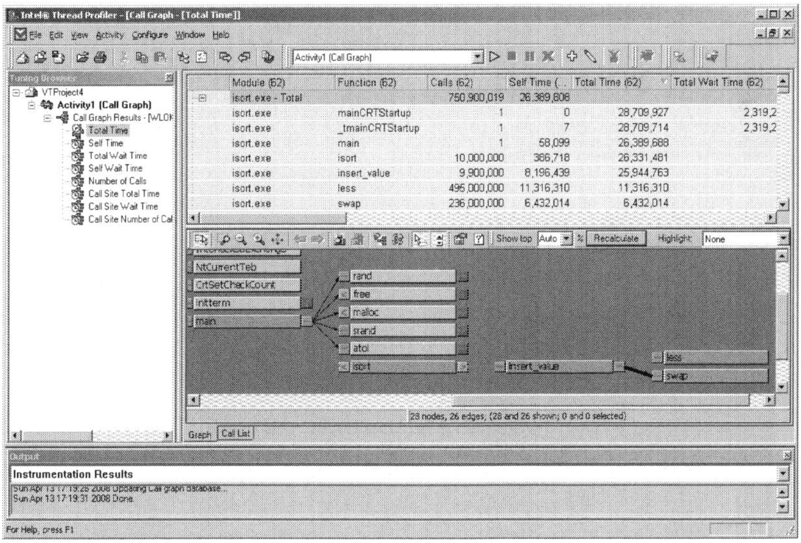

Fig. 6.7 VTune profile data of `isort.c`, Call Graph mode

83

Lessons learned:

- There are different approaches how a profiler can collect data. They vary in terms of setup, accuracy, reproducibility and runtime overhead.
- *Sampling*: interrupt the program at regular intervals and analyze the call stack. Simple setup, low overhead, but not very accurate and not well reproducible (reported numbers vary from one run to the next). This technique is used by `gprof` and VTune in sampling mode.
- *Instrumenting object files*: more complicated setup, high runtime overhead (multiple 10x slowdown), high accuracy, reproducible numbers. This technique is used by Quantify and VTune in call graph mode.
- *Instrumentation during emulation of the CPU*: simple setup, high runtime overhead (multiple 10x slowdown), high accuracy, reproducible numbers. This technique is used by Callgrind.

6.3 Analyzing I/O Performance

In this section, we show how to analyze performance problems caused by incorrect or inefficient I/O (read/write) operations to external memory systems. These memory systems can be hard disk drives, USB memory sticks, flash memory, CD ROM drives, and network file servers. The properties shared by these devices is that they provide permanent storage of large amounts of data, at several orders of magnitude lower data access speeds than the registers, cache and main memory of a computer.

We will use a simple example for a step-by-step approach. Please refer to the `filebug.c` program given in Appendix C.4. When called as follows:

```
./filebug s xxx.log 2000000
```

the program will write 2000000 characters to the file `xxx.log`, using the buffered I/O functions `fopen()`, `fclose()`, and `fputc()`. The s argument circumvents the built-in buffering, by calling the `fflush()` function after each character, thus causing separate system calls and I/O operations to disk for each individual character.

The example obviously is simple enough that the unnecessary call to `fflush()` will be caught by a code review. However, keep in mind that in practice such code will be well hidden in a large software program, so a systematic approach is needed to locate and isolate the problem.

The first step to do is a measurement with the `time` command:

```
> time ./filebug s xxx.log 200000000
73.724u 444.128s 8:40.78 99.4%
```

We make two observations from this measurement: First, only 14% (73.7s) of the total runtime ($73.7 + 444.1 = 517.8$s) is spent inside the user process, the rest is system call time. This is a marked difference to the time results measured for the isort.c example, which only did computations, but no I/O.

6.3.1 Do a Sanity Check of Your Measurements

Second, a rough sanity-check calculation shows that the test program wrote 200 million characters in 520 seconds, or 0.38 MB/s. The computers available at the time of writing this book were capable of 10-100X faster disk I/O, so something is suspicious with this data rate. Further investigation shows that the location of the file xxx.log is on a remote file server, connected to the computer by a network.

To rule out the effect of either low network bandwidth or low file server performance, we rerun the experiment on a different computer with a local disk, where a separate disk benchmark tool claimed a maximum transfer rate of 40MB/s. The result is 451s real time. This is a slight improvement but at 0.46 MB/s still below expectations.

```
Function+descendants time (secs)
4.77    main
4.70    fflush
0.05    fputc
0.00    fopen
0.00    fclose
```

Fig. 6.8 Quantify Function List of I/O performance example

The next step is to rerun the experiment and look inside the program with a profiler. As was stated above, the gprof profiler does not instrument system calls, and is therefore not a good tool to investigate I/O problems. Therefore, we use Quantify next. Since Quantify is known to slow down the program, the size of the output file is reduced by a factor of 100, to 2 million, to make the test case more manageable, and to get a result quickly. The **Function List** view of the data is shown in Figure 6.8. We can already see that most of the program execution time is spent in fflush().

To get additional data about the number of function calls, the **Function Detail** display is shown in Figure 6.9. This confirms that the program contains code to call fflush() with the same frequency as fputc(), so the program does a buffer flush for every character, and that the cost for doing this is very high.

We change the code so that fflush() is no longer called. This is conveniently done in the example program simply by passing f instead of s as the first command line argument. Then, and this is important, the experiments are rerun to verify that the code change does have the intended effect of speeding up the program. For the filebug.c example, rerunning the first experiment, using the network disk, gives:

```
> time filebug f xxx.log 200000000
9.179u 1.363s 0:10.89 96.6%
```

```
Function name:                     main
Distribution to callers:
1 time    __libc_start_main
Contributions from descendants:
2000000 times (98.64%)   fflush
2000000 times ( 1.07%)   fputc
      1 time ( 0.06%)   fopen
      1 time ( 0.01%)   fclose
```

Fig. 6.9 Quantify Function Detail of I/O performance example

This is a 47x speedup for the measured real time, and translates to a disk transfer rate of 18.2MB/s. The experiment is also rerun on the computer with the local disk, where the experiment runs in 24s real time, which translates to a speedup of 19x. The experiment is then rerun inside the Quantify profiler, where it can be seen that the total time spent by the program is much smaller, and most of it is spent inside fputc(), as can be seen in Figure 6.10.

```
Function+descendants time (secs)
0.08    main
0.07    fputc
0.00    fopen
0.00    fclose
```

Fig. 6.10 Quantify Function List of I/O performance example, after removing fflush()

For our small example, there are no further changes needed, but in a large application program, there are usually multiple performance bottlenecks that have to be removed one by one.

Lessons learned:

- Profiling I/O performance is quite similar to profiling run time: select a good, scalable test case, do an upfront analysis/sanity check before finally using a profiling tool.
- Check that the profiling tool of your choice works well for profiling time that is spent inside calls of the operating system.

Chapter 7
Debugging Parallel Programs

In this chapter we give an introduction to debugging parallel programs written in C or C++. We will first look at the two most prominent classes of parallel programming errors: *race conditions* and *deadlocks*. We then take a look at thread analysis tools and conclude this chapter by discussing asynchronous events and interrupt handlers.

7.1 Writing Parallel Programs in C/C++

Concurrency in software can take a number of different forms. There are low-level variants such as bit-level and instruction-level parallelism. Then there are programs written for specialized systems such as vector or array processors. This chapter, however, focuses on more coarse-grain parallelism. In particular, we consider multiple communicating executables written in C or C++, possibly running on different hosts, multi-threaded executables including applications running on embedded (real-time) operating systems, and code such as signal or interrupt handlers that is inherently asynchronous in nature.

There is a number of libraries and language extensions available to write parallel programs. Please see Appendix B.7 for more information, references, and links to documentation. *Posix Threads* and *Windows threads* are libraries that offer low-level access to the thread capabilities of a modern OS. *Threading Building Blocks (TBB)* is a C++ template library to write OS-independent multi-threaded code. *OpenMP* is a C/C++ and Fortran language extension based on preprocessor directives, usually implemented on top of threads. The thread libraries and OpenMP are based on the concept of shared memory: each parallel thread has access to all global variables and all dynamic memory on the heap. Each thread has stack with local variables.

Going beyond shared memory, the *MPI (Message Passing Interface)* standard is based on the model of cooperating processes, each with its own memory, running on a cluster of machines. Google's *MapReduce* is a framework for parallel computations spread over widely separated clusters with unreliable nodes.

Debugging these parallel applications adds further complexity. Unexpected behavior can be due to bugs that would affect sequential programs as well. In addition, there are new challenges. The two most prominent categories of bugs are *race conditions* and *deadlocks*.

A race condition is a bug in a system where the result critically depends on a proper sequential ordering of computation steps. The outcome of breaking this ordering can be incorrect data or behavior, or just an annoyance such as log files that keep changing their contents with every run. Race conditions are caused by incorrect or missing synchronization on shared variables and program code. Mechanisms such as mutexes, semaphores, critical regions or barriers, and atomic operations are available to prevent race conditions. For a general introduction to these mechanisms, proofs of equivalence, and implementation details, please refer to the standard books by [Tanenbaum01] and [Silberschatz04]. We will discuss in Section 7.2 how to debug a race condition.

Deadlocks are representative of problems related to thread or process activations. The most common case is a set of processes waiting for each other. Other cases include premature process termination – often the result of accidentally returning from the top-level routine of a thread – and processes that get triggered far too often. We will cover these cases in Section 7.3.

7.2 Debugging Race Conditions

A race condition can occur when two or more threads share one variable, and there is no synchronization mechanism to block one thread while the other one executes a *atomic transaction* on the shared variable. An atomic transaction is a sequence of operations that should not be interrupted.

A simple example for a *data race condition* is shown in Figure 7.1: two parallel threads t_beancounter0, t_beancounter1 access the variable beans allocated in line 19. The access occurs in the increment statement (*beans)++ in line 11.

When you run the program, you will observe occasionally that the result is less than the expected 200000. The reason is that the statement in line 11 is not an atomic operation: it is translated into a sequence of machine operations: a read of the variable, an addition in a CPU register, followed by a write to the variable. The C/C++ language does not guarantee that statements or even variable increments are executed as atomic operations. Now, the following can happen in line 11:

- t_beancounter1 executes the read operation.
- t_beancounter2 gains access to the shared variable and does one or more increments.
- t_beancounter1 completes the increment and writes back the result.
- The increments made by t_beancounter2 are lost.

```
1   #include <stdio.h>
2   #include <stdlib.h>
3   #include <pthread.h>
4
5   void* beancounter(void* beans_arg)
6   {
7     int counter;
8     int* beans = (int*)beans_arg;
9
10    for (counter=0; counter<100000; counter++) {
11      (*beans)++;
12    }
13    return beans_arg;
14  }
15
16  int main(void)
17  {
18    pthread_t t_beancounter0, t_beancounter1;
19    int beans = 0;
20
21    pthread_create(&t_beancounter0,0,beancounter,
                    (void*)(&beans));
22    pthread_create(&t_beancounter1,0,beancounter,
                    (void*)(&beans));
23    pthread_join(t_beancounter0,0);
24    pthread_join(t_beancounter1,0);
25
26    printf("The sum of all beans is %d\n",beans);
27    return 0;
28  }
```

Fig. 7.1 Calling the function `beancounter()` from two different threads

Please note that the frequency of failure will depend on your environment such as the operating system, compiler, CPU load, etc. You may want to run the test repeatedly either from a script or using the UNIX `csh` command `repeat`:

```
repeat <nr_or_repetitions> <path_to_exe_file>
```

The symptom – non-predictable behavior, occuring infrequently – is typical for data races. If you see this kind of failure in a program containing parallel processes, then identify the shared memory variables, and look for potential flaws in the code that accesses them.

7.2.1 Using Basic Debugger Capabilities to Find Race Conditions

Stepping through or setting breakpoints in parallel programs is intrusive; it changes timing. The application might behave differently if running under control of a debugger. Similarly, adding trace code or I/O code such as a `printf()` statement will alter the timing of the program.

Do not expect too much from stepping through the code with a source code debugger and displaying the content of the shared variables. Attaching the debugger changes the scheduling behavior of the threads so much that the error may be not observable any more. Still, it is a first step to try. Attaching the debugger to the program may influence the execution in such a way that the error occurs more frequently, so that you are able to identify the bug.

Most debuggers will permit you to analyze the threads of the program. This includes analysis of the current thread ID, the stack of the thread, and other useful information.

You can also *mimic the scheduling*, that is you can arbitrarily switch from one thread to the other. If you are able to localize a few small spots in your program where the common variables are read from and written to, then this capability can be used to identify potential issues. You should step through the code with the debugger and ask yourself the following question at each step:

"What happens if the scheduler switches right here?"

In case you cannot answer the question, you can just switch to another thread and see what happens.

However, if you step through the above example line by line, you will realize that you can switch threads at any place or time without breaking the correct functionality of the program. You are doing line-by-line steps in the C/C++ code, while the scheduler can switch threads anywhere in the machine code, which can be in the middle of a C/C++ statement.

You can tell your debugger to display and step through the machine code instead of the C/C++ code. For GDB, the command `disassemble` shows the disassembled content of the memory around the current position of the program counter, and the command for stepping to the next machine instruction is `stepi`. In Visual Studio, use the **Dissassembly** window, as described in Section 10.11.4.

Here is the sequence of machine operations for the `(*beans)++` operation on an Intel x86 CPU:

```
0x08048452 <beancounter+30>:   mov   0xfffffff8(%ebp),%eax
0x08048455 <beancounter+33>:   incl  (%eax)
0x08048457 <beancounter+35>:   lea   0xfffffffc(%ebp),%eax
```

If you let the debugger switch threads between step 2 and step 3, you can reproduce the incorrect result. The next time the suspended thread gets scheduled it will continue its execution right where it was suspended. It will write back the content of the local register, which overwrites any changes the other thread made.

7.2.2 Using Log Files to Localize Race Conditions

As we mentioned in Section 7.2.1 using a debugger as if you were debugging a sequential program often does not work as expected, since attaching a debugger, pausing the execution of the program and stepping through the code is heavily influencing the timing of the application. A typical case of a *Heisenbug*: the harder you try to debug the better the bug is hiding.

In addition, the debugger's view is in many cases too narrow and detailed, especially if you do not know what you are looking for. It may make more sense to let the program run without interrupting it, collect all required data during runtime, and then post-process the gathered data. This can be done via *log files* or *trace files*, or by displaying the debug information in a console window. For this approach you have to instrument the code with *logging instructions* as shown in Figure 7.2. You may still have the Heisenbug situation, that after instrumentation the failure is less frequent or not observable any more.

```
1 void* beancounter(void* beans_arg)
2 {
3   int counter;
4   int* beans = (int*)beans_arg;
5
6   for(counter=0; counter<100000; counter++) {
7     printf("%x before next bean %d|",(int)clock(),(*beans));
8     fflush(stdout);
9     (*beans)++;
10    printf("%x after next bean %d\n",(int)clock(),(*beans));
11    fflush(stdout);
12  }
13  return beans_arg;
14 }
```

Fig. 7.2 Using logging instructions to collect debug information on the fly

The printf() commands display the relevant data to observe the flow and intermediate results of the program, which allows you to spot places of unexpected behavior from the log files or terminal output after the simulation run. Here are some rules you should obey when instrumenting your code:

- Make sure you are using *thread safe* and *atomic* functions and commands to instrument parallel code – otherwise you will end up debugging your instrumentation instead of your actual program.
- printf() and fprintf() work reliably on most operating systems. Call fflush() after every I/O statement to write the stream buffers to terminal or file immediately. The error stream stderr is unbuffered and hence preferable for logging. The C++ streams are the least preferable, since they may produce completely interleaved text output from the different threads.

- Use time-stamps when dumping information from threads in large programs. This helps you later on to review and post-process the collected information. You can use either *wall clock* timing information, using the function time() or the *CPU time* – using the function clock(). Both functions time() and clock() are in the standard C library, and their function prototypes are declared in the header file time.h. The wall clock time you get from the function time() has a maximum granularity of one second, which might not be sufficient for some programs, but the wall clock time is a good common reference if you are debugging a program running on more than one processor. The CPU ticks you get back from the function clock() have more fine grain resolution, but might not be suited as common time ordering reference on multi-processor systems.
- The wall clock time on 2 separate machines is never in sync, so you can't use it to reconstruct an ordering of events when merging log files from the 2 machines. Check the documentation of your parallel processing library if a clock synchronization mechanism is provided.
- If you are frequently debugging parallel programs, it is a good approach to create helper *trace functions* or *trace buffer* variables that automatically capture useful information such as time-stamps or thread IDs.
- In some cases, *assertions* – code that immediately checks the correctness of the data of the program – make sense, especially if the amount of logged data would become huge otherwise. Be aware though that the more code you add for debugging purposes, the more you deviate from the original timing behavior of the program that has shown the defect you are actually searching. Sometimes this makes the root cause of the problem untraceable. The alternative, especially if the collected data is extensive, is to use scripts or utilities to post-process and filter the data.

In many cases, the logged data can point you exactly to the source of the problem, in other cases it may just give you a better idea where exactly the program behaves unexpectedly. This is the place where you have to dig deeper, either using further code instrumentation, using a debugger, or in rare cases even by restructuring the code.

The log produced by the example in Figure 7.2 contains the following patterns for those cases where the race condition occurs:

```
    . . .
1   7530 before next bean 791|7530 after next bean 792
2   7530 before next bean 792|7530 after next bean 793
3   7530 before next bean 793|7530 after next bean 794
4   7530 after next bean 790
5   7530 before next bean 790|7530 after next bean 791
6   7530 before next bean 791|7530 after next bean 792
7   7530 before next bean 792|7530 after next bean 793
    . . .
```

You can see from the log that in rows 3 and 4 you have two consecutive executions of code line 10 of Figure 7.2, implying that the program switched threads. We also see in line 4 of the log file that the `beans` variable is reset to 790. This should be indication enough to cast doubts on the thread-safety of the `(*beans)++` operation in line 9. The next step would be to either use a debugger to analyze the machine code and play with the scheduling as described in Section 7.2.1 to understand the nature of the failure so you can fix it.

The methodology of collecting data during the execution of the program has built-in support in some debuggers. You can set *tracepoints* with the GDB `trace` and `collect` commands. Along with a tracepoint, you can specify the data that shall be logged each time the tracepoint is hit; you can count the number of hits, and collect other information useful for the post-processing.

You can do something similar with breakpoints as well, if you assign commands to the breakpoints to dump the required data, and then continue the execution. However, be aware that these debugging methods are intrusive and influence the timing of the program being debugged. It might lead to different behavior in the presence of race conditions. In practice, most experienced developers use both methods: debugger tracepoints as well as the `printf()`-logging.

7.3 Debugging Deadlocks

Deadlocks in a program can occur if a resource required by one thread or process is not released and hence causes the thread or process to wait on the resource forever. A condition like this occurs when a *mutex* or *semaphore* is applied but never unlocked appropriately. The root causes for the deadlock situation in most cases are:

- Circular mutex locking, where two or more threads start reserving resources, but can not continue because they are mutually waiting on resources currently locked by the other threads. The most famous example for this is probably the *dining philosophers' problem.*
  The dining philosophers' problem consists of five philosophers sitting at a table and trying to eat. The five philosophers sit at a circular common table with a large bowl of spaghetti in the center. A fork is placed in between each philosopher, so that each philosopher has one fork to his left and one fork to his right. As Edsger Dijkstra considered it difficult to eat spaghetti with a single fork, in order for a philosopher to eat, he must have possesion of two forks, and can only use the fork on his left or right. If all five philosophers try to eat at the same time by taking the fork on their right hand side and then wait for the left hand fork to become available, they will all die of starvation.
- Protocol mismatches, where two or more processes or threads are synchronized via mutexes or semaphores that are not unlocked as required. This is commonly encountered in *producer-consumer* scenarios. If you have a fixed-size communication buffer, you need to make sure the producer stops writing if the buffer is full, and the consumer stops reading if the buffer is empty. This can be done for example via semaphores. If there is a protocol error or race condition leading to a

missing increase or decrease of the semaphore, it might lead to one of the threads going to sleep forever.

The first analysis you can do when your program is stuck is to use a debugger to see at what state the program and the single threads are, as described in Section 7.3.2. If the information you can get from using the debugger interactively is not sufficient – for example because attaching the debugger makes it impossible to reproduce the error – you can apply logging methods as described in Section 7.2.2.

As an example how a debugger can help you to find the reason for a deadlock we can take almost the same code as in Figure 7.1, with the only difference that we tried to use a mutex to eliminate the race condition described in Section 7.2. The modified beancounter() function is shown in Figure 7.3. Unfortunately we "forgot" to unlock the mutex in line 16 after locking it before in line 12 – to make it a good example for deadlock debugging.

```
 1  #include <stdio.h>
 2  #include <stdlib.h>
 3  #include <pthread.h>
 4
 5  pthread_mutex_t mutex = PTHREAD_MUTEX_INITIALIZER;
 6
 7  void* beancounter(void* beans_arg)
 8  {
 9    int counter;
10    int* beans = (int*)beans_arg;
11
12    pthread_mutex_lock(&mutex);
13    for (counter=0; counter<100000; counter++) {
14      (*beans)++;
15    }
16    /* oops, forgot to unlock the mutex here... */
17    return beans_arg;
16  }
```

Fig. 7.3 Defining and using a global mutex

If you run the example with this modified beancounter() function it will run into a deadlock situation and will never exit. Starting the program in a debugger will get you into the same deadlock situation. Instead of starting the program in the debugger right away, you can also attach a debugger to the running program.

7.3.1 How to Determine What the Current Thread is Executing

The debugger can tell you which thread was last executed by the CPU and what the stack of this thread looks like. The probability is high that you immediately get the root cause for the deadlock this way. If you interrupt our example program in GDB (e.g. by typing Ctrl-C) and issue an `info stack` command you will see that the current thread is waiting for `mutex` to be unlocked:

```
^C
Program received signal SIGINT, Interrupt.
[Switching to Thread -172106832 (LWP 18839)]
0x.. in __lll_mutex_lock_wait() from /lib/tls/libpthread.so.0

(gdb) info stack
#0  0x.. in __lll_mutex_lock_wait () from ...
#1  0x.. in _L_mutex_lock_28 () from ...
#2  0x.. in __JCR_LIST__ () from ...
#3  0x.. in ?? ()
#4  0x.. in ?? ()
#5  0x.. in beancounter at beancounter_deadlock.c:12

(gdb) frame 5
#5  0x.. in beancounter at beancounter_deadlock.c:12

(gdb) list 12,15
12    pthread_mutex_lock(&mutex);
13    for (counter=0; counter<1000; counter++) {
14      (*beans)++;
15    }
```

The debugger information above reveals that the current thread is waiting for a mutex, and that the user code line containing this command is line 12 of the file `beancounter_deadlock.c`.

7.3.2 Analyzing the Threads of the Program

The debugger can tell you the state of each thread, and which code each thread was executing when the program was suspended. This is quite helpful to get an overview of the program's state and often reveals which of the threads is – in terms of program flow – running behind the others and therefore a good candidate for further investigation.

In GDB you can use the command `info threads`. It lists all threads with their unique ID and marks the currently active thread with a `*`. In our example the current thread has the ID 3 and is at line 12 of the file `beancounter_deadlock.c` – as we could also see from the stack trace of the previous section – and that the second thread is in the function `pthread_join`. This thread is obviously waiting for the other thread to finish its execution. You can also switch from one thread to the other using the GDB command `thread` along with the ID of the thread to that you want to switch. This allows you to analyze the stacks of all other threads as well.

```
(gdb) info threads
* 3 Thread in __lll_mutex_lock_wait () from ...
```

```
    1 Thread in pthread_join () from ...

(gdb) thread 1
[Switching to thread 1] #0 in pthread_join () from ...

(gdb) info stack
#0  0x.. in pthread_join () from /lib/tls/libpthread.so.0
#1  0x.. in main () at beancounter_deadlock.c:45
```

With the information displayed here it is rather straightforward to analyze that
Thread 3 was waiting for mutex to be unlocked, and that Thread 1 has already passed the locking of mutex at line 12. The next logical step would be to
analyze why Thread 1 never unlocked mutex. With this question you arrived
at the solution of the issue, that is, the function beancounter() as shown in
Figure 7.3 is completely missing a statement to unlock mutex. Inserting a
pthread_mutex_unlock(&mutex) statement after line 15 will fix this issue.

7.4 Familiarize Yourself with Threading Analysis Tools

There are a number of sophisticated tools on the market to analyze parallel programs
and find potential sources of misbehavior. Threading analysis tools can help you
find hidden potential errors, such as deadlocks and data races, mapping them to the
memory reference and to the source-code line.

Examples for useful tools are the commercial Intel Parallel Studio (see Appendix B.8.1), and the Open Source tool Helgrind (see Appendix B.4.2).

Helgrind is part of the Valgrind instrumentation framework, and at the time of
writing this book still in an experimental, but nevertheless quite useful stage. Running Helgrind with the beancounter.c example shown in Figure 7.1 we will get
a valuable hint that there is a potential data race:

```
> gcc -g beancounter.c -lpthread -o beancounter
> valgrind --tool=helgrind beancounter

== Helgrind, a thread error detector.
== Using valgrind-3.3.0
==
== Thread #2 was created
==    at 0x48CDD0C: clone (in /lib/tls/libc-2.3.2.so)
==    by 0x80484BB: main (beancounter.c:40)
==
== Thread #3 was created
==    at 0x48CDD0C: clone (in /lib/tls/libc-2.3.2.so)
==    by 0x80484DD: main (beancounter.c:41)
==
== Possible data race during write of size 4 at 0xFEFF6D4C
==    at 0x8048475: beancounter (beancounter.c:11)
==    by 0x48CDD19: clone (in /lib/tls/libc-2.3.2.so)
==    Old state: shared-readonly by threads #2, #3
```

```
==     New state: shared-modified by threads #2, #3
==     Reason:    this thread, #3, holds no consistent locks
==     Location 0xFEFF6D4C has never been protected by any lock
The sum of all beans is 200000
==
== ERROR SUMMARY: 1 errors from 1 contexts
```

In this case Helgrind correctly points out that the increment operation in line 11 of beancounter.c represents a shared access to the same memory location, and that this access is not protected by any locks.

Using the deadlocking example beancounter_deadlock.c shown in Figure 7.3 we can also get some valuable information from Helgrind:

```
> valgrind --tool=helgrind beancounter_deadlock

== Helgrind, a thread error detector.
== Using valgrind-3.3.0
==
== Thread #2 was created
==    at 0x48CDD0C: clone (in /lib/tls/libc-2.3.2.so)
==    by 0x8048507: main (beancounter_deadlock.c:25)
==
== Thread #2: Exiting thread still holds 1 lock
==    at 0x47E5E24: start_thread (/lib/tls/libpthread-0.60.so)
==    by 0x48CDD19: clone (in /lib/tls/libc-2.3.2.so)
==
...
```

The one hint of vital importance is that Thread #2 exits, but still holds a lock. Situations like this are usually not intended and very likely the source of a deadlock.

Helgrind's basic mechanism is to do bookkeeping of all memory accesses. Helgrind identifies memory locations which are accessed by more than one thread. For each such location, Helgrind records which of the program's locks were held by the accessing thread at the time of each access.

One small difficulty is that even the action of locking a mutex represents a potential data race. Locking a mutex is always accessing a memory location from more than one thread – otherwise the mutex wouldn't be required in the first place. Since typically the access to such a locking mechanism is not secured by another lock, Helgrind reports this pattern as possible data race. (At least there must be one outermost locking mechanism that cannot be secured by a surrounding lock). This means that even for a perfectly bug-free program containing locks you will get a lot of error reports. Luckily those *don't care* potential data races are easy to spot in the Helgrind report, since they refer to the method to set the lock (pthread_mutex_lock) as well as to the location in the program code where this locking function is called. In the example below, this is line 12 of the file beancounter_fixed.c:

```
> valgrind --tool=helgrind beancounter_fixed

== Helgrind, a thread error detector.
== Using valgrind-3.3.0
==
```

```
== Thread #2 was created
==     at 0x48CDD0C: clone (in /lib/tls/libc-2.3.2.so)
==     by 0x8048553: main (beancounter_fixed.c:25)
==
== Thread #3 was created
==     at 0x48CDD0C: clone (in /lib/tls/libc-2.3.2.so)
==     by 0x8048575: main (beancounter_fixed.c:26)
==
== Possible data race during write of size 4 at 0x80497F0
==     at 0x47E78D1: pthread_mutex_lock
==     by 0x80484EB: beancounter (beancounter_fixed.c:12)
==     by 0x48CDD19: clone (in /lib/tls/libc-2.3.2.so)
==   Old state: shared-readonly by threads #2, #3
==   New state: shared-modified by threads #2, #3
==   Reason:   this thread, #3, holds no consistent locks
==   Location 0x80497F0 has never been protected by any lock
==
== Possible data race during write of size 4 at 0x80497E8
==     at 0x47E78D4: pthread_mutex_lock
==     by 0x80484EB: beancounter (beancounter_fixed.c:12)
==     by 0x48CDD19: clone (in /lib/tls/libc-2.3.2.so)
==   Old state: owned exclusively by thread #2
==   New state: shared-modified by threads #2, #3
==   Reason:   this thread, #3, holds no locks at all
==
...
```

In general there are a large number of *don't care* potential data races reported by Helgrind: during thread creation and exiting, lock acquisition and release, or inter-thread communication.

7.5 Asynchronous Events and Interrupt Handlers

How parallel is parallel, actually? Well, it depends. One could argue that, on a simple single-core processor system, even a multi-threaded program is not truly "parallel." After all, there's only a single thread active at any given point in time. What makes it challenging is the fact that task switches are mostly asynchronous – unless you don't take special precautions you cannot be sure to reach the next line of your program's source code without interruptions.

This brings us to other types of asynchronous events, and the context switches they can trigger. Two key examples are signal handlers and low-level interrupt service routines. A signal handler is a function that is invoked by the operating system as a result of delivering a signal to a process (see section 10.7). Signals are inherently asynchronous; they can, for instance, be generated as a result of a user or an executable trying to communicate with your program (SIGINT, SIGIO, SIGTERM, ...). As a result, the corresponding signal handler can interrupt your program at any point in time unless you (temporarily) blocked the respective signal.

Now things get tricky. On one hand, we are dealing with asynchronous execution, which demands properly guarded access to shared resources. On the other hand, interrupt and signal handlers are supposed to run extremely swiftly in order to reduce the time when delivery of further events is masked. This means that any "slow" operation such as making OS calls to access semaphores or I/O operations can not be used. Now you are stuck between a rock and hard place: you have to deal with asynchronous accesses but cannot rely on standard synchronization schemes, and good old `printf()` debugging has been declared questionable too.

This book will not tell you how to write a good signal handler. Please refer to a good textbook on OS level software development instead. We can give hints when it comes to debugging though:

First, you may want to look at Section 10.7, which explains what type of support you can expect from a source code debugger. Of course, you can always place a breakpoint in a routine handling interrupts or OS signals. Using breakpoint commands can be a powerful tool in this context. Next, consider using watchpoints (see Section 10.6 to determine if and when other parts of the program access the same variables. The set of variables should be very small, or else your handler is of debatable "greatness." Hardware-assisted watchpoints are preferable in order to reduce the likelihood of Heisenbugs.

Lessons learned:

- Use trace files to debug race conditions.
- Make sure that your tracing mechanism is thread safe.
- Check if your parallel processing library has a clock synchronization mechanism before using time stamps to order events.
- Use a simple example to learn how to switch threads and inspect synchronization code in your debugger.
- Familiarize yourself with threading analysis tools: Helgrind, Intel Thread Checker.

Chapter 8
Finding Environment and Compiler Problems

The behavior of a program is dependent not only on its code and input data files and user input, but also on the environment in which it runs. For example, a program may run fine in the controlled environment where it was developed, but it can fail on some user systems. Maintenance work such as an OS update, a new software installation, or a service pack update to the development system will cause seemingly unrelated program failures. In this chapter we discuss the effect of environment changes, and list some tools that visualize what the processes of a program are doing. We also address compiler bugs, and incompatibilities between the debugger and compiler.

8.1 Environment Changes – Where Problems Begin

An environment dependency can manifest itself in many unpredictable ways. The following sections list typical environment dependencies, including environment variables and installation dependencies. We show how to diagnose such a dependency, and how to either anticipate or avoid them in a program.

8.1.1 Environment Variables

User-defined *environment variables* are a frequent reason why a program behaves differently on different systems and for different users. The variables that have the most influence are `PATH` and `LD_LIBRARY_PATH` on UNIX, and `PATH`, `LIB`, and `INCLUDE` on Windows. `PATH` is used to locate other programs. On UNIX, `LD_LIBRARY_PATH` variable is used to locate the shared libraries that are dynamically loaded into the program. On Windows, the operating system uses the `PATH` variable to find programs and *dynamic link libraries* (DLLs). Picking up the wrong version of a DLL can have fatal consequences.

If you observe that a program behaves correctly in one environment, and changes behavior in another, the program may switch internal behavior depending on one or more environment variables. Make sure the difference is consistent and can be reproduced, by running the program multiple times. Print out all environment variables, and compare the settings in both environments. On UNIX, use the `env` command. On Windows, open a DOS box by going to **Start/Run** and entering `cmd`. In the DOS box, use the command `set`. Compare the two sets of variables, change the variables that differ one by one, and check at each step if the program behavior changes. If you find the variable that caused the change in program behavior, make sure to document the dependency, or modify the program to remove or anticipate the dependency.

8.1.2 Local Installation Dependencies

A program bug may be triggered by differences in the local installation of a machine: operating system, patches, tools, C/C++ runtime libraries, etc. If so, try to capture the significant differences of the installation, and build a similar system for inhouse testing. Make sure you can reproduce the failure. Then, either put code in your software that supports the new installation, or put in a guard that prevents the program's execution in new installation, and document the incompatibility. A good example for this is the Windows Vista SP1 operating system, which warns the user that the Visual C++ 7.0 compiler is not supported.

8.1.3 Current Working Directory Dependency

The behavior of the program may depend on the current working directory. On UNIX, this is the directory from which the program is started. The directory is registered in the environment variable `CWD`. For example, a program may expect to read or write files located relative to a certain working directory. To make the program work from another directory, either use absolute path names, or make the program change the current working directory.

8.1.4 Process ID Dependency

The process ID (PID) of the current process may also have an effect. The PID is an integer number and automatically assigned to a program's process when the program is started. UNIX programs occasionally create temporary files with names such as `/tmp/myprog.<pid>`. The program may not always delete these temporary files, and it may incorrectly assume that no previous file with the same name existed before opening the file for writing. When you run the program and are unlucky enough to get the very same PID, your program cannot create the file, and fails.

PID-related problems are fixed by adding good error messages to your software, so that a clear trace of the occasional collision is created. Also, the software should be modified to use a better unique identifier.

8.2 How else to See what a Program is Doing

An application may not be just a single program. It may consist of multiple programs and scripts that work together. To debug the application, you need to determine which program is running, what the program arguments are, and to what process to attach the debugger.

8.2.1 Viewing Processes with top

On UNIX and Linux, you can use the utility top (see also Appendix B.9.5) to see a list of which processes are running on your computer. The process list is updated every few seconds. The utility shows you which programs need the most CPU time or memory. On Windows, use the Task Manager to display processes.

```
Tasks:  78 total, 4 running, 74 sleeping, 0 stopped, 0 zombie
Cpu(s): 60.5%us, 38.1%sy, 0.0%ni, 0.0%id, 0.0%wa, 1.3%hi, 0.0%s
Mem: 276616k total, 271224k used,   5392k free,  48328k buffers
Swap:321260k total,      0k used, 321260k free, 111272k cached

 PID USER    PR  VIRT  RES  SHR S %CPU %MEM    TIME+ COMMAND
7606 zaphod 23 26704  22m 2256 R 54.7  8.2  0:22.44 havoc
7491 arthur 25  2252  680  592 R 14.0  0.2  0:16.40 survive
5597 root   15 34096  13m 2716 S  1.7  5.0  0:09.85 X
5959 mice0  15 31772  15m  12m S  0.3  5.7 56:06.00 find_pol
7604 mice9  19  5120 2352 1588 S  0.3  0.9  0:00.01 test.human
   1 root   16   680  248  216 S  0.0  0.1  0:00.62 init
 ...
```

The output of top is shown above.

8.2.2 Finding Multiple Processes of an Application with ps

The UNIX utility ps (see Appendix B.9.3) shows a snapshot of the processes running on a computer. ps has command line arguments to provide different types of information. Note that the actual command line arguments vary on different operating systems. A particularly useful feature of ps is to check the parent/child relationship of processes for a specific user, and to show the command line arguments of the processes. On Linux, this is done with ps -u <username> -H -opid,cmd where <username> refers to the user name.

In the following example, the program myprogA takes a long time before it returns, and we want to understand why.

```
> ps -u someone -H -opid,cmd
...
8804          ./myprogA MyFile 123
8805            /bin/csh -f ./myshellB MyFile 123
8806              ./myprogC MyFile abc 123
8807                sleep 100
...
```

The indentation shows that myprogrA calls myshellB, which calls myprogrC, which executes a sleep command.

8.2.3 Using /proc/<pid> to Access a Process

Some Linux and UNIX operating systems allow you to access processes through file system /proc/.... Each process has its own directory in this file system. Note that the kind of information available under /proc/..., and how to access it, varies greatly with the operating system. The proc functionality is not available on Windows.

On Linux Red Hat and Suse, it is possible to access command line arguments (/proc/8806/cmdline), environment variables (/proc/8806/environ), a symbolic link to the executable (/proc/8806/exe), and other information.

8.2.4 Use strace to Trace Calls to the OS

The Linux utility strace (truss on Solaris) logs all accesses to the operating system, such as memory allocation, file I/O, system calls, and launching sub-processes. The option -f will also log information about any sub-process. On Windows, install Cygwin to get an strace command.

strace is a debugging tool that still works when you need to debug a program or a linked-in library that has no available source code. It is simple to use, and does not require drastic changes to your source code, such as putting a code wrapper plus tracing code around every system call. Plus, it really captures all calls to the OS. With a hand-written wrapper around each OS call, you have to worry about completeness and correctness of your tracing code.

Among the drawbacks of strace are that it produces a lot of output, and the output is hard to read. strace will show you the raw error codes of the system calls, so you need to refer to the man pages or do an Internet search to understand what went wrong.

We recommend the use of strace for the following debugging scenarios.

- File I/O: Use strace to find out which files were opened. Programs often use setup files during initialization, and will open them silently.

- Uncaught errors or interrupts in OS routines. strace will show the return status of the OS call. A common bug is to ignore the return status of OS calls, so look for error values being returned, and cross-check your source code for correct handling of these values.

- Frequency of OS calls: when you debug performance problems, strace can indicate whether the bottleneck was caused by too many expensive (in terms of CPU time) OS calls. Re-factoring of the code to move the OS call(s) out of an inner loop may help.

- Memory allocation/deallocation/mapping: strace will show calls to dynamic memory management. Useful when a memory debugger such as Purify or Valgrind is not available.

In the following example we will use strace to get more information about myprogA and its sub-processes. Note that we have condensed the output to show only the most interesting activities:

```
> strace -f -o strace.log ./myprogA MyFile 123

File trace.log:
8804   execve("./myprogA", ["./myprogA", "MyFile", "123"],
          [/* 82 vars */]) = 0
8804   uname({sys="Linux", node="linux", ...}) = 0
8804   brk(0)                               = 0x804a000
8804...
8804   open("MyFile", O_RDONLY)        = -1 ENOENT
          (No such file or directory)
8804   fstat64(1, {st_mode=S_IFCHR|0600, ...}) = 0
8804...
8804   write(1, "About to call ./myshellB MyFile "...) = 36
8804...
8804   clone(child_stack=0, flags=CLONE_PARENT_SETTID|SIGCHLD,
          parent_tidptr=0xbfffed68) = 8805
8804...
```

The line open("MyFile", O_RDONLY) reveals that myprogA was trying to open a file, but it was not found. Next the program prints About to call ./myshellB MyFile to stdout and then clones itself. Process 8805 becomes active and spawns more sub-processes:

```
8805   execve("/bin/sh", ["sh", "-c", "./myshellB
          MyFile 123\n"], [/* 82 vars */]) = 0

...
```

```
8805   read(16, "#!/bin/csh -f\n./myprogC $1 abc $"...,
4096) = 34
8805...
8805   clone(child_stack=0, flags=...) = 8806

8806   execve("./myprogC", ["./myprogC","MyFile","abc","123"],
       [/* 82 vars */]) = 0
8806...
8806   write(1, "C called with \'MyFile\', \'abc\', \'"...) = 37
8806...
8806   clone(child_stack=0,flags=...) = 8807

8807   execve("/bin/sh", ["sh", "-c", "sleep 100"],
       [/* 82 vars */]) = 0
8807...
8807   nanosleep({100, 0}, NULL)          = 0
```

8.3 Compilers and Debuggers have Bugs too

One part of the environment of a program is the development system. In this section we discuss the two major sources of time-consuming bugs due to the development system: compiler bugs and incompatibilites between debugger and compiler. The third source of bugs in the development chain, the linker, is discussed in Chapter 9.

8.3.1 Compiler Bugs

When you hit a bug while using a new or advanced language feature in C++, you need to consider the possibility that the compiler itself has bugs. This was quite common in the past, when C++ underwent a lot of new development and standardization, but it still occasionally happens today. We recommend the following approach in case a compiler bug is suspected:

- Use *divide and conquer* to reduce the size of the test case. Try to isolate the compiler feature that is broken, ideally down to just a few lines of code.
- Experiment with the compiler options to see if the problem goes away: turn off optimization or switch to a less aggressive optimization level. Turn debug support on/off, this will also alter memory layout and initialization for variables.
- Use a previously published example of the language feature, to cross-check that you are not using the feature incorrectly.
- Search the Internet to see if other developers have run into the same problem.
- Try a different compiler and see whether the problem persists.
- Report the compiler bug.

Once you have determined that a problem is due to a compiler bug, you have to recode. Typically compiler bugs take a while to get fixed, so you can not put your project on hold to wait for the bug fix. Find a work-around for your own software, by not using certain language features, or by adapting a restricted coding style. Also, document the problem, and save the test case. Once a new compiler version becomes available, you can quickly test if the bug has been fixed. This way your work-arounds and coding style restrictions won't have to become permanent.

8.3.2 Debugger and Compiler Compatibility Problems

There are many different C/C++ compilers and debuggers. Each of the compilers and debuggers have many different major and minor versions. Not all compiler-debugger combinations work together. It is impossible to test all combinations, and backward and forward compatibility can not always be ensured. Further complications can arise from debugger incompatibilities with the OS, system libraries such as pthreads, and specific language features. If a debugger incompatibility occurs, you may see one of these symptoms:

- The debugger dumps core while loading the program, or in the middle of a debug session.
- The debugger is unable to set a breakpoint in a C++ class member specified by function name.
- The debugger sets a breakpoint in a specific source file/line location but never stops there although the location is executed.

There are a number of things you can do if a compiler-debugger incompatibility occurs:

- Check the documentation: what is the recommended debugger version? Are there known incompatibilities?
- Experiment by installing several debugger versions, and keep track of what incompatibilities you encounter. This is a common approach for users of GDB and GCC. In Visual Studio, debugger and compiler are integrated, so you are limited to using a different major version.
- Document what combination worked. Incompatibilites are often forced by major updates to the development system: compiler, OS, debugger. You may have to roll back a software update to ensure a working debugging environment.
- Do not assume that the default debugger and compiler that came with your OS distribution is the right one for your project.

Lessons learned:

- A program bug can be due to the environment: environment variables, OS installation dependencies, interrupt handlers, etc. Consider these bug sources when deploying new software on computers different from the development system.
- There are tools to let you debug the environment of a program: `top`, `ps`, `env`, `/proc/<pid>`, `strace`.
- An incorrect search path for dynamic libraries can be the source of environment-dependent crashes. Look for wrong or missing variable values of `PATH` and `LD_LIBRARY_PATH`.
- Compilers have bugs too. Use divide-and-conquer to isolate the problem, and look for work-arounds to continue your project.
- Debuggers can be incompatible with particular compilers, language features, OS, and system library versions. Keep track of what worked, before doing a major change to your development system.

Chapter 9
Dealing with Linking Problems

This chapter describes how to find bugs introduced at the link stage of a program. Linking problems are numerous, occur frequently, are time-consuming to fix, and not well supported by debugging tools. We will give examples of link problems that can not be detected at link time, but will result in program crashes or wrong program behavior. Also, in practice, linker error message can be cryptic: they indicate a mismatch of the pieces that should form a program, often without any further explanation where this mismatch comes from. These aspects led to the decision to make the debugging of linking problems an integral part of this book.

We start by shortly describing some principles of linking. Then, we go step-by-step through the most common link problems, and show how to detect and fix them.

9.1 How a Linker Works

Linking is the process of building an executable file from object files and object file libraries. A compiler or assembler translates source code into machine code, and produces object files as output. An object file contains *symbols* which represent functions or variables *defined* in the source code. If a symbol is associated with an address and a segment containing its definition in the same object file, it is called a *defined* or *resolved* symbol. A symbol not yet associated with an address is called an *undefined* or *unresolved* symbol. The basic idea of linking is to associate each unresolved symbol with its corresponding definition. This process is also referred to as *resolving symbols*. Please refer to [Levine00] for more details on how a linker works.

The linker keeps resolved and unresolved symbols in two different lists. Its main job is to turn unresolved symbols into resolved symbols when assembling the object files and libraries into a program. In the final executable every symbol has to have one valid definition – if this is not the case then you have a problem.

9.2 Building and Linking Objects

During the following sections we will use a modified `factorial.c` code example, similar to the one used in Chapter 3. The difference here is that we placed the `main()` functions and the `factorial()` function into different source files.

```
1  /* factorial.h */
2  extern int factorial(int n);
```

```
1  /* factorial.c */
2  #include "factorial.h"
3  int factorial(int n) {
4    int result = 1;
5    if(n == 0)
6      return result;
7    result = factorial(n-1) * n;
8    return result;
9  }
```

```
1  /* main.c */
2  #include <stdlib.h>
3  #include <stdio.h>
4  #include "factorial.h"
5
6  int main(int argc, char **argv) {
7    int n, result;
8    if(argc != 2) {
9      fprintf(stderr, "usage: factorial n, n >=0\n");
10     return 1;
11   }
12   n = atoi(argv[1]);
13   result = factorial(n);
14   printf("factorial %d!=%d\n", n, result);
15   return 0;
16 }
```

We can do the compilation of these source code files into object files and the subsequent linking in one step:

```
> gcc -g -o calc_factorial factorial.c main.c
```

The two steps of compilation and linking can be separated – and for large projects it is a good idea to build an executable file in a modular way, that is, to cleanly separate the phases of building each object file and subsequently building the executable file or library from the object files. Code changes in one of the source code files would otherwise require all source code to be re-compiled, while the modular approach permits to only re-compile those parts affected by the code changes.

A command such as `gcc` is actually not a plain compiler – it manages multiple phases around the build process of a program – preprocessing, compilation, assembling, and linking. It is often called a *compiler driver*. The linker program `ld` is called by the compiler driver, and the compiler driver provides the linker with the relevant arguments derived from the arguments to the compiler driver plus a number of platform specific object files and system libraries.

Separating the object file creation and link steps for the above example means to first compile the source files into object files and subsequently linking these object files to an executable. In the command lines below we are using the GCC compiler with flag `-c` to build the object files. Then, we link the object files to an executable `calc_factorial`:

```
> gcc -g -c factorial.c  (builds object file factorial.o)
> gcc -g -c main.c       (builds object file main.o)
> gcc -o calc_factorial factorial.o main.o
```

9.3 Resolving Undefined Symbols

The most frequent link problems are caused by unresolved symbols. We will take a look at the most common cases in the following sections.

9.3.1 Missing Linker Arguments

If an object file containing a required symbol definition is missing from the linker command line arguments, the linker will complain about the missing symbol(s). For example, here is what happens if we leave out the argument `factorial.o`:

```
> gcc -o calc_factorial main.o
  main.o: In function 'main':
  [...]/linking_issues/example1/main.c:13:
      undefined reference to 'factorial'
```

We see that the linker does provide enough information on what is missing:

- the link error is caused by an unresolved symbol named `factorial`
- the symbol is unresolved in the object file `main.o`
- the object file `main.o` belongs to the source file `main.c`
- the `factorial()` function was used in line 13 of this source file

In the following example we compile the source file `main.c` without the debug information, to show that the linker error messages still contain enough information to search for the object file or library containing the definition of the missing symbol. We can see that the level of details provided in the linker error message is reduced: the location of the source file is missing, and the line number is replaced by a location inside the object file.

```
> gcc -c main.c
> gcc -o calc_factorial main.o
  main.o: In function 'main':
  main.c:(.text+0x4): undefined reference to 'factorial'
```

9.3.2 Searching for Missing Symbols

Depending on the size of the project, it can be quite difficult to find the missing definition of a symbol. In the best case the programmer knows what the symbol refers to and where it is defined – either in an object file or library, or in a source file that still needs to be compiled.

In case one does not know the symbol or where it is defined, the first approach is to search for it. If the symbol is a function or method, you should try to look it up in the documentation. Good candidates are the documentation belonging to your computer system, project, or third-party contributed software. As an alternative, you can have your computer search for it. On UNIX you can use the utilities grep and find to locate files. On Windows you can use the Explorer Search dialog.

There are utilities to analyze the symbols of object files, libraries, and programs. On UNIX the utility nm provides a list of symbols. On Windows you can use for example the utility DUMPBIN. A symbol that needs to be resolved is marked as such with the token U or UNDEF, and defined symbols are preceded by tokens indicating the object file section that contain the symbol definition. For example, the letter T corresponds to the text section of an object file that contains the instructions of the compiled code. Symbols representing functions are contained in a text section of an object file.

Our factorial example is small enough that one could use the utility nm on the object files unfiltered and read the entire symbol table. In real-life projects this is almost impossible, so one needs to use search or filter utilities such as grep on top of that:

```
> nm -o *.o | grep factorial
   factorial.o:00000000 T factorial
   main.o:        U factorial
```

In this example the nm utility shows a list of all symbols in all object files in the current directory, and the grep utility filters out the function name that we are interested in. We use the -o option of the nm command to precede each line with the file name – otherwise the result of the grep command would not be very helpful. The result shows that the symbol factorial is defined in the object file factorial.o. Adding this file to the list of linker arguments will enable the linker to build the program correctly.

If none of the object files or libraries in the project contains the missing symbol, one can use the same strategy to search in different places for the definition:

- In the source code for the program: if the code was not compiled into an object file, the build system needs to be fixed.
- In the system libraries: Since there are usually a large number of system libraries on a computer, it is often easier to consult the online documentation. For example, if one gets an undefined symbol sqrtf on UNIX, the command man sqrtf will show this function is part of the math library and that -lm is needed as linker argument.

- In third-party software libraries: when the program is planned to include software from other companies or developers, the missing symbols might be found here as well.
- Outside of your computer or network: in case the object file with the system definition is not on your system at all, you may need to use an Internet search engine to locate the missing library or symbols. It is amazing to discover how many other programmers have encountered and solved the same issues that you have.

9.3.3 Linking Order Issues

One important aspect of providing an object file *directly* as argument to the linker is that all its symbols will be linked into the executable. Especially when linking in object files containing various service functions that are typically used for multiple projects it can have the undesired effect of producing an unnecessarily large executable file. You can use *libraries* or *archive files* instead of object files to avoid this. From a library the linker picks only those object files containing symbols that are currently undefined in its current list of defined and undefined symbols. It is important to note that most linkers process the provided object files and libraries only once, according to the following algorithm:

- First the linker loads the object file(s) that contain the initialization code for the executable. The initialization code also calls the `main` routine of a C program, that is, the linker starts at least with the undefined symbol `main`. The object file(s) containing the initialization routines are provided to the linker by the compiler driver automatically.
- Then the linker sequentially walks through the object files and libraries specified, in the order of the link line arguments. From each library the linker picks only those object files that satisfy at least one symbol that is currently still unresolved. From an object file it picks all symbols, regardless whether it resolves symbols that are currently marked as undefined in the linkers list. Including a new object file can create new undefined symbols for the linker.
- The link process is successful if at the end of the link line all symbols are resolved.

In our example we generate a library `libfactorial.a` from the object file `factorial.o` using the UNIX utility `ar`. `ar` is a program that creates or modifies libraries, or extracts objects from libraries. In the following link step we now ignore the importance of ordering the linker arguments correctly. Even though every piece of information the linker needs is present, the linker complains about missing symbols:

```
> ar -r -o libfactorial.a factorial.o
  ar: creating libfactorial.a
```

```
> gcc -o calc_factorial libfactorial.a main.o
  main.o:main.c:(..): undefined reference to 'factorial'
```

With the knowledge how a linker works, this behavior is easily explained: when the linker arrives at the library `libfactorial.a` it has only the undefined symbol `main` in its list. There is no object file in the library `libfactorial.a` that provides a definition for this symbol, and the symbol `factorial` that *is* defined in the library is not picked up, since the linker does not have an unresolved symbol for it. In the next step the linker loads the object file `main.o` – here the symbol `main` is defined, but the `main()` routine also calls the function `factorial()`. Hence it creates a new unresolved item in the list of undefined symbols. Since the linker has reached the end of the argument list now, it terminates with an error message and a list of missing symbols.

If the order of the object file `main.o` and the library `libfactorial.a` is changed, the linking process succeeds:

```
> gcc -o calc_factorial main.o libfactorial.a
```

9.3.4 C++ Symbols and Name Mangling

The C++ features such as namespaces, classes, templates, or overloading of functions have made compilation and linking far more complex. The potential for linking issues due to symbol mismatches is increased. Even compiling the same C source code with a C compiler and then with a C++ compiler results in different symbols:

```
> gcc -c main.c
> nm main.o | grep factorial
         U factorial

> g++ -c main.c
> nm main.o | grep factorial
         U __Z9factoriali
```

While for C it is sufficient to compile the function `factorial()` into a symbol with the name `factorial`, it is not sufficient for C++. In C++ one can *overload* functions, i.e. there can be more than one function with name `factorial` that differ in their number and types of arguments and the type of the return value. To produce a unique symbol for C++ code elements, the compiler uses a technique called *name mangling* where the exact specification of an object or function (e.g. namespaces, and type and number of function arguments) are encoded into the symbol. Unfortunately almost every compiler has its own rule-set for name mangling, and even different versions of the same compiler can produce incompatible object code.

9.3.5 Demangling of Symbols

To track down these incompatibilities it is necessary to observe the name-mangled symbols carefully. Reading the name-mangled symbols is often very tedious and error prone, so it is better to *demangle* these symbols. One can do this either by using analysis utilities that can switch between mangled and demangled output, or using filters such as c++filt. The nm utility can be called with the option -C or --demangle to obtain the actual user level names of the symbols. These filters translate the cryptic argument and type encoding back into the source code, so it is easier to see the original form of a symbol.

Note that name mangling is compiler dependent, so one needs to make sure that the matching utilities and tools are used:

```
> nm main.o | grep factorial
        U __Z9factoriali

> nm main.o | grep factorial | c++filt
        U factorial(int)
```

9.3.6 Linking C and C++ Code

As we have seen, compiling a piece of code with a C++ compiler produces different symbols as compiling the same code with a C compiler. This often leads to link errors as well:

```
> gcc -c factorial.c
> g++ -c main.c
> gcc -o calc_factorial main.o factorial.o
  main.o:main.c:(..): undefined reference to 'factorial(int)'
```

It is noteworthy that only using the C compiler driver does by no means ensure that the source is really compiled as C code – the compiler drivers may decide by the file extension whether C or C++ style symbols will be produced. If, for example, the compiler driver gcc is called for a file with extension .c, then it is compiled as C code, while the same code in a file with extension .cc compiles as C++ code. Other examples for commonly used file extensions for C++ files are .C, .cpp, or .cxx.

```
> gcc -c main.c
> nm main.o | grep factorial
        U factorial
> cp main.c main.cc
> gcc -c main.cc
> nm main.o | grep factorial
        U __Z9factoriali
```

To avoid linking issues such as those described here it is a good idea to be very strict about the file extensions or to provide explicit compiler directives to pick the target format.

Nevertheless, it is not always possible to have all source code compiled by the same compiler. It is common to have a C++ program that needs to link in symbols defined in a C object file – which would normally cause the linking issue we have seen earlier in this section. The solution here is to tell the C++ compiler explicitly not to name-mangle the undefined symbols that need to be resolved by the symbols in the C object file. One can do so by using the extern "C" compiler directive in the declaration of the appropriate elements. In the example in Figure 9.1 we have only enclosed the declaration of the function factorial() in an extern "C" block, which enables us to compile main.cc with a C++ compiler and the resulting object file can still be linked to the C library defining the required symbol factorial. Linking the program then no longer results in undefined
symbols.

```
> g++ -c main.cc
> nm main.o | grep factorial
          U factorial


1   extern "C" {
2   unsigned factorial(unsigned n);
3   }
```

Fig. 9.1 Header file factorial.h with extern "C" declaration

9.4 Symbols with Multiple Definitions

The opposite of missing symbols during the linking phase is that the linker discovers multiple definitions of the same symbol. In the best case the linker complains about this, so there is a chance of locating the source of the bug when linking the program. In many other cases the linker just picks the first definition it finds in the object and library files specified in the command line. If we are lucky the first definition is the intended one and the program works as expected. Often enough we are not lucky.

As an example let us assume that besides the definition of factorial in the library libfactorial.a there is also a stub function factorial() defined in the file sfactorial.c.

```
1   #include <stdio.h>
2
3   int factorial(int n)
4   {
```

```
5        fprintf(stderr,"Stub for factorial is called\n");
6        return 0;
7   }
```

If one specifies the linker arguments in an order that forces the linker to pick both symbols it will issue an error message indicating that two symbols of the same name are conflicting, along with the information where these symbols have been defined:

```
> gcc -o calc_factorial main.o libfactorial.a sfactorial.o
sfactorial.o:sfactorial.c: multiple definition of 'factorial'
libfactorial.a(factorial.o):factorial.c:4: first defined here
```

9.5 Symbol Clashes

Let us change the order of command line arguments, so the linker is free to pick the first symbol definition and ignore all following ones. The linking process will succeed, but we end up with unintended program behavior:

```
> gcc -o calc_factorial main.o sfactorial.o libfactorial.a
> ./calc_factorial 5
  Stub for factorial is called
  factorial 5!=0
```

The calc_factorial program in this case always displays the result 0, no matter which number is specified as input.

The code snippet above is also a good example to show that it is a wise idea to clearly mark stub functions that are not intended to be called with safety bolts, such as assertions, debug output, or invalid return values. Otherwise it may take rather lengthy debug sessions to find that the wrong functions are executed.

The problem we observe is called a *symbol clash*; multiple definitions of the same symbol exist yet this ambiguity has not been detected at link time.

How can we analyze a symbol clash?

Calling the wrong function is likely to result in memory corruption. The symptoms are strange core dumps which do not seem to make any sense; the program suddenly crashes at a location which looks fine, data members of class objects suddenly have corrupt values, yet memory checkers cannot find a statement that corrupted the memory.

If the function is a C function then the number and type of arguments may be different in caller and callee. If the symbol is a class method then accessing any class members will be wrong because the memory layout of both classes is almost certainly different. This may lead to an immediate error such as a segmentation fault or a memory corruption detected much later.

Once you have identified symbol clashes in your application, there are different ways out:

- The obvious solution – especially if you have access to the source code – is to rename the variables and functions causing the symbol clashes in your code.
- You may also want to consider introducing C++ namespaces.
- It may be possible to suppress exporting certain symbols using `static` qualifiers in the source code or, later in the flow, linker flags. This process is also referred to as *localizing symbols*.
- As a last resort you may want to look at tools such as `objcopy` (part of the GNU `binutils`), and, on Windows, `EDITBIN` or `LIB`. In addition to localizing symbols these tools can be used to rename both symbol references and definitions.

9.6 Identifying Compiler and Linker Version Mismatches

When we talk about mismatching compiler or linker versions, we are actually referring to the fact that different C++ compilers generate code for different *application binary interfaces* or *ABIs*. An ABI is the set of runtime conventions followed by all of the tools that deal with binary representations of a program, including compilers, assemblers, and linkers. One obvious difference is the different C++ name mangling conventions by the C++ compilers. Another difference can be the *system library symbols* that are defined in the libraries that come with the C++ compiler and linker installation, such as `libstdc++.a`. During linking the defined and used symbols will no longer match. The linker will complain about *undefined symbols*, although all the linker arguments, and their order appear to be correct. To illustrate this, we have used different compiler/linker versions, contemporary and outdated, in this section. Of course "contemporary" refers to the time of writing this book – but the principles (and problems) when using different compilers and versions are likely to stay around for coming compiler generations as well.

It is noteworthy that these incompatibilities in name mangling are often introduced intentionally by compiler developers to prevent the compiler users from running into more subtle problems of mismatching ABIs. This way incompatible libraries are detected at link time rather than at run time when the program crashes for no obvious reason.[1]

Symbol mismatches are mainly a C++ issue: C compilers and linkers do not have to support concepts such as function overloading, templates, and all those other features that were the reason for introducing name mangling for C++ compilers in the first place. Still, you can run into issues with inconsistent ABI even for pure C compilation and linking.

---

[1] Cited from GNU On-line docs, http://gcc.gnu.org/onlinedocs/gcc-4.0.3/gcc/Interoperation.html

9.6.1 Mismatching System Libraries

The problem of mismatching system libraries occurs when compiling all object files with the same compiler, but use a different compiler (version) for linking.

C++ compilers implement some of the C++ specific features, for example dynamic cast, by including system libraries. The GCC 3.x compiler links a library libstdc++ into the executable. Object files and library must match to make the feature of dynamic cast work.

When you generate object files with GCC 2.95.3 but use GCC 3.3.5 for linking, then you will get a large number of undefined symbols similar to the following:

```
undefined reference to '__throw'
undefined reference to '__builtin_delete'
undefined reference to '__builtin_new'
undefined reference to '__rtti_user'
undefined reference to 'cout'
undefined reference to 'endl(ostream &)'
undefined reference to 'ostream::operator<<(char const *)'
```

If the linker complains about missing symbols for internally used functions and methods such as cout or __throw it is very likely that the reason is a mismatch between the object files and the system libraries. Functions used internally by the C++ compiler usually start with two leading underscores, for example __dynamic_cast.

9.6.2 Mismatching Object Files

This problem occurs when trying to link object files that were generated with different compilers – or compiler versions. The most frequent situation for this issue is that one has to include object files or libraries, where no corresponding source code is available – such as third party libraries. In this case the easy fix of building everything from scratch using the same compiler and linker is not applicable.

The symptom for a compiler mismatch is that the linker complains about missing symbols, but the symbols are present in the object files or libraries, and link order appears to be correct.

Using tools such as nm on UNIX or DUMPBIN on Windows to analyze the symbol tables of the object files with the unresolved symbols and those with the corresponding defined symbols will reveal that the demangled user level symbols are the same while the name-mangled symbols differ. The next step toward fixing this issue is to find out the compiler versions that have been used to generate the different object files – see Section 9.6.4 on page 120 – and decide which compiler to use to compile and link *all* object files and libraries.

Note that even small differences in the compilers, such as a different release version, can cause the above link problems.

9.6.3 Runtime Crashes

Even if the executable links without error messages, there's still a chance that *something* went wrong during the linking process – usually this *something* surfaces later at runtime and produces a core dump. How can you distinguish these core dumps from other issues that are likely to lead to core dumps, for example memory problems described in Chapter 4? The core dump happens usually when some C++ specific function is used. These functions start with a leading double underscore. That is, you should check for this in the stack trace of the core or when running the program in the debugger. Of course it is no guarantee that C++ specific functions in the stack trace always indicate a compiler or linker mismatch. You will still need to check your source code with the memory debugging tools described in Chapter 4.

For example, when you compile a source code with GCC 2.96 but use GCC 2.95.3 for linking, this may trigger a core dump when a dynamic cast is used.

Fixing the problem is rather simple: re-compile *all* source files with the *same* compiler, and use this compiler also for linking.

9.6.4 Determining the Compiler Version

One of the questions raised above is how to find out which compiler version has been used to generate existing object files. This is of special interest if the sources are not available for these object files or libraries, and the solution to rebuild everything just from scratch with the same compiler is not possible.

One approach that works well on almost all UNIX-like platforms is to search in the object files for certain strings that provide a hint regarding the compiler version. Possible ways are to use UNIX tools such as `strings` and `egrep` or an editor such as `emacs`.

What strings do we look for? This depends on the compiler that has been used – we cannot supply a complete list for all past, current, and future compilers. But we can provide some hints for the most frequently used ones. This also gives an idea of what type of information to look for when other compilers come into play:

- GNU compilers contain a string "`(GCC)`" followed by the version number.
- Sun compilers contain a string "`Forte Developer`" or "`Sun`" followed by the compiler version number and the patch level.
- HP compilers do not include version strings directly, but typically supply complete path names to system files that have been included. These paths contain the compiler version of the compiler as well.

Here is one example of searching for the compiler version string on UNIX/Linux:

```
> strings -a factorial.o | egrep "(GCC|GNU|Sun|Forte|HP)"
GCC: (GNU) 3.3.2
```

Another approach to guessing the compiler that produced an object file is to observe the generated symbols in the object files, for example using the UNIX utility nm. Different compilers use different symbols for certain C++ language constructs or standard C++ classes. In case of doubt, create a small test file like the following, compile it with the compiler that should be used throughout the entire program and check the generated object files with nm. If the same sort of symbols shows up in the object file and test file, then chances are good that this compiler was also used to create the object file.

```
 1  #include <iostream>
 2
 3  struct B { virtual int foo(); };
 4  struct D: public B { virtual int foo(); };
 5  void test() {
 6    std::string S("abc");      // std::string::string(...)
 7    std::string S2(S);         // ditto
 8    int* a = new int[4];       // operator new
 9    delete [] a;               // operator delete []
10    D* d1 = new D;
11    B* b = d1;
12    D* d2 = dynamic_cast<D*>(b); // dynamic_cast
13  }
```

Fig. 9.2 Example file test_file.cc

Compile the file and check symbol name with nm:

```
> g++ -c test_file.cc
> nm test_file.o | grep " T "            # output in mangled form
  000000c4 T _Z4testv
> nm -C test_file.o | grep " T "          # output in C++ notation
  000000c4 T test()
```

Different compiler families such as GCC and Sun Forte compiler CC have different mangling schemes. Each one has its own version of c++filt which works differently. This can already give a clue about the compiler. If one tries to translate a mangled symbol from an object file with the c++filt tool of the currently used C++ environment and the result does not resemble a C++ signature then it is quite likely that the object file was compiled with a different compiler.

In the following example the file test_file.cc has been compiled with a Sun Forte compiler, and we are using the c++filt utility of the GCC installation.

```
> /opt/SUNWspro/bin/CC test_file.cc
> nm test_file.o | grep " T "
  00000010 T __1cEtest6F_v_
> nm test_file.o | grep " T " | c++filt
  00000010 T __1cEtest6F_v_
> nm test_file.o | grep " T " | /opt/SUNWspro/bin/c++filt
  00000010 T void test()
```

The example shows that using a non-matching version of `c++filt` has no effect at all. In other cases error messages are issued by `c++filt` saying there is no information available how to treat the current format.

Using `c++filt` to test for link-incompatible compiler versions only works reliably when testing for different compiler families. For different versions of the same compiler family, such as GCC, we have to be extra careful: some `c++filt` versions are trying to be smart and detect the format of the input automatically. So you even get correct looking C++ names as `c++filt` output even though there is a version mismatch.

9.7 Solving Dynamic Linking Issues

Libraries with object code can be linked *dynamically* instead of *statically* into the executable. Such *dynamic link libraries (DLLs)* or *shared object files* typically have the extension `.so` on UNIX and Linux, and the extension `.dll` on Windows. Explaining the creation of DLLs for various compilers is not in the scope of this book – please refer to your compiler documentation.

DLLs have several advantages, such as shorter link times and smaller executable sizes. In addition to slightly slower program execution, DLLs also have DLL-specific link and runtime problems. These problems are the focus of this section.

9.7.1 Linking or Loading DLLs

There are two different ways how a DLL can be tied to an executable: it can be *linked* to an executable, or it can be *loaded* with an explicit call at runtime.

Here is an example with GCC how you can specify a DLL as an argument to the linker:

```
> gcc -o myprog main.o libA.so
```

The linker will not link the real content of `libA.so` into the executable `myprog` but it will create a reference to it. Whenever the executable is started, then `libA.so` will automatically be loaded.

In Visual Studio you don't use the actual DLL (file extension `.dll`) for linking, but, instead, a special *import library*, which has the same file extension as a static library (`.lib`).

You can access a DLL at runtime via `dlopen()` on Linux or `LoadLibrary()` on Windows. This puts the decision if and when to load the DLL under user control. It can be loaded early during program startup, in the middle of the program, or not at all.

After loading a DLL one gains access to its symbols via system calls: `dlsym()` on UNIX or Linux, and `GetProcAddress()` on Windows. These return pointers to the respective variables and routines, or null pointers if no symbol with the given name is exported by the DLL.

The example in Figure 9.3 shows both techniques for GCC: function `show1()` is located in `libutil1.so` which is linked into the program. Function `show2()` is located in `libutil2.so` which is loaded in line 13 of `main.c`. The commands in Figure 9.4 show the compilation and linking command lines for the DLLs and the executable `myprog`. If you want to build shared object files with GCC you have to use the `-fPIC` flag to create *position-independent code* suited for *dynamic linking*. To generate shared objects with GCC you have to use the `-shared` flag. Note that at link time only `libutil1.so` is supplied as linker argument, but not `libutil2.so`, which is loaded instead.

```
 1 /* dll_issue_example.c */
 2 #include <dlfcn.h>
 3 #include <stdio.h>
 4 void show1(char* msg, int value);
 5
 6 int main(int argc, char* argv[])
 7 {
 8   void *dll;
 9   void (*fn)(char*,int);
10
11   show1("pol", 42);
12
13   if((dll=dlopen("./libutil2.so",RTLD_NOW|RTLD_GLOBAL))==0){
14       fprintf(stderr,"%s\n",dlerror());
15       return 1;
16   }
17   if((fn = dlsym(dll,"show2")) == 0) {
18       fprintf(stderr,"%s\n",dlerror());
19       return 2;
20   }
21   (fn)("pol", 42);
22   return 0;
23 }
```

Fig. 9.3 Using DLLs through linking and loading

```
> gcc -g -c -fPIC util1.c
> gcc -shared -o libutil1.so util1.o
> gcc -g -c -fPIC util2.c
> gcc -shared -o libutil2.so util2.o
> gcc -o myprog -g main.c libutil1.so -ldl
```

Fig. 9.4 Building and linking shared objects

9.7.2 DLL Not Found

A very common problem with using DLLs is that the program issues an error message about not being able to load or find a DLL or shared object during startup. This applies to DLLs that are linked into the executable. For example, this can happen when trying to run the code example of Figure 9.3:

```
> ./myprog
./myprog: error while loading shared libraries:
     libutil1.so: cannot open shared object file:
     No such file or directory
```

When the program is started, a startup routine automatically tries to load all DLLs that are linked into the executable. How does the program know which DLLs have to be loaded and where to find them? Most development environments have default library directories that are searched for DLLs. In addition, you can specify additional search paths to the linker when building the program. Last but not least, you can also set environment variables such as LD_LIBRARY_PATH on UNIX or PATH on Windows to add directories to the search path of the loader.

The exact rules governing the search order for DLLs are more complex but for user-defined DLLs the environment variables LD_LIBRARY_PATH on UNIX and PATH on Windows are most important.

Utility programs help finding out which DLLs are used in an executable. For example, on UNIX the command ldd prints a list of dynamic libraries required by a program and where they are taken from.

```
> ldd myprog
     linux-gate.so.1 =>  (0xffffe000)
     libutil1.so => not found
     libdl.so.2 => /lib/libdl.so.2 (0x4002d00)
     libc.so.6 =>/lib/tls/libc.so.6 (0x4003100)
     /lib/ld-linux.so.2 (0x4000000)
```

Note that libutil1.so is not found while all other required libraries could be located on the system.

If a specific library is not found then one should check whether the library is really not in the library search path of the executable. The DLL search path consists of

- a list of directories specified by the environment variables LD_LIBRARY_PATH or PATH
- a list of OS and machine dependent system library directories such as /lib or /usr/lib

It should be noted that incorrect search order can result in problems too; specifically if different versions of the same DLL are stored on your system. Please refer to the documentation of your linker for details.

9.7.3 Analyzing Loader Issues

Problems with missing or wrong library search paths as described in Section 9.7.2 are often hard to debug without appropriate tools. Most UNIX-like systems offer runtime analysis support for the loader, which logs or traces each step of the loader during the runtime of the program. From such traces or log files you can, for example, see which directories are searched, and where a DLL was finally found. You can enable this loader debug feature by setting the environment variable LD_DEBUG. If you set the variable to libs and then call a program using a loader, it will report every step related to finding the required DLLs.

Setting the environment variable LD_DEBUG to libs and running the executable myprog described in Section 9.7.1 will produce a trace similar to the one shown below. The first number represents the ID of the process using the loader. Then, for each DLL that is needed by this process, you see first the name of the DLL followed by the search path. Next you see the loader looking into all of the directories until it finds the required DLL or reports a failure.

```
> setenv LD_DEBUG libs
> ./myprog
    2420:  find library=libutil1.so [0]; searching
    2420:   search path=./tls/i686/sse2:./tls/i686:
                        ./tls/sse2:./tls:./i686/sse2:
                        ./i686:./sse2:. (LD_LIBRARY_PATH)
    2420:    trying file=./tls/i686/sse2/libutil1.so
    ...
    2420:    trying file=./i686/libutil1.so
    2420:    trying file=./sse2/libutil1.so
    2420:    trying file=./libutil1.so
    2420:
    2420:  find library=libdl.so.2 [0]; searching
    2420:   search path=./tls/i686/sse2:./tls/i686:
                        ./tls/sse2:./tls:./i686/sse2:
                        ./i686:./sse2:. (LD_LIBRARY_PATH)
    2420:    trying file=./tls/i686/sse2/libdl.so.2
    ...
    2420:    trying file=./i686/libdl.so.2
    2420:    trying file=./sse2/libdl.so.2
    2420:    trying file=./libdl.so.2
    2420:   search cache=/etc/ld.so.cache
    2420:    trying file=/lib/libdl.so.2
    2420:
    ...
```

Most loaders offer even more analysis capabilities that you can enable by setting the environment variable LD_DEBUG to different values. If you set LD_DEBUG to help you will also get a short list of the supported features:

```
> setenv LD_DEBUG help
> ./myprog
Valid options for the LD_DEBUG environment variable are:
```

```
libs        display library search paths
reloc       display relocation processing
files       display progress for input file
symbols     display symbol table processing
bindings    display information about symbol binding
versions    display version dependencies
all         all previous options combined
statistics  display relocation statistics
unused      determined unused DSOs
help        display this help message and exit
```

To direct the debugging output into a file instead of standard output a file name can be specified using the LD_DEBUG_OUTPUT environment variable.

9.7.4 Setting Breakpoints in DLLs

As explained before, DLLs can either be *linked* into the program or they can be *loaded* during runtime with an explicit dlopen() call. Most debuggers have different modes and commands related to DLLs.

The default setting is to load debug information for a DLL as soon as possible. Debug information for linked DLLs is read during startup, debug information for DLLs that are loaded is read when the DLL is opened with a dlopen() or LoadLibrary() call. When a debugger is attached to a program, the debug information is read for all DLLs that are opened at this point in time. The GDB command shared library displays which DLLs are already loaded and loads debug information for them if not already done. In Visual Studio, pause execution, and go to the menu item **Debug/Windows/Modules**, to open a window that shows all loaded DLLs.

The dynamic nature of loading DLLs has the effect that the source code contained in a DLL can only be debugged after the DLL is loaded. No debug information is available before that point in time, so it is not possible to set breakpoints directly. This is especially confusing when starting to debug a completely new and hence not well known program. In particular it is not always easy to identify which parts of the source code are compiled into the static part of the program and which parts are compiled into DLLs. A frequent symptom for the latter is that one tries to set a breakpoint in a specific function and this fails for no obvious reason.

Most of the newer debuggers have features to cope with this situation: the breakpoint is set as *pending* . Whenever a new DLL is loaded the debugger tries to resolve pending breakpoints.

We can try this out with the code example shown in Figure 9.3: setting a breakpoint in show1 is possible right away but a breakpoint in show2 is *pending* until the DLL is loaded in line 13:

```
> gdb myprog
...
(gdb) break show2
```

```
Function "show2" not defined.
Make breakpoint pending on future shared library load?
(y or [n]) y

Breakpoint 1 (show2) pending.
(gdb) run
Starting program: [...]/linking_problems/example4/myprog
Breakpoint 2 at 0xa7a882: file util2.c, line 5.
Pending breakpoint "show2" resolved
util1, pol:value=42

Breakpoint 2, show2 (msg=0x.. "pol", value=42) at util2.c:5
5           printf("util2, %s:value=%d\n", msg, value);
(gdb)
```

9.7.5 Provide Error Messages for DLL Issues

If loading a dynamic library or accessing its symbols fails then one can make use of *error reporting functions* to produce a human-readable explanation of what actually went wrong. On UNIX this error handling function is called dlerror(). On Windows you can use the functions GetLastError() and FormatMessage() to provide meaningful error messages. These error reporting functions can also be called from the debugger.

We make use of dlerror() in lines 14 and 18 of the example in Figure 9.3. If we remove the DLL that needs to be loaded in line 13 before starting the program myprog then we observe the following:

```
> rm libutil2.so
> ./myprog
  util1, pol:value=42
./myprog: error while loading shared libraries: libutil2.so:
  cannot open shared object file: No such file or directory
```

Without the error message issued by the dlerror() call in line 14, the program would silently return from the main() routine without any error message.

Lessons learned:

- If a linker reports undefined symbols, identify where those symbols are defined and make sure the appropriate compilation units (object files or libraries) are supplied as linker arguments.
- The order of the linker arguments is important. This holds both for the compilation units – such as object files and libraries – and for the search paths.
- C and C++ compilers produce different symbols for the same functions.
- If a linker reports undefined symbols even though you can not find any obvious flaws in the linking process, the error might be caused by the use of different ABIs (application binary interfaces) in the compilation units. This can occur if the compilation units were created with different compilers, or with different environment settings.
- Do an Internet search on the missing symbols; chances are good that other developers have encountered the same link issues.
- Multiply-defined symbols can cause problems too, with runtime symbol clashes being particularly hard to analyze. Renaming symbols in the source code, introducing namespaces, or mangling the symbols after compilation can be part of the solution.
- DLLs pose specific challenges. Be aware of search pathes and debugging aids provided by your linker and runtime loader. Often, breakpoints can only be set after the corresponding DLLs are loaded.

Chapter 10
Advanced Debugging

In this chapter you will find a collection of advanced debugging topics. We will address each topic in a stand-alone section. Some of the topics are general, whereas some are specific to a particular debugger.

In Sections 10.1 – 10.5 we show how to navigate with the debugger in C++ code. We will concentrate on function overloading, implicit functions, templates, and static constructors/destructors. We will look at data-dependent breakpoints called *watchpoints* in Section 10.6, followed by sections on how to debug signals and exceptions, how to read *stack traces*, how to modify a running program, and how to debug a program that was compiled without debug information.

10.1 Setting Breakpoints in C++ Functions, Methods, and Operators

An important debugging skill is to force a program stop at a location that is of interest to you. We do this by setting a breakpoint in a specific function or line, as explained in Chapter 3. However, when setting breakpoints in C++ methods, functions and operators, the debugger may refuse to set a breakpoint, reporting that there is no such function, or there are too many functions to select.

C++ supports *function overloading*, so there may be multiple C++ functions with the same name, but with differences in the type and number of arguments. The debugger needs to know the exact *signature* of the C++ function in order to find it. In C++, the signature of a function contains the name, class name, the types of all arguments, and namespace. For a template function specialization, the signature also includes the template arguments. The purpose of the signature is to let the debugger distinguish between multiple versions of functions. The signature of a function is also used when a program is linked (see Chapter 9).

Since typing the correct signature of a C++ function into the debugger can be time-consuming, you should let the debugger assist you in selecting the desired

C++ function names. GDB and Visual Studio provide several useful features, which
we will explain with the help of the following example:

```
1   class C {
2   public:
3       C(int a)            : n(a)  {}
4       int foo(int a)              {return n=a;}
5       int foo() const             {return n;}
6       int foo(char c, bool b)  {return n+=b+c;}
7       C& operator=(const C& r) {n=r.foo(); return *this; }
8   private:
9       int n;
10  };
11
12  int main(int argc, char* argv[]) {
13      C ca(0);
14      C cb(1);
15      ca.foo(-23);
16      cb=ca;
17      return cb.foo('A',false);
18  }
```

For GDB, we start the program and then set a breakpoint in member function `foo`
on line 4. We first try to set a breakpoint with the `break  C::foo` command:

```
(gdb) break C::foo
[0] cancel
[1] all
[2] C::foo(char, bool) at main.cpp:6
[3] C::foo() const at main.cpp:5
[4] C::foo(int) at main.cpp:4
```

The method name `foo` does not specify the arguments, so the name is ambiguous
and GDB prints a list of all matching methods. One solution is to enter one of the
candidate signatures proposed by GDB. Example: `break  C::foo(int)` will
break in line 4.

You can also type in a partial signature, and then let GDB do the rest. GDB has a
convenient completion feature that is similar to file completion in a command shell.
Use a single quote ' as a prefix for a function and the TAB key or the sequence
ESC ? to trigger the automatic completion. For example, type `break  'C::foo`
followed by TAB.

A different way to find out more about class methods is to use the `ptype` command of GDB. This command lists all elements of the class including the methods:

```
(gdb) ptype C
type = class C {
  private:
    int n;

  public:
    C(int);
```

```
    int foo(int);
    int foo() const;
    int foo(char, bool);
    C & operator=(C const&);
}
```

The GDB command `info functions <expr>` will find all global and member functions that match <expr>:

```
(gdb) info functions C::foo
All functions matching regular expression "C::foo":

File main.cpp:
int C::foo() const;
int C::foo(char, bool);
int C::foo(int);
```

In the Visual Studio debugger, go to the **Debug** menu, click on item **Breakpoint/Break at Function...**. Enter `C::foo`. This will create 3 breakpoints, one for each function named `C::foo`. For overloaded functions, you can enter the function name followed by the argument types. For example, `C::foo(int)` will create a breakpoint in line 4.

Lessons learned:

- Setting breakpoints in C++ code is complicated by function overloading. Use a simple C++ example to familiarize yourself with debugger commands and features to list the complete signature of functions, and to cope with incomplete signatures.

10.2 Setting Breakpoints in Templatized Functions and C++ Classes

A problem particular to GDB is handling breakpoints in templates. When you set a breakpoint in a specific line of a templatized function or C++ class, the program may not stop there. We will explain why this happens, and how to circumvent the problem. Consider the following example containing a templatized function `myFunction`:

```
1  #include <iostream>
2
3  template <class T>
4  void myFunction(T value)
5  {
6      std::cout << "got " << value << std::endl;
7  }
```

131

```
 8
 9  int main(int argc, char* argv[]) {
10      myFunction(100);
11      myFunction('A');
12      myFunction(true);
13      return 0;
14  }
```

We want to stop on each call of myFunction, so we put a breakpoint at line 6.
GDB accepts the breakpoint command, but when we run the program, we find that
the debugger stops only once and not three times:

```
(gdb) break main.cpp:6
Breakpoint 1 at 0x8048882: file main.cpp, line 6.
(gdb) run
got 100

Breakpoint 1, myFunction<char> (value=65 'A') at main.cpp:6
6      std::cout << "got " << value << std::endl;
(gdb) cont
got A
got 1
```

Why did GDB fail to stop on the first call? The C++ compiler creates different
object code when a template is instantiated with a new argument. The debugging information in every template instance will refer back to the same source
line in the template code. Setting a breakpoint in a specific *line* in a template
causes GDB to set the breakpoint in just *one* instance. In the example, break
main.cpp:6 sets the breakpoint in myFunction<char>. No other instances,
such as myFunction<int>, get a breakpoint, so GDB will not stop there.

You should use the info breakpoints command to find out which template
instance GDB really did select:

```
(gdb) info breakpoints
Num Type           Disp Enb Address    What
1   breakpoint keep y   0x..     in void  myFunction<char>(char)
                                  at main.cpp:6
breakpoint already hit 1 time
```

In order to stop in a different template instance, you must set breakpoints at *function
signatures* and not at source code lines. See the previous Section 10.1 on how set
breakpoints in C++ functions.

```
(gdb) info functions myFunction
All functions matching regular expression "myFunction":

File main.cpp:
void void myFunction<bool>(bool);
void void myFunction<char>(char);
void void myFunction<int>(int);
```

Following this approach, we can set breakpoints in all three template instances of
myFunction and we will now see that GDB stops in all three function calls:

```
(gdb) break void myFunction<bool>(bool)
Breakpoint 2 at 0x80488b6: file main.cpp, line 6.
(gdb) break void myFunction<int>(int)
Breakpoint 3 at 0x80488e8: file main.cpp, line 6.
```

Note that we have discussed a GDB issue that exists in GDB 6.5 and previous versions; newer versions of GDB may have fixed this problem. However, independent of the debugger used, it is important to be aware of the subtle rules that apply to template instantiations and breakpoints. Different instantiations will result in multiple functions at different memory addresses. A specific breakpoint always applies to just one instance.

If you use Visual Studio and set the breakpoint in line 6, then it will create three breakpoints, one for each template instance, which is more intuitive than GDB.

Lessons learned:

- Setting a breakpoint at a specific *line* in a template can be ambiguous. Specifying breakpoints by *function signature* removes the ambiguity.
- Be careful with templatized functions or members. A GDB breakpoint applies to only one instantiation of the template, not to all.

10.3 Stepping in C++ Methods

In C++, a simple statement of C++ code may contain many implicit or "hidden" function calls. For example, the statement A=B; could contain calls to an assignment operator or a type conversion operator. Class constructors, operators, implicit conversions, and so on, allow us to express complex operations with a very compact piece of source code. This gives us good abstraction, high code density, and the ability to extend the language with class libraries. The drawback of the compact C++ source code is in debugging: all those implicit functions have to be made visible if they do not work as intended. In this section, we will show how to find out which implicit functions are called, and how to navigate the debugger into a specific function.

Consider the following example, an intentionally less-than-well-written string class STR.

```
1   /* class STR example */
2   #include <string>
3   #include <iostream>
4
5   class STR {
6   public:
7       STR(const char* a) {
8           s=a;
9           num++;
```

```
10          }
11          STR(const STR& a) {
12              s=a.s;
13              num++;
14          }
15          ~STR() {
16              num--;
17          }
18          const char* c_str() const {
19              return s.c_str();
20          }
21          const STR& operator+ (const STR& a) {
22              s += a.s; return *this;
23          }
24          int num_objs() const {
25              return num;
26          }
27          STR operator* (int num_copies) const {
28              std::string tmp("");
29              for (int n=0; n<num_copies;n++)
30                  tmp += s;
31              return STR(tmp.c_str());
32          }
33  private:
34      static int num;   // total #objects of this class
35      std::string s;
36  };
37  int STR::num=0;
38
39  void show( STR z )
40  {
41    std::cout <<z.num_objs() <<": " <<z.c_str() <<std::endl;
42  }
43
44  int main(int argc, char* argv[]) {
45      STR x="abc";
46      show(x);
47      show((x+"def") * 3);
48      return 0;
49  }
```

10.3.1 Stepping into Implicit Functions

Take a look at the show(x) statement in line 46. Function main() seems to directly call function show() but there is a hidden call to a constructor of class STR. The reason for this constructor call is that the function show() uses STR arguments, instead of references to STR objects, so the compiler must create a copy of the argument before calling the function. By advancing the debugger to line 46 and stepping into the function call, the constructor of STR is called. We then continue to use step-into commands to proceed until we are in function show ():

```
...
46      show(x);
(gdb) step
STR (this=0xbfffee00, a=@0xbfffee10) at main.cpp:11
11      STR(const STR& a) {
...
(gdb) step
show (z= ... 0x804b014 "abc" ... ) at main.cpp:41
41      cout <<z.num_objs() <<": " <<z.c_str() <<endl;
```

The step-into command will go down into any implicit function call, so it is a good way to locate implicit functions. It is important to understand that a step-into will usually only stop in code that is compiled with debug information. That means implicit functions compiled without debug information are not easy to find.

Note that a step-into command may occasionally go into functions or methods provided by the C++ compiler or the various included libraries. This can happen in the above example when a step-into goes into the constructor of class std::basic_string<...>.

10.3.2 Skipping Implicit Functions with the Step-out Command

Let us now debug the function call to show (x + "def") in line 47 of example 10.3. Line 47 is really a sequence of implicit function calls equivalent to (but not necessarily identical to) the pseudo code statements that we labeled 47-1 ... 47-6 in Figure 10.1

```
47        show((x+"def") * 3);
  47.1      tmp1=STR::STR("def");
  47.2      tmp2=STR::operator+(x,tmp1);
  47.3      operator*(tmp2,3);
  47.4      show(tmp2);
  47.5      STR::~STR(tmp2);
  47.6      STR::~STR(tmp1);
48        return 0;
```

Fig. 10.1 Implicit functions calls

We can reach the body of function show() with repeated step-into commands, but this will walk through the function bodies of statements 47-1 to 47-3, including any function calls performed in those lines. It takes a large number of step-into commands to do it this way, and it is easy to get lost in low-level implementation details. Is there a faster way to step from line 47 into function show() in line 41?

One way to speed things up is to *step-out* of the current function. In GDB, this is the `finish` command. In Visual Studio, use the **Step-Out** button.

Let us see how that works. We start at line 47, which translates to line 47-1 of our imaginary pseudo-code. The step-into command brings us into the body of the STR constructor in line 7. The step-out command brings us out of the constructor and will stop at statement 47-2. Note that GDB will report the location as `0x<address> ... at main.cpp:47`. All pseudo-code lines 47-1 ... 47-4 belong to the same source line 47 but all have different program addresses, so there is a way to distinguish them. The next step-into then goes into the function call of 47-2.

It is difficult to keep track of which implicit function is called, but a sequence of commands step-into, step-out, step-into, ... will eventually lead into function `show()`. A look at the call stack is helpful if you lost track. In this example, it takes 4 step-into commands, plus 3 step-out commands, which is considerably faster than a large number of consecutive step-into commands.

10.3.3 Skipping Implicit Functions with a Temporary Breakpoint

In some cases, you may want want to go from line 47 directly into the function `show()`, without stepping through all the implicit functions that compute the function arguments. This can be done by setting a *temporary breakpoint* with the GDB command `tbreak`:

```
(gdb) tbreak show
Breakpoint 2 at 0x8048a06: file main.cpp, line 41.
(gdb) cont
show (z=..."abcdefabcdefabcdef"...) at main.cpp:41
41    cout <<z.num_objs() <<": " <<z.c_str() <<endl;
```

Note that GDB removes temporary breakpoints automatically the first time they are hit. The GDB debugger also does not report the breakpoint number when it is hit.

In Visual Studio, set a breakpoint by left-clicking on line 41, and hit the F5 function key to continue. Once the debugger stops in line 41, remove the breakpoint by left-clicking on line 41 again.

10.3.4 Returning from Implicit Function Calls

Temporary breakpoints are also useful if you get lost in nested implicit function calls. Let us start again in line 47 and use repeated step-into commands until we reach the second constructor call in line 7. Assume that by now, you have lost track of what is going on, and you just want to get back to line 47 to start stepping into implicit functions again. You can combine the stack navigation command `up` and `tbreak` in the following way to get to the next pseudo statement in line 47:

```
47           show((x+"def") * 3);
(gdb) step  (repeatedly until you reach line 7 again)
...
(gdb) step
7            STR(const char* a) {
(gdb) where
#0  STR (..."abcdefabcdefabcdef"...) at main.cpp:7
#1  in STR::operator* (...) at main.cpp:31
#2  in main (...) at main.cpp:47
(gdb) up
(gdb) up
(gdb) tbreak
Breakpoint 4 at 0x8048b1d: file main.cpp, line 47.
(gdb) cont
47           show((x+"def") * 3);
(gdb) step
show (z=..."abcdefabcdefabcdef"...) at main.cpp:41
41      cout <<z.num_objs() <<": " <<z.c_str() <<endl;
```

When used without an argument, the command `tbreak` instructs the debugger to stop on the next address in the selected stack frame, which happens to be line 47-4 of our imaginary pseudo-code.

Lessons learned:

- To locate hidden function calls, compile all code with debug information, and use the step-into command repeatedly.
- To bypass stepping through all source code lines of implicit functions, do step-out, step-into repeatedly.
- To bypass stepping through hidden functions, set a temporary breakpoint in the target function, and then continue.
- If you get lost stepping through implicit functions, navigate up in the stack until you are back to the calling statement, and set a temporary breakpoint.

10.4 Conditional Breakpoints and Breakpoint Commands

You will frequently encounter the situation where the program stops at too many breakpoints before it reaches the place that you want to debug. The question is how to make the program stop when it is most interesting, and automatically continue in all other cases. The answer is to use *conditional breakpoints* and *breakpoint commands*, which we discuss in this section.

We will explain the use of conditional breakpoints first using GDB in the STR class example from Section 10.3 on page 134 above. The class has a STR constructor for string literals. String literals are constants of type const char* in the source code, for example "abc" in line 45. We will use a breakpoint command to find out the time and location of the constructor call. We want to print one line per constructor call, and thereafter the program should continue automatically. We will then add a conditional breakpoint that will pause the program when the constructor is called with the argument "def".

Let us first do this with the GDB debugger. We use commands to specify a sequence of commands that will be executed whenever a particular breakpoint is hit. The sequence starts with silent, which prohibits printing the subsequent commands, so the screen is not cluttered with too much output. We want to print only one line to the screen and use the GDB command printf to create a nicely formatted output. The continue command resumes the execution of the program. The command sequence is terminated with end:

```
(gdb) break main.cpp:7
Breakpoint 1 at 0x8048c3a: file main.cpp, line 7.
(gdb) commands 1
Type commands for when breakpoint 1 is hit, one per line.
End with a line saying just "end".
> silent
> printf "STR CTOR with a=0x%x \"%s\"\n", a, a
> continue
> end
(gdb)
```

The argument in commands 1 refers to breakpoint number 1. Each breakpoint can have only one sequence of commands attached. If we specify commands 1 again, it will override the previous command sequence.

Running the program will now print the memory addresses and string literals of all STR constructors, and we see that there are three constructor calls.

```
(gdb) run
...
STR CTOR with a=0x8048f3b "abc"
2: abc
STR CTOR with a=0x8048f3f "def"
STR CTOR with a=0x804b51c "abcdefabcdefabcdef"
3: abcdefabcdefabcdef
```

In Visual Studio, create the breakpoint by right-clicking on line 7 of the example, and select **Breakpoint/Insert Breakpoint**. Then, go to the **Breakpoints** window, right-click on the breakpoint, and select the **When Hit...** dialog. Select **Print a message**. Make sure the **continue execution** check mark is set.

Next in our GDB example, we will create a *conditional breakpoint* to stop at the call with string literal "def", by using the condition command of GDB:

```
(gdb) break main.cpp:7
...
Breakpoint 2 at 0x8048c3a: file main.cpp, line 7.
(gdb) condition 2 a[0]=='d' && a[1]=='e' && a[2]=='f' &&a[3]==0
(gdb) run
...
```

```
Breakpoint 2, in STR (... a=0x8048f3f "def") at main.cpp:7
7          STR(const char* a) {
```

Choosing the right condition here is tricky because we have a string literal. The conditional expression a=="def" is never true, since the debugger compares the value of pointer a with the address of another string literal "def". Both string literals have the same content ("def") but are stored at different addresses. We also cannot call function strcmp() inside the condition. As a compromise, we compare individual characters of the string.

In Visual Studio, right-click on the breakpoint in line 7, and select **Breakpoint/Condition**. Enter a[0]=='d' && a[1]=='e' && a[2]=='f' && a[3]==0 in the dialog.

An alternative method to create a conditional breakpoint in GDB is to use a regular breakpoint, but then attach a command containing a conditional statement.

```
(gdb) break 7
Breakpoint 2 at 0x8048c3a: file main.cpp, line 7.
(gdb) commands 2
Type the commands for when breakpoint 2 is hit, one per line.
End with a line saying "end".
> silent
> print strcmp(a,"def")
> if $$0==0
>    print "FOUND the right BP!"
> else
>    printf "STR CTOR with a=0x%x \"%s\"\n", a, a
>    continue
> end
> end
(gdb)
```

Expression $$0 refers to the result returned by the previous line, in this case the command print strcmp(a,"def").

Note that conditional breakpoints or breakpoint commands can slow down program execution. CPU time is needed for GDB whenever the breakpoint is reached, regardless of whether the condition is met or not.

Lessons learned:

- You can add print statements without recompiling the program, by using breakpoint commands.
- A conditional breakpoint can catch a specific function call and ignore all others.
- Breakpoints can significantly slow down program execution.

10.5 Debugging Static Constructor/Destructor Problems

In this section, we show how to debug problems with static constructors and destructors. In C++, a class object instantiated in global scope or a static class member will cause a call to the object's constructor at program startup. In addition, C++ allows you to initialize global and static objects with a function or method called *static initializer*. Here is an example:

```
MyClass otherGlobal;
int MyClass::veryImportantStatic = somefunction();
```

An unusual aspect is *when* these function and constructor calls take place. They happen during the *static initialization phase* which takes place before function main() is called. Similarly, destructors are called for static or global class objects during the shut-down phase of the program, after main() has returned.

If the static constructors are part of a shared library, then they take place when the library is dynamically loaded at runtime. This happens either during startup time, or later, if the shared library is explicitly loaded from the program's code. Destructors are executed when the program exits, or when the shared library is explicitly closed.

Static initializers can cause some particularly ugly bugs, and create special debugging challenges. The most common source for bugs is program code that relies on a certain order of static initialization. Stack traces will look different because these calls are not invoked from main(). Finally, there is an additional complication if you have to attach the debugger to a running program; the initialization may have already taken place by the time the debugger is connected.

10.5.1 Bugs Due to Order-Dependence of Static Initializers

The following example has two variables with static initializers, the global variable otherGlobal and the static variable veryImportantStatic.

```
1   /* MyClass.h */
2   class MyClass {
3   public:
4       MyClass() {
5           int i;
6           for(i=0;i<10;i++)
7               a[i]= veryImportantStatic+i; }
8       int a[10];
9       static int veryImportantStatic;
10  };
```

```
1   /* MyClass.cc */
2   #include "MyClass.h"
3
4   int somefunction()
```

```
 5  {  return 42;  }
 6
 7  int MyClass::veryImportantStatic = somefunction();

 1  /* static_conflict.cc */
 2  #include <stdio.h>
 3  #include "MyClass.h"
 4
 5  MyClass otherGlobal;
 6
 7  int main() {
 8      printf("otherGlobal.a[3]=%d\n", otherGlobal.a[3]);
 9      return 0;
10  }
```

Both variables are initialized by functions that are called during the startup of the program. There is a hidden requirement that veryImportantStatic must be initialized before otherGlobal. However, the programmer failed to take care of the necessary precautions, so the program relies on mere luck that the initialization order is correct.

In addition to the compiler, the initialization order also depends on the linker and link order. The sequence how linkers arrange static initializer code is not standardized, and subject to change. For the above example, GCC 3.4.4 will compute the intended result by initializing veryImportantStatic first. The result in Visual Studio 2008 will depend on the order in which you list the source files in the project. Keep in mind that it is also possible to create examples with cyclic dependencies that will never work.

10.5.2 Recognizing the Stack Trace of Static Initializers

Bugs related to order-of-construction or order-of-destruction problems tend to be very obscure, so they are not easily recognized. The first useful indication when searching for these bugs is the stack trace:

```
> g++ -g -o static_conflict static_conflict.cc MyClass.cc
> ./static_conflict
otherGlobal.a[3]=45
> gdb ./static_conflict
...
(gdb) break MyClass.cc:5
Breakpoint 1 at 0x4010e0: file MyClass.cc, line 5.
(gdb) run
(gdb) where
#0  somefunction () at MyClass.cc:5
#1  0x.. in __static_initialization_and_destruction_0 (
    __initialize_p=1, __priority=65535) at MyClass.cc:7
#2  0x.. in global constructors keyed to _Z12somefunctionv ()
    at MyClass.cc:8
#3  0x.. in do_global_ctors () from /usr/bin/cygwin1.dll
#4  0x.. in _check_for_executable () from /usr/bin/cygwin1.dll
```

Note that function `main()` is not part of the stack trace because it has not yet been called. The call of `somefunction()` was initiated from functions provided by the compiler and operating system. The exact names of such functions may vary with the compiler and OS but their names will be similar to those above. From here on, you can set breakpoints in the constructors and initialization routines, and proceed debugging as usual.

10.5.3 Attaching the Debugger Before Static Initialization

In some situations, you may have to attach the debugger to a running process, and then debug the initialization routines. Because static initialization routines are called during the startup phase, they are already executed by the time you are ready to attach the debugger. It is therefore necessary to slow-down program execution at the init phase. We add another static initializer call that introduces enough delay to the program to allow you to attach the debugger. The following piece of code gives an example of how to do this:

```
File initial_delay.cpp
  1  #include <unistd.h>
  2
  3  static int delay_done=0;
  4  static int ask_mice() {
  5      while(!delay_done)
  6          sleep(10);
  7      return 42;
  8  }
  9 static int pol = ask_mice();
```

We attach to the running process, and then set up all the breakpoint in the debugger that we need. Then we change the `delay_done` variable to let the program continue.

```
> g++ -o test -g main.cpp inital_delay.cpp
> ./test &
[1] 20189

> gdb test 20189
(gdb) ...
(gdb) set var delay_done=1
(gdb) continue
```

Note that this approach also relies on the particular execution order of static initialization code, namely that `ask_mice()` is called first. The linker influences the order, so it may require some experimentation to place this code into the file that the linker initializes first.

> ## **Lessons learned:**
>
> - C++ uses functions to initialize global objects. These functions are called before `main()`, and have no predefined order of execution. Use the provided example to learn how to debug these initialization functions.
> - Use the provided code fragment to attach to a running process, and then debug the static initialization functions.

10.6 Using Watchpoints

Watchpoints or *data breakpoints* stop the program if the value of an expression changes. In GDB, the expression for the `watch` command can be a variable, a memory address, or an arbitrary complex expression. The debugger will now constantly monitor the expression and stop the program at the statement where the expression changes.

In Visual Studio, use the dialog **Debug/New Breakpoint/New Data Breakpoint** to set a watchpoint. Here, it is not possible to attach a watchpoint to a variable of local scope: only addresses can be watched.

In the example below, we will again use the `STR` class program from Section 10.3, page 134. We want to find all occasions when the variable `x.num` changes. The debugger should stop whenever `x.num` changes, and print which statement modified it. We will use GDB here.

```
(gdb) start
(gdb) watch x.num
Hardware watchpoint 2: x.num
(gdb) cont
...
9    num++
(gdb) where
#0  0x08048c62 in STR::STR (...) at break_str.cc:9
#1  0x08048a92 in main (...) at break_str.cc:45
```

As we can see, the program is paused when the value of the watchpoint expression changes.

If possible, the GDB debugger will implement the watchpoint with *hardware assistance*. If a watchpoint is *not* hardware assisted, it can seriously slow down the program, whereas hardware breakpoints impose almost no slow-down of the execution.

Note that GDB deletes watchpoints that contain variables of local scope, when the program leaves that scope. For example, if you stop in one of the constructors and set a watchpoint on `num`, the watchpoint is lost as soon as you leave the constructor.

For both GDB and Visual Studio, you can set the watchpoint on the *address* of the variable that you want to watch. This expression will remain valid in all scopes, so the watchpoint is not deleted:

```
(gdb) start
... run program till line 13
13            num++;
(gdb) p &num
$1 = (int *) 0x804a360
(gdb) watch *0x804a360
Hardware watchpoint 2: *134521696
```

Do not forget the `*` in front of the address. If you accidentally type `watch 0x804a360` instead of `watch *0x804a360`, the watchpoint will check a constant hex address value that never changes.

Watching addresses is not recommended for objects on the program stack, such as a local variable. Once the current function is exited, the stack will be used to store other variables. There is also no guarantee that the local variable that you want to watch will be assigned the same stack address on the next call to the function.

Lessons learned:

- Watchpoints offer an effective way to find all statements that modify a specific variable.
- Watchpoints that are not hardware assisted have a significant impact on performance.
- The use of watchpoints is not recommended for local variables.

10.7 Catching Signals

This section deals with debugging signals. Signals allow communication between processes. A signal is sent from one process to another, or within the same process. Signals are asynchronous. The set of available signals varies with the operating system. Fewer signals are available on Windows. On UNIX or Linux, use the command `kill -l` to list all available signals. A widely known application is the Ctrl-C keystroke that interrupts a running program. Typing Ctrl-C in a shell sends a SIGINT signal to the program running in the foreground.

The process that receives a signal *must* react to it. The process may have a C function called a *signal handler* registered for a specific signal type. Whenever a signal of this type comes in, and is not temporarily blocked, the handler is called, irrespective of what the process is currently doing. In the absence of a user-defined handler, the operating system takes a predefined action, which, depending on the signal, either aborts the program, ignores the signal, or suspends the process.

Problems arising from signal handling are hard to debug, since we cannot predict when the event occurs. System calls may be interrupted, and can return with an unanticipated error code. Also, we could be in the middle of constructing a data structure, so reading or writing values to that structure from the signal handler can produce unpredictable results.

Most debuggers allow the user to specify how to handle each individual incoming signal. In GDB, this is done with the `handle` command. It is possible to print a message to the screen, and/or to stop execution of the program. We can also instruct the debugger to ignore the signal, so it will be handled by the registered interrupt handle. There is also a command that tells the debugger to produce and deliver a signal to the program. For GDB, this is the `signal` command.

We can use the following strategies to debug signal related problems:

- Improve visibility: instruct the debugger to print a message when it receives a signal (for example, SIGUSR1), and then propagate it to the program. The signal will leave a visible trace on the screen, which makes it easier to understand what is going on:
  `handle SIGUSR1 print nostop pass`.
- Disable disturbing signals: a signal handler may interfere with some other aspect of the program that you want to debug. Use the debugger to ignore all incoming signals so that there are no more calls to the signal handler:
  `handle SIGUSR1 noprint nostop nopass`.
- Provoke a bug: produce a signal and send it to the program to test whether or not it triggers the bug: `signal SIGUSR1`.

The following example has a simple signal handler that counts how often the signal SIGUSR1 is received while the program is busy in some inner delay loop. Note that this program will not compile on Windows, as signal SIGUSR1 is not supported on this platform.

```
1   #include <signal.h>
2   #include <stdio.h>
3
4   static int  num_sigusr1=0;
5
6   void handler(int sig) {
7       num_sigusr1++;
8       signal(SIGUSR1,&handler);
9   }
10
11  int main(int argc, char** argv) {
12      int n,m, pol=0;
13      signal(SIGUSR1,&handler);
14      printf("- program starts\n"); fflush(stdout);
15      for (n=0; n<10; n++) {
16          raise(SIGUSR1);
17          for (m=0; m<1000000000; m++)
18              pol++;
19      }
20      printf("- program ends: received SIGUSR1 %d time(s)\n",
```

```
21            num_sigusr1);
22        fflush(stdout);
23        return 0;
24  }
```

The program will send itself 10 signals of type SIGUSR1. While it is running, send more signals from another shell with the help of UNIX command `kill -USR1 <pid>`. Run the program under GDB and use the GDB command `handle` to configure how GDB should react to an incoming signal. First, we make the signal visible:

```
(gdb) handle SIGUSR1 print nostop pass
Signal   Stop Print Pass to program Description
SIGUSR1  No   Yes   Yes              User defined signal 1
(gdb) run
```

As soon as the handler receives the signal, GDB prints a message:

```
Program received signal SIGUSR1, User defined signal 1.
Program received signal SIGUSR1, User defined signal 1.
Program received signal SIGUSR1, User defined signal 1.
...
program ends: received SIGUSR1 10 time(s)
```

Next, we disable SIGUSR1 so that it will no longer reach the program:

```
(gdb) handle SIGUSR1 noprint nostop nopass
Signal   Stop Print Pass to program Description
SIGUSR1  No   No    No               User defined signal 1
(gdb) run
program ends: received SIGUSR1 0 time(s)
```

Finally, use the GDB `signal` command to produce a signal to test how the program reacts:

```
(gdb) break handler
Breakpoint 1 at 0x894842f: file main.c, line 7.
(gdb) run
... Interrupt program with Ctrl-C
(gdb) signal SIGUSR1
Continuing with signal SIGUSR1

Breakpoint 1, handler (sig=10) at main.c:7
 7            num_sigusr1++;
...
program ends: received SIGUSR1 11 time(s)
```

We see that the handler receives the signal in line 7, and is accounted for.

Lessons learned:

- Debuggers are able to deal with signals such as SIGUSR1, SIGALRM, SIGSEGV, SIGINT.
- You can make signals visible, filter them out, or create them with the help of the debugger.

10.8 Catching Exceptions

C++ has a feature called *exceptions*. It is used for error handling, as well as for handling exceptional situations, as the term suggests. An exception is thrown (generated) and caught (consumed) within the same process. The GDB `catch throw` command makes the debugger stop when any exception is thrown. The `catch catch` command makes the debugger stop when any exception is caught. Consider the following example:

```
 1  #include <iostream>
 2
 3  void f1() {
 4      throw 42;
 5  }
 6  void f2() {
 7      throw "pol";
 8  }
 9
10  int main(int,char**) {
11      try {
12          f1();
13      } catch (int E) {
14          std::cout << "caught E=" << E << std::endl;
15      }
16      f2();
17      return 0;
18  }
```

```
(gdb) start
...
(gdb) catch throw
Catchpoint 2 (throw)
(gdb) catch catch
Catchpoint 3 (catch)
(gdb) cont

Catchpoint 2 (exception thrown)
0x400c1ea5 in __cxa_throw () from /usr/lib/libstdc++.so.5
(gdb) where
#0  0x400c1ea5 in __cxa_throw () from /usr/lib/libstdc++.so.5
#1  0x08048955 in f1 () at main.cpp:4
#2  0x800489a2 in main () at main.cpp:12
```

Note that the GDB `catch` and `throw` commands may only work after the C++ runtime library (DLL) has been loaded. Therefore, make sure the program is running before entering these commands. One convenient way to achieve this is to stop the program at the first line of `main()` with the `start` command.

If a debugger cannot be applied, then an alternative debugging strategy would be to modify the program, and insert a `catch` statement. When an exception is thrown, the program will continue at the next surrounding `catch` statement that has a matching type. Note that `catch(...)` will catch any exception regardless of the type. This tells you that an exception has occurred and, if the type is known, what value the exception has. However, this strategy does not reveal the location of where the exception was thrown, so using a debugger should always be the first choice.

In Visual Studio, go to the **Debug** menu, and select **Exceptions....** A dialog window will pop up, giving you the choice to break the program when certain exceptions are thrown. Select **C++ Exceptions** to enable a program breakpoint for the C++ throw statements in your code.

Lessons learned:

- Use the GDB catch command to debug C++ exceptions.
- In Visual Studio, go to menu **Debug** and use the **Exceptions...** window to enable a program breakpoint when an exception is thrown.

10.9 Reading Stack Traces

This section focuses on the skill of reading stack traces. Chapter 3.4 has already introduced these and has shown you how to navigate stack frames with a debugger. A stack trace is a list of frames, where each frame corresponds to a called function. The function name may be readable, and the frame may have additional information about function arguments.

10.9.1 Stack Trace of Source Code Compiled with Debug Information

Let us start with the STR class example from Section 10.3, page 134. We modify the code for operator+ in line 22 such that it references a null pointer and thus causes a segmentation fault:

```
file main.cpp
21   const STR& operator+ (const STR& a) {
22       int* dummy=0;
23       (*dummy)++;                        // <== BUG
24       s += a.s; return *this;
25   }
```

We compile the program with debug information, and then run it up to the crash:

```
...
Program received signal SIGSEGV, Segmentation fault.
0x08048d24 in STR::operator+ (...) at break_str.cc:23
23               (*dummy)++;
```

```
...
(gdb) where
#0  0x.. in STR::operator+ (...) at break_str.cc:23
#1  0x.. in main (argc=1, argv=0xbfffee44) at break_str.cc:51
```

The signal SIGSEGV is a *segmentation fault* and happens when the program tries to access a memory address for which it does not have permission. In this example, we access address 0x0, a common reason for a segmentation fault. Other fatal signals are SIGBUS (illegal bus address), SIGILL (illegal instruction) and SIGFPE (floating point exception).

The stack trace has two frames, each with source and line information and the list of actual arguments. We see that function main() was calling function STR::operator+ in line 23. This example is as good as a stack trace ever gets.

10.9.2 Stack Trace of Source Code Compiled Without Debug Information

Quite often, stack traces will not contain as much information. If we compile the same source file without debug information, then the stack trace will look like this:

```
> g++ -o break_str break_str.cc
> gdb ./break_str
...
(gdb) where
#0  0x08048d24 in STR::operator+ ()
#1  0x08048b11 in main ()
```

Note that the source and line information are missing, which makes it harder to find the faulty source code line. The good news is that it is clear that function main() was still calling function STR::operator+. Next, you should search sources for class definition STR and then inside that for operator+, which will bring you close to line 23. For further information on how to debug programs that were compiled without debug information, see Section 10.11.

10.9.3 Frames Without Any Debug Information

It is possible that the debugger will not find any information whatsoever for a particular frame. We will construct this situation by stripping the executable, which will remove all debug information:

```
> g++ -o break_str -g break_str.cc
> strip break_str
> gdb break_str
...
Program received signal SIGSEGV, Segmentation fault.
```

149

```
0x08048d24 in ?? ()
(gdb) where
#0  0x08048d24 in ?? ()
#1  0x08048b11 in ?? ()
#2  0x4012ae80 in __libc_start_main () from /lib/tls/libc.so.6
#3  0x08048961 in ?? ()
```

This stack trace is now almost useless, since there are no function names other than __libc_start_main. All other frames report the function name ??, which indicates that the debugger does not have any debug information for the given address.

Note that the number of stack frames increased to four. This is correct, the lower two frames are functions that belong to the C/C++ standard library, and call main(). The debugger normally does not report any frames below main(), so they were simply not reported before.

Frames reported as ?? will be encountered whenever the debugger has no debug information about object code at a specific address. This problem can happen in many situations, including the following:

- The executable was stripped, and all debug information was removed on purpose.
- Debug information is located in a shared library and the debugger has not yet loaded it.
- The debugger was unable to understand the debug information. This frequently happens when different compilers are mixed, for example, Sun Forte and GCC on Solaris.
- The memory where the stack frames are stored is corrupted.

10.9.4 Real-Life Stack Traces

The example below is a stack trace of a real-life application. Try to guess which application it is (hint: start reading from the bottom) and what it is doing at that moment (hint: start reading from the top):

```
#0  0x.. in ?? ()
#1  0x.. in ?? ()
#2  0x.. in ?? ()
#3  0x.. in ?? ()
#4  0x.. in select () from /lib/tls/libc.so.6
#5  0x.. in XtAddTimeOut () from /usr/X11R6/lib/libXt.so.6
#6  0x.. in _XtWaitForSomething () from ..
#7  0x.. in XtAppProcessEvent () from /usr/X11R6/lib/libXt.so.6
#8  0x.. in emacs_Xt_handle_widget_losing_focus ()
#9  0x.. in event_stream_resignal_wakeup ()
#10 0x.. in Fnext_event ()
#11 0x.. in Fcommand_loop_1 ()
#12 0x.. in Fcommand_loop_1 ()
#13 0x.. in condition_case_1 ()
#14 0x.. in Frecursive_edit ()
```

```
#15 0x.. in internal_catch ()
#16 0x.. in initial_command_loop ()
#17 0x.. in xemacs_21_5_b18_i386_suse_linux ()
#18 0x.. in main ()
```

Frames 17 and 8 reveal that this is the XEmacs editor (the one used to write this chapter). Frames 4..6 indicate that the editor was waiting for new input, for example a key stroke. Note that frames 5..7 belong to the X library. Function `select()` is part of the standard C library and is probably calling some function of the OS. Frames 0..3 probably belong to the OS, and no debug information is available for them.

10.9.5 Mangled Function Names

If we use different compilers to compile C++ source code, there is a chance that the function names of some frames are reported in their mangled form. Debuggers usually demangle such names automatically but occasionally get confused. See Section 9.3.4, page 114 for details of how to read mangled C++ function names.

10.9.6 Broken Stack Traces

When a program corrupts memory due to a bug, it may also overwrite the call stack. This frequently happens with local fixed-size arrays. Writing over the boundary of the array will corrupt the stack, and it is probable that the program will run into a fatal bug soon afterward. Furthermore, when the debugger tries to report the stack trace, it will also see corrupted data instead of the correct call stack information. We can construct this scenario with the following example:

```
1   int n;
2   int *p;
3   int F(int a) {
4       p = &a;
5       for (n=a; n>0; n--)
6           *p-- = 0x42;
7       return a;
8   }
9   int main(int argc, char* argv[])
10  {
11      return F(10);
12  }
```

```
> g++ -o broken_stack -g broken_stack.cc
> gdb broken_stack
...
(gdb) run
...
```

```
Program received signal SIGSEGV, Segmentation fault.
0x0000002a in ?? ()
(gdb) where
#0  0x00000042 in ?? ()
#1  0x00000042 in ?? ()
#2  0xbfffee4c in ?? ()
#3  0xbfffedb8 in ?? ()
#4  0x08048491 in __libc_csu_init ()
Previous frame inner to this frame (corrupt stack?)
```

The important point is that GDB reports that the stack is probably corrupt. Note that frames 0..1 have values 42 which gives you more evidence that the program corrupted the stack.

> ### Lessons learned:
>
> - Learn to read stack traces.
> - Broken stack traces can be a symptom of memory corruption, such as writing over the end of a local array. Run the program with a memory debugger.

10.9.7 Core Dumps

If a program runs into a bug and triggers a segmentation fault, the operating system will create a *core dump file*. The core dump provides data for post-mortem debugging, and lets us find out why the program failed.

The following program will cause a segmentation fault:

```
 1   /* answer.c */
 2   #include <stdio.h>
 3
 4   void runexperiment() {
 5       int *answerp;
 6       answerp = (void *) 42;
 7       printf("The answer is %d\n", *answerp);
 8   }
 9
10   void createplanet() {
11       runexperiment();
12   }
13
14   int main() {
15       printf("Hello Universe! Computing answer ...\n");
16       fflush(stdout);
17       createplanet();
18       return 0;
19   }
```

Run the program. It will fail in line 7 with a segmentation fault:

```
> ./myprog
Hello Universe! Computing answer ...
Segmentation fault
```

Note that you may not get a core dump file, if, for instance, you have a `limit coredumpsize 0` command in your `.cshrc` shell initialization file. Check the documentation of your command shell to see how to enable core dumps.

We use the command `gdb myprog core` to load the core dump along with the executable into the debugger.

```
> gdb myprog core
...
#0 0x080c1368 in runexperiment ()
#1 0x080bff8f in createplanet ()
#2 0x080bfc0f in main ()
(gdb)
```

The core dump contains a copy of all the data allocated by the program. Part of this data is the stack, which we can use to view the stack trace with a debugger *after* the program terminates.

If you run the program on Windows, it will crash with a segmentation fault. A window will pop up, asking you whether you want to debug using the selected debugger. Click **Yes** and Visual Studio will be started. There are 2 possibilities to work on the crashed process: you can immediately debug it, or you can generate a core dump file and debug it later. To save a core dump file in Visual Studio, go to menu item **Debug** and select **Save Dump As....** A `.dmp` file will be written. To load the core dump file back into Visual Studio, double-click on the `.dmp` file.

Lessons learned:

- The core dump files allow for post-mortem debugging. You can see where the segmentation fault occurred, including a full stack trace listing the function that caused the crash, and all functions that led to this function.
- You can also move the stack frame up or down, and query values of variables and memory.

10.10 Manipulating a Running Program

A debugger is useful for following the control flow of a program and for analyzing data. However, debuggers can do much more than this. It is possible to manipulate the behavior of the program by changing the content of variables, or by calling functions from within the debugger. Such program manipulations are the focus of this section. These debugger capabilities are helpful for testing the effect of a bug fix without going through a lengthy recompilation process, and for driving the program into a state that is not normally covered by the testing process.

The standard approach of changing the behavior of the program is to change the source code and then to recompile. We can use the debugger to achieve the same result. This is an alternative if recompilation takes too long, or when it is difficult to recreate the current state of the program. You need to keep in mind that manipulations performed with a debugger are lost when the debugger exits, and there are limits to manipulations, but it is always worth knowing what you can do.

Debuggers usually offer all, or at least some, of the following commands to manipulate the program behavior:

Manipulating data

- Changing variable values or actual arguments of functions: In GDB use the command `set var <varname>=<expr>`, for example `set var MyVar=17`. In Visual Studio you can edit the value in the **Variables** window.
- Changing return argument values of functions: In GDB, step to the last instruction of a function, and then use command `return <expr>`.
- Modifying the contents of heap memory, as shown in Section 10.10.6.
- Changing environment variables: In GDB, use the command `set environment <var> <value>`. In Visual Studio, click on menu item **Project** and go to **Properties / Configuration Properties / Debugging / Environment** to override environment variables. Altered environment variables will only have an effect on the next start of the program.

Manipulating the flow of control

- Invoking functions: In GDB, use the commands `call` or `print`. In Visual Studio, use the **Immediate** window.
- Getting out of functions, skipping their remaining statements: In GDB, use the `return [<expr>]` command. There is no Visual Studio equivalent command.
- Skipping or redoing statements in the current function: In GDB, use the `jump` command. There is no Visual Studio equivalent command.

You can make these modifications semi-permanent, by adding the commands to breakpoints. The modifications will remain effective throughout multiple runs of the executable, as long as the debugger does not exit. See Section 10.4 on conditional breakpoints on how to do this.

We will now explain the manipulations using the following example. The program in the example searches for names in an input string, turns them into upper case, and counts how many strings were changed:

```
1   /* capitalize.c */
2   #include <stdio.h>
3   #include <ctype.h>
4   #include <string.h>
```

```
 5  #include <stdlib.h>
 6  #ifdef _MSC_VER
 7  #define strncasecmp strnicmp
 8  #endif
 9
10  void change_word ( char* str, int len ) {
11      int i;
12      for (i=0; i<len; i++)
13          str[i]=toupper(str[i]);
14  }
15
16  int capitalize_str( char* str, const char* name ) {
17      int n;
18      int hits=0;
19      int len=strlen(str);
20      int len_name=strlen(name);
21      int lastpos = len-len_name;
22      for (n=0; n<=lastpos; n++) {
23          if (strncasecmp(str+n,name,len_name)==0) {
24              change_word( str+n, len_name );
25              n += len_name;
26              hits++;
27          }
28      }
29      return hits;
30  }
31
32  int main( int argc, char* argv[] ) {
33      int hits_total=0;
34      int na;
35      char *mycopy;
36      if (argc<3) return 1;
37      mycopy = strdup(argv[1]);
38      for(na=2; na<argc; na++)
39          hits_total += capitalize_str( mycopy, argv[na] );
40      printf("Total %d hits:\n", hits_total);
41      printf("original: %s\n", argv[1]);
42      printf("modified: %s\n", mycopy);
43      free(mycopy);
44      return 0;
45  }
```

Running the program exposes a bug:

```
> myprog "Foofoo, foobar and Bar!" foo bar
Total 4 hits:
original: Foofoo, foobar and Bar!
modified: FOOfoo, FOOBAR and BAR!
```

The program somehow fails to turn the second "foo" within "Foofoo" into uppercase. The reason is a bug in line 25 where n is incremented by len_name, instead of len_name-1, to account for the loop increment n++ in line 22.

10.10.1 Changing a Variable

Changing the source code and recompiling the program is fast for this small program but may take a long time for a larger project. Before starting a slow re-compilation, it is worth testing whether the proposed bug fix has the right effect. In our example, we can do this by decrementing the variable n with the debugger. The program then shows the correct results, so we have identified a fix for the bug.

```
(gdb) run "Foofoo, foobar and Bar!" foo bar
... run program until it stops in line 23 for the 2nd time
23              if (strncasecmp(str+n,name,len_name)==0) {
(gdb) print n
$1 = 4
(gdb) print str+n
$2 = 0x804a00c "oo, foobar and Bar!"
(gdb) set var n=3
(gdb) print str+n
$3 = 0x804a00b "Foo, foobar and Bar!"
(gdb) continue
...
Total 5 hits:
original: Foofoo, foobar and Bar!
modified: FOOFOO, FOOBAR and BAR!
```

All debuggers provide some way to change variables because this is an important and frequently used feature. In Visual Studio, enter n=3 in the **Immediate** window, or change the value in the **Variables** window.

10.10.2 Calling Functions

Another important feature provided by a debugger is the ability to manipulate a program by calling a C or C++ function. In GDB, you can use the call or print commands. In Visual Studio, use the **Immediate** window. We will demonstrate this feature by calling capitalize_str one extra time to turn the string and into upper case:

```
... navigate the program to line 39
39              hits_total += capitalize_str( copy,argv[na] );
(gdb) call capitalize_str( copy,"and")
$3 = 1
(gdb) cont
Continuing.
Total 4 hits:
original: Foofoo, foobar and Bar!
modified: FOOfoo, FOOBAR AND BAR!
```

Note that AND is now capitalized. The call or print commands allow you to call any C/C++ function. You need to make sure that you call C functions with the correct number and types of arguments because GDB cannot check this, at least, not for C functions. If a call leads to a fatal error, then GDB can react in two different modes, depending on the setting of `unwindonsignal`:

- `set unwindonsignal off`: GDB stops where the crash happened. This is useful when you want to test a function to understand why it crashes. The stack frames will show you where the call starts with a frame named `<function called from gdb>`. If you want to continue executing the program, then use the `return` command described above to return from there.
- `set unwindonsignal on`: GDB will print that a signal was received, and returns automatically.

Calling member functions of a C++ class is also possible to some extent. For example, you can call simple members such as `mystr.c_str()` that take no arguments, or only arguments with ANSI C types. Calling members that take other class objects as arguments is more difficult, and calling class constructors or operators is next to impossible.

10.10.3 Changing the Return Value of a Function

Next, we want to override the return value of function `capitalize_str` with the `return` command, just when the function is about to return in line 30:

```
... run program till line 30
30      }
(gdb) return 40
Make capitalize_str(char*, char const*) return now? (y or n) y

#0  0x080486cd in main (argc=4, argv=0xbffffee44) at main.c:39
39          hits_total += capitalize_str( copy,argv[na] );
(gdb) cont
Continuing.
Total 42 hits:
original: Foofoo, foobar and Bar!
modified: FOOfoo, FOOBAR and BAR!
```

The normal return value is 4, however, the program now prints 42. This shows that manipulating the return value worked.

10.10.4 Aborting Function Calls

We can use the GDB `return` command to manipulate the program behavior more drastically. It will return out of the selected stack frame and thus skip all inner stack frames. We will use this when we are in the middle of `change_word` to return out of `change_word` and `capitalize_str` and get back to `main`:

```
... run the program until it reaches line 12 for the 2nd time
12          for (i=0; i<len; i++)

(gdb) up
#1  0x08048639 in capitalize_str (...) at main.c:24
24          change_word( str+n, len_name );

(gdb) return 0
Make capitalize_str(char*, char const*) return now? (y or n) y

#0  0x080486cd in main (...) at main.c:39
39          hits_total += capitalize_str( copy,argv[na] );

(gdb) cont
Continuing.
Total 2 hits:
original: Foofoo, foobar and Bar!
modified: FOofoo, fooBAR and BAR!
```

The `return` command will clean up the stack frame, so the chances are good that the program can continue to run. Keep in mind that the program does not execute any more statements of the inner frames when you bail out of them with a `return` command. This can produce memory leaks or corrupted class objects because we may have skipped implicit destructor calls.

10.10.5 Skipping or Repeating Individual Statements

The GDB `jump` command causes a jump from the current stack frame to an arbitrary line. You can jump forwards, and therefore skip some statements, or jump backwards, and repeat some statements. We will use the command to jump over line 24, thus avoiding the change_word(...) call:

```
... navigate program to line 24
24          change_word( str+n, len_name );
(gdb) jump 25
Continuing at 0x804863c.
Total 4 hits:
original: Foofoo, foobar and Bar!
modified: Foofoo, FOOBAR and BAR!
```

Note that the modified string now begins with "Foofoo..." instead of the usual "FOOfoo...", so the `jump` command effectively skipped function call change_word(...) in line 24.

10.10.6 Printing and Modifying Memory Content

This section describes how to print and modify memory content. All debuggers offer a feature that allows you to inspect, and sometimes to modify, the content of memory. The relevant GDB commands are whatis, print, x and set var. In Visual Studio, you can use the windows for displaying variables and memory, or the **Immediate** window. Memory locations are addressed through addresses such as 0xbf7a5b4 or by variables that point to heap memory, for example, argv[1].

We will once again use the STR class example from Section 10.3, page 134 to demonstrate how these debugger features manipulate the program behavior. Our aim is to read and then modify the argc and argv variables of main(). Variable argc is an integer and hence easy to change. But argv is an array of char* strings that are allocated somewhere in memory, so modifying it is more challenging.

The first step is to determine the type of argv with the whatis command and the current value of argv with the print command:

```
(gdb) start "foofoo, FooBar and Bar!" foo bar
...
(gdb) whatis argv
type = char **
(gdb) print argv
$1 = (char **) 0xbfffee54
```

Variable argv is an array of strings, so we can use expression argv[<n>] to access an individual array element:

```
(gdb) whatis argv[0]
type = char *
(gdb) print argv[0]
$2 = 0xbffff05e "/home/someone/myprog"
(gdb) print argv[1]
$3 = 0xbffff08a "foofoo, FooBar and Bar!"
```

The @ operator plus the argument 5 can be used to tell GDB that argv is an array and that we want to see the first 5 elements. Note that the array is terminated with a null pointer, so there are actually argc+1 elements:

```
(gdb) print argc
$4 = 4
(gdb) print *argv@5
$20 = {0xbffff05e "/home/someone/myprog",
       0xbffff08a "foofoo, FooBar and Bar!",
       0xbffff0a2 "foo",
       0xbffff0a6 "bar",
       0x0}
```

You can also access the memory directly with the x command, which needs only an address and an optional format:

```
(gdb) x/5xw 0xbfffee54
0xbfffee54:   0xbffff05e  0xbffff08a  0xbffff0a2  0xbffff0a6
0xbfffee64:   0x00000000
```

See the GDB documentation or type `help x` to get a full description of the format. The `x/5xw` command will print five 4-byte words. We can also print the string `argv[1]` with `x/40c`, which is a command to print 40 bytes as characters:

```
(gdb) p argv[1]
$38 = 0xbffff08a "foofoo, FooBar and Bar!"
(gdb) x/40c 0xbffff08a

0xbffff08a: 102 'f'  111 'o'  111 'o'  102 'f'  111 'o'  111 'o'   44 ','   32 ' '
0xbffff092:  70 'F'  111 'o'  111 'o'   66 'B'   97 'a'  114 'r'   32 ' '   97 'a'
0xbffff09a: 110 'n'  100 'd'   32 ' '   66 'B'   97 'a'  114 'r'   33 '!'    0 '\0'
0xbffff0a2: 102 'f'  111 'o'  111 'o'    0 '\0'  98 'b'   97 'a'  114 'r'    0 '\0'
0xbffff0aa:  76 'L'   69 'E'   83 'S'   83 'S'   75 'K'   69 'E'   89 'Y'   61 '='
```

We now want to create new values for `argc` and `argv`, by changing the order of "Foo" and "Bar", and by adding a new argument "and" between "Foo" and "Bar". There is not enough allocated memory in `argv` for `argv[5]`, so we have to reallocate memory for `argv` by calling `malloc` to allocate six 4-byte words.

```
(gdb) set var argc=5
(gdb) print/x malloc(6*4)
$23 = 0x804a048
(gdb) set var argv=0x804a048
```

Next, set all pointers in `argv`. We copy the pointers of the original `argv[0]` and `argv[1]` and use string literals for the other arguments. Note that GDB allocates string literals used in expressions on the heap and does not free them, so we don't have to worry that the memory will suddenly be released.

```
(gdb) set var argv[0]=0xbffff05e
(gdb) set var argv[1]=0xbffff08a
(gdb) set var argv[2]="BAR"
(gdb) set var argv[3]="and"
(gdb) set var argv[4]="Foo"
(gdb) set var argv[5]=0
(gdb) print *argv@6
$24 = {0xbffff05e "/home/someone/myprog",
       0xbffff08a "foofoo, FooBar and Bar!",
       0x804a068 "BAR",
       0x804a078 "and",
       0x804a088 "Foo",
       0x0}
```

The last exercise is to modify the string `"foofoo, FooBar and Bar!"` into `"ABCDEF, FooBar and Bar!"`. The first two characters are overwritten by accessing `argv[1][0]` and `argv[1][1]` referring to single characters. This is possible, but tedious. We will therefore modify the remaining 4 characters with a `strncpy` call:

```
(gdb) set var argv[1][0]='A'
(gdb) set var argv[1][1]='B'
(gdb) call strncpy(argv[1]+2,"CDEF",4)
$25 = -1073745779
(gdb) print *argv@6
```

```
$27 = {0xbffff05e "/home/someone/myprog",
       0xbffff08a "ABCDEF, FooBar and Bar!",
       0x804a068 "BAR",
       0x804a078 "and",
       0x804a088 "Foo",
       0x0}
```

The memory modifications are now complete and we can let the program run to its end to check whether it works out:

```
(gdb) cont
Continuing.
Total 4 hits:
original: ABCDEF, FooBar and Bar!
modified: ABCDEF, FOOBAR AND BAR!
```

We have shown that you can modify more than just a few variables. With enough effort and care, you can change the entire memory content. Of course, it is also easy to corrupt the memory by accident.

Lessons learned:

- A debugger will let you change a running program, by changing variables, calling functions, overriding the return value of a function, aborting function calls, skipping or repeating statements, and by directly modifying memory contents.
- Combining the above features with breakpoint commands leads to very powerful debugging techniques.

10.11 Debugging Without Debug Information

This section is on how to debug a program where some or all of the source code was compiled without debug information. When you debug a program with GDB or some other debugger, you typically compile the program with debug information, for example, with `gcc -g`. However, there are occasions when the debug version of the program is not available but only the optimized (non-debug) version. One example for such a situation is when you are debugging at a customer site, and your visit will end before there is time to create a debug build.

Assume that you have to debug such a program with what you have. This is definitely an unpleasant situation, but not hopeless. This section gives some hints on how to make the best of it, and how to extract as much information as possible using a debugger. We will use the following example to print the value of function arguments, find the approximate statement in the source code, and step through the source code.

```
1  #ifndef NODEBUG_H
2  #define NODEBUG_H
3  /* nodebug.h */
4  int size(const char* S);
5  int F (int A, const char* B, char* C);
6  #endif
```

```
1  /* nodebug.c */
2  #include "nodebug.h"
3
4  int F (int A, const char* B, char* C) {
5      int R = size(B+A);
6      R *= size(C+A);
7      return R;
8  }
```

```
1  /* main.c */
2  #include "nodebug.h"
3  #include <string.h>
4
5  int size(const char* S) {
6      return strlen(S);
7  }
8
9  int main(int argc, char* argv[]) {
10     return F (2,               /* A */
11              "AABBCCDD",        /* B */
12               argv[1] );        /* C */
13 }
```

We prepare the example so that main() and size() are compiled with debug information, but F() is compiled without it. The command line arguments are chosen so that the program crashes:

```
gcc -O -c nodebug.c
gcc -g -c main.c
gcc -o test main.o nodebug.o
./test
Segmentation Fault
```

The debugger reveals that the crash occurs in function strlen():

```
gdb test
(gdb) run
Program received signal SIGSEGV, Segmentation fault.
0x400938db in strlen () from /lib/tls/libc.so.6
(gdb) where
#0  0x400938db in strlen ()
    from /lib/tls/libc.so.6
#1  0x080483cd in size (S=0x2 <Address 0x2 out of bounds>)
    at main.c:6
#2  0x0804842f in F ()
#3  0x08048405 in main (argc=1, argv=0xbfffeeb4)
    at main.c:10
```

Function `size()` was called with an illegal argument `S=0x2` from `F()`, which itself was called from `main()`. We will first check with the debugger that `main()` works correctly, because `main()` was compiled with debug information and is therefore easy to debug. A bug in `strlen()` is unlikely, because it is a well-tested function from the standard C library. That leaves only `F()` as the place where the bug was introduced. We need to collect as much information as possible about what happened inside `F()`.

10.11.1 Reading Function Arguments From the Stack

We first need to check the function arguments of `F()`. The debugger cannot show them directly, because `F()` was compiled without debug information. But the debugger may still be able to give enough information, which we will combine with our knowledge of the source code to achieve the same result. The way to connect this information depends on the CPU type, operating system and compiler. This example was compiled on a Pentium CPU, running under Suse9 Linux and compiled with GCC 3.3.5. In this case, all function arguments are stored on the stack. Using the GDB `info frame` command, we first locate the memory address where the stack is located:

```
(gdb) frame 2
#2  0x0804842f in F ()
(gdb) info frame
Stack level 2, frame at 0xbfffee00:
 eip = 0x804842f in F; saved eip 0x8048405
 called by frame at 0xbfffee30, caller of frame at 0xbfffede0

 Arglist at 0xbfffedf8, args:        <== MOST INTERESTING PART
 Locals at 0xbfffedf8, Previous frame's sp is 0xbfffee00

 Saved registers:
  ebx at 0xbfffedf0, ebp at 0xbfffedf8, esi at 0xbfffedf4,
  eip at 0xbfffedfc
```

The frame starts at address `0xbfffee00`. All three arguments of `F()` are located at this, and the consecutive, addresses. We can use the GDB commands `print sizeof(int)` and `print sizeof(char* )` to find out how much space the arguments require. Each argument needs 4 bytes, so we will find all data by accessing the three words starting at `0xbfffee00`:

```
(gdb) p sizeof (int)
$1 = 4
(gdb) p sizeof (char*)
$2 = 4
(gdb) x/3x 0xbfffee00
0xbfffee00:  0x00000002  0x08048558  0x00000000
```

The second argument is `char* B`, so we check the string content as well:

```
(gdb) x/s 0x08048558
0x8048558 <_IO_stdin_used+4>:      "AABBCCDD"
```

Now we have all the required information:

```
0xbfffee00: int A   = 2
0xbfffee04: char* B = 0x08048558 "AABBCCDD"
0xbfffee08: char* C = 0x00000000
```

The way of passing the function arguments from calling function to callee may vary
with the CPU architecture, operating system and compiler. It may require some
experimentation to find out where function arguments are stored. The arguments
may be stored in main memory on the stack, or in CPU registers. If the arguments
are stored on the stack, use the commands shown above to locate the values. If
they are stored in registers, use the GDB command info reg to print them out.
Unfortunately, the compiler is free to overwrite the registers during execution of a
function for the sake of optimization; that means that the initial value (passed down
from the calling function) can be safely accessed only at the begin of the function.

Here are some examples that illustrate the platform dependency: On a Sparc
V9 CPU running under Solaris 5.10 and GCC 3.3.5 compiler, the arguments are
accessible as registers i0, i1, and i2. GDB gives access to them with prefix $,
for example with print $i0. On a 64bit AMD Opteron processor under Linux
Red Hat 3.0 with GCC 3.3.5, the function arguments can be found in registers rdx,
rsi and rdi. In both cases, registers will be overwritten during execution of the
function F(), so set a breakpoint in F() and read the values immediately when the
breakpoint is hit.

This highlights that there is no simple, common way to locate the function arguments. Things are likely to change, and the register names we have mentioned
may not hold for future CPU types and compilers. However, the methodology of
searching for valuable data in memory and registers should remain valid. You can
use these commands in the middle of a debugging session to find out what they are:

```
(gdb) break strncmp
Breakpoint 17 at 0x400451fa
(gdb) call strncmp("AAAAAA","BBBBBB",0x77777777)
Breakpoint 17, 0x400451fa, in strncmp () ...
(gdb) info frame
...
(gdb) info reg
...
(gdb) return
(gdb) delete 17
```

Function strncmp() is probably linked into the program. strncmp() is part of
the standard C library which most programs contain, so there is no need to modify
and recompile the program. A value such as 0x77777777 is easy to locate in memory dumps. Once you have found out how arguments are passed to strncmp()
then the same method can be used for other functions. Do not forget the return
statement, which ends the strncmp() call, and turns the stack back to its previous
state.

This approach to retrieving the value of function arguments is especially useful during post-mortem debugging if the program was compiled without debug info, and only a core dump file is available. See also Section 10.9.7 on debugging core dumps.

10.11.2 Reading Local/Global Variables, User-Defined Data Types

There is, unfortunately, no easy way to read the value of local variables. The compiler is free to store variables arbitrarily on the stack, or in registers. In the example for Pentium CPU, Suse 9, GCC 3.3.5, local variable S is stored in register eax which can be printed with p $eax. But there is generally no guarantee that the variable will be stored in the same register throughout the entire function.

Global variables are stored in fixed memory addresses, and the debugger might find them from a variable name. If the address is known, then a global variable can be accessed from that address throughout the entire program.

User-defined data types also present a difficult problem. It is possible to access every single byte, but correlating each byte to the corresponding field is tedious and error prone.

10.11.3 Finding the Approximate Statement in the Source Code

Next, we want to find out which statement within F() is causing the crash. A quick review of the source code combined with the function arguments will reveal this information, but we do it the hard way for demonstration purposes.

The where command has already revealed that the current address within F() is 0x0804842f. Now, disassemble the entire function F() and check where this address is:

```
(gdb) disassemble F
0x0804840c <F+0>:    push    %ebp
0x0804840d <F+1>:    mov     %esp,%ebp
0x0804840f <F+3>:    push    %esi
0x08048410 <F+4>:    push    %ebx
0x08048411 <F+5>:    mov     0x8(%ebp),%ebx
0x08048414 <F+8>:    sub     $0xc,%esp
0x08048417 <F+11>:   mov     0xc(%ebp),%eax
0x0804841a <F+14>:   add     %ebx,%eax
0x0804841c <F+16>:   push    %eax
0x0804841d <F+17>:   call    0x80483bc <size>   <== 1st size() call
0x08048422 <F+22>:   mov     %eax,%esi
0x08048424 <F+24>:   add     0x10(%ebp),%ebx
0x08048427 <F+27>:   mov     %ebx,(%esp)
0x0804842a <F+30>:   call    0x80483bc <size>   <== 2nd size() call
0x0804842f <F+35>:   imul    %eax,%esi          <== current adr
```

```
0x08048432 <F+38>:   mov    %esi,%eax
0x08048434 <F+40>:   lea    0xfffffff8(%ebp),%esp
0x08048437 <F+43>:   pop    %ebx
0x08048438 <F+44>:   pop    %esi
0x08048439 <F+45>:   pop    %ebp
0x0804843a <F+46>:   ret
0x0804843b <F+47>:   nop
0x0804843c <F+48>:   nop
0x0804843d <F+49>:   nop
0x0804843e <F+50>:   nop
0x0804843f <F+51>:   nop
End of assembler dump.
```

While most assembly instructions may look cryptic, some instructions usually stand out. For example, the calls to function `size()` can be easily located, and correlated back to lines 5 and 6 of file `nodebug.c` of `F()`. The current address of this frame is located just after the second call, and the next instruction will be a multiplication. We can conclude with reasonable certainty that the crash occurred in line 6.

As before, the assembly code will vary greatly with the host CPU type, so reading the assembly code will always be a challenge. Other complicating factors include the presence of inlined functions, the freedom of the compiler to arrange basic blocks, and so on. However, there is always a good chance that you will be able to locate the statement where the crash occurs.

10.11.4 Stepping Through Assembly Code

The final part of this process is to step through the code of function `F()`. We cannot directly step through the C source code because the debug information linking addresses to source lines is missing. However, we can step through the machine instructions and correlate back to the source code as shown above. All good debuggers have features to disassemble machine instructions and step through them. For GDB, the commands are `disassemble`, `stepi`, `nexti`.

A useful feature of GDB allows you to step from code compiled with debug information into function calls compiled without debug information. This feature is enabled with `set step 1`. Combining this command with disassembling and machine code stepping, we can step through the code in `F()` as follows:

```
(gdb) start
main (argc=1, argv=0xbfffeeb4) at main.c:10
10      return F (2,          /* A */
(gdb) set step 1
(gdb) step
0x0804840c in F ()
(gdb) disas $pc $pc+5
0x0804840c <F+0>:   push   %ebp
0x0804840d <F+1>:   mov    %esp,%ebp
0x0804840f <F+3>:   push   %esi
```

```
0x08048410 <F+4>:    push    %ebx
(gdb) nexti
0x0804840d in F ()
(gdb) nexti
0x0804840f in F ()
(gdb) nexti
0x08048410 in F ()
```

This approach to debugging is tedious, but you can follow the approximate flow of the program, which may be good enough to help you locate the bug.

To debug our example above in Visual Studio, right-click on the program's project, and select **Properties**. In the **Properties** dialog, go to **Configuration Properties/C/C++/General** and set the item **Debug Information Format** to **Disabled**. The compiled program will then have no debug information. To debug a program without debug information in Visual Studio, start the program with a click on **Step-Into**. You will get a tabbed window **Call Stack**, where you right-click on the entry for the program executable, and select `Go To Disassembly`. You will get another window with the disassembled code for the program. The entry points for function `main` and `F` will be visible as:

```
_main:
...
_F:
...
```

You can step through the code, set breakpoints, and inspect register and memory values by pointing the cursor at the desired item. It is also possible to change the assembly code.

Lessons learned:

- A debugger is useful even if the program has no debug information. You can read function arguments, examine the call stack, and step through the code.
- If you happen to know the assembly language of your processor well and understand calling conventions for C/C++ functions then you actually have almost everything you need. Determining addresses of local variables can be quite challenging, but you may be able to locate them adjacent to the function call arguments.

Chapter 11
Writing Debuggable Code

When a program starts being used then chances are high that it will eventually run into a bug. Therefore, it needs to be debugged at which point you or someone else will find out how well it is suited for being debugged. Not all programs score equally high in this respect. This chapter deals with hints and techniques how to make a program more debuggable right from the beginning.

Debugging means to a large extent reverse engineering, especially if you did not write the program in the first place. Consequently, the first two Sections 11.1, 11.2 deal with comments and coding style. The easier the source code can be read and understood, the more debuggable it is. How to write source code is a question of personal style and philosophy, but some general recipes stand out and we will explain them.

Take macros such as `#define INCR 20` as an example. They are a nuisance for interactive debugging. We show in Section 11.3 how one can often replace them with different language constructs.

Build a number of helpful debugging functions into the program, as shown in Section 11.4. If you expect that a noteworthy amount of time will be spent later for debugging your program, which you should, then why not spend some small effort early on and be prepared? Chances are high that you and others will be glad to see these helper functions some day.

The final aspect covered in Section 11.5 is preparing the program for post-mortem debugging, by writing hints about ongoing activities into a log file, so there will be enough information to read after the crash.

11.1 Why Comments Count

There are two extreme opinions about comments in source code and whether they are helpful in the process of debugging or not. The first faction claims that comments in the source code are an integral part of software, and that software would not be maintainable – or intelligible – without them. The second faction claims that comments are extremely dangerous. Comments tend to be written initially with the first version of the source code and they become easily stale, as code changes do not necessarily go hand in hand with changes in the comments. This often results in wrong comments, which is worse than no comments at all. Thus, the second faction pleads for writing code in a self-documenting way, rendering additional comments unnecessary. The authors believe that the truth lies somewhere in between both of these extreme views: source code should be as self-explanatory as possible. But nevertheless comments are vital to the maintainability and debug-ability of the code, as long as they add information to the self-documenting source code. This also determines of what type these comments have to be: they describe the intention (*what*) of a function or piece of code and potentially also the motivation (*why*) for choosing a certain solution. Non-obvious tricks in the source code also deserve some comments.

Debugging requires to a large extent the skill of reverse engineering; after all you will frequently debug source code that someone else wrote some time ago. Good comments that make understanding the source code easier are always welcome.

The following sections provide some examples where comments have proved helpful for debugging.

11.1.1 Comments on Function Signatures

The description should clearly state the following:

- What a function is supposed to do: this behavioral description should be independent from the actual implementation. For example, the comment on a function such as `data* get(content *list, const char* key)` should explain that it retrieves the first address entry from a data structure that matches the provided string key, rather than elaborating on an underlying mapping algorithm from the C++ standard library.
- Function arguments and how they are dealt with in exceptional cases. Example: `data* get(content *list, const char* key)` tolerates if `list` is a NULL pointer and returns NULL itself in this case.
- Assumptions on the interface usage: are there special format requirements for the provided string key in the search function `data* get(content *list, const char* key)`, such as forbidden white spaces or line breaks? Are there programming sequences, for example "*call* `get()` *only after you called* `init()`"?
- Memory allocation: in case the function returns a pointer to a class object, what is the lifetime of that object and who is responsible for deleting it later on?
- Side effects: having side effects is bad enough. Not documenting them in a comment makes them a nightmare.
- Document all known pitfalls and temporary workarounds.

11.1.2 Comments on Workarounds

Defects in library functions, compilers, or even hardware bugs sometimes require a programmer to use rather odd-looking workarounds in the code to get things working. Those constructs sometimes turn into buggy code once the root cause is fixed. A comment describing what the workaround is doing, and why it was needed, will be highly appreciated by anybody in charge of debugging the code.

11.1.3 Comments in Case of Doubt

It definitely helps if the programmer was honest enough to state his or her doubts about certain pieces of code. Something that was not entirely clear to the programmer is always a good candidate for a debugging hypothesis. A comment such as

```
delete[] a; /* not sure if we can really deallocate here */
```

can be a good hint on the way to hunt down a segmentation fault.

11.2 Adopting a Consistent Programming Style

One can get fanatic about programming style – about capitalization, indentation, placing of braces, and many more things. What really matters is not which particular style is picked, but that the overall style serves the purpose of making code more readable and thus understandable. A consistent coding style makes it easier to read and understand source code written by other people. That is why you should strive to maintain the coding style when doing modifications of an existing software project; new coding styles should be introduced only with new projects or with new software modules.

11.2.1 Choose Names Carefully

Variable and function names should be descriptive. If one follows this guideline, the code becomes in fact considerably more self-documenting. There is no *single* standard on naming conventions. Nevertheless, *one* de facto standard is to follow the rules established by the C++ standard library, for example:

- Classes, structs, enums, typedefs, functions, variables, constants, and namespaces all use lowercase with words separated by an underscore.
- Template argument names start with an upper-case letter, with words separated by beginning each word with an upper-case letter.

- Macro names should be in all caps, with words separated by underscores.
- Avoid creating identifiers starting with underscores - they are reserved for compilers, system libraries, and operating systems.

11.2.2 Avoid Insanely Clever Constructs

Brian W. Kernighan once wrote

> *"Debugging is twice as hard as writing the code in the first place. Therefore, if you write the code as cleverly as possible, you are, by definition, not smart enough to debug it."*

Keep in mind that software tends to have bugs and eventually someone, quite often not the original author, will have to debug it. His or her efforts will comprise to a large extend reverse engineering the code in order to find out what it was supposed to do. The cleverer the code is, the harder it will be to reverse engineer.

11.2.3 Spread Out Your Code

Do not squeeze too many statements into a single line as this may hinder debugging. In the following code example, both the if-statement and then-clause are written into the same line:

```
1   if (is_this_true() || is_that_true()) expr1 = expr2++;
```

When you step through the source code, then the debugger will stop only once in line 1, whether the then-clause of the if-statement is executed or not. This makes it unnecessarily complicated to find out if the condition was met or not. It is better to rewrite the code and use an extra line:

```
1   if (is_this_true() || is_that_true())
2       expr1 = expr2++;
```

Debugging is now easier. If the debugger goes into line 2, then the expression was true.

11.2.4 Use Temporary Variables for Complex Expressions

Think about a complex expression that is composed of other sub-expressions, some of them being function calls or operator calls. How can you find out the value of sub-expressions? One approach is to follow the program flow with the debugger using *step-into* and *step-out* commands but that is very tedious. The other approach, directly printing the value of a sub-expression, may not be possible in case inlined functions or operator calls are involved.

In the following example it is not very convenient to analyze the return values of the two functions `is_this_true()` and `is_that_true()` - and it is completely impossible once you have passed line 1:

```
1   if ( is_this_true() || is_that_true() )
2     expression1 = expression2++;
```

If the same code is rewritten with temporary variables to hold the return values of those two functions, this analysis will become rather simple:

```
1   int this_is_true = is_this_true();
2   int that_is_true = is_that_true();
3
4   if ( this_is_true || that_is_true )
5     expression1 = expression2++;
```

Note that the code is no longer exactly identical to the previous versions. Function `is_that_true()` is now always called, instead of only when `is_this_true()` returns false. This difference may affect the runtime speed. It may also affect the program behavior in case the called functions have side effects.

11.3 Avoiding Preprocessor Macros

Macros make debugging harder, so try to avoid preprocessor macros as much as possible. The preprocessor replaces the macro by its content before the code is fed into the compiler. That is, for the compiler they do not exist any more and hence they are invisible or unknown to the debugger. When you step through source code and reach a place where a macro is used then you hit by all practical means a blind spot.

Although there are cases where a macro is the most practical solution (for example when using concatenation, "##"), there are often other ways to achieve the same. We will describe these alternatives and the reasons why they are preferable in the following sections.

11.3.1 Use Constants or Enums Instead of Macros

It is a rather common habit to use preprocessor `#define` statements to define constants that are used in one or more code files. The preprocessor will replace them before compilation – hence, the macro name does not represent a symbol to the debugger and thus cannot be displayed. An alternative to defining constants via preprocessor macros is to use *enums* or *constants*.

The following example defines four macros, NUM_REGISTERS, INCR, DECR, and INVERT. They are used in function execute_unary() which executes unary operations as part of a CPU simulation program:

```
1   #include <assert.h>
2   #include <stdlib.h>
3
4
5   #define NUM_REGISTERS  8
6   #define INCR          16
7   #define DECR          20
8   #define INVERT        22
9
10  int* registers;
11
12  void execute_unary( int opcode, int reg )
13  {
14    assert(0 <= reg && reg < NUM_REGISTERS);
15
16    if (opcode == INCR)
17      ++registers[reg];
18    else if (opcode == DECR)
19      --registers[reg];
20    else if (opcode == INVERT)
21      registers[reg] = ~registers[reg];
22    else
23      assert(0); /* illegal unary opcode */
24  }
```

None of the four macros is visible to the debugger:

```
(gdb) ... run till line 14 ...
14    assert(0 <= reg && reg < NUM_REGISTERS);
(gdb) p NUM_REGISTERS
(gdb) No symbol "NUM_REGISTERS" in current context.
(gdb) p opcode
(gdb) $1 = 20
(gdb) p INCR
(gdb) No symbol "INCR" in current context.
```

We rewrite the same program to make it easier to debug. Macro NUM_REGISTERS is replaced with a constant (const int num_registers = 8) and macros INCR, DECR, and INVERT are replaced with an enum:

```
1   #include <assert.h>
2   #include <stdlib.h>
3
4
5   const int num_registers = 8;
6   enum UnaryOpcodeEncoding {incr=16, decr=20, invert=22};
7
8   int* registers;
9
10  void execute_unary( enum UnaryOpcodeEncoding opcode,
```

```
                                 int reg )
11   {
12     assert(0 <= reg && reg < num_registers);
13
14     if (opcode == incr)
15       ++registers[reg];
16     else if (opcode == decr)
17       --registers[reg];
18     else if (opcode == invert)
19       registers[reg] = ~registers[reg];
20     else
21       assert(0); /* illegal unary opcode */
22   }
```

All four definitions are now fully accessible with the debugger:

```
(gdb) ... run till line 12 ...
12    assert(0 <= reg && reg < num_registers);
(gdb) p num_registers
(gdb) $1 = 8
(gdb) p opcode
(gdb) $2 = decr
(gdb) p (int)incr
(gdb) $4 = 16
```

Defining the constants in form of enums not only makes debugging easier, it also improved the readability of the source code because type `UnaryOpcodeEncoding` gives an extra hint about the purpose of the constants.

There are, however, also a few minor penalties to using `const` definitions. A `const` definition introduces a symbol to the symbol table, so the generated object file gets a little bit larger. The symbol may also clash during linking with another symbol of the same name but this can be avoided by either using a namespace in C++ or by adding `static` to the constant declarations, thus making the constant available only at file scope. A macro defined with `#ifdef`, on the other hand, may also clash with another macro definition, so the chances for a clash stay more or less the same.

11.3.2 Use Functions Instead of Preprocessor Macros

Even worse than using the preprocessor to define constants is the frequently encountered habit of using the preprocessor to define functions. Similar to the use of preprocessor constants described in the previous section, the debugger is not able to find a symbol for the macro function and cannot step through the code of the function, making it very hard to debug. The reason for using preprocessor macro functions might have been that the code executes faster than a normal function since it is inlined into the code by the preprocessor. In C++ you can achieve the same effect with better debugger support by using `inline` functions, which instructs the compiler to inline the code of the function. The following example shows a macro function MAX and an `inline` function min that both are effectively *inlined* by the compiler:

```
1   #define MAX(x,y)  ((x)>(y))?(x):(y)
2
3   inline int min(int x,  int y)
4   {
5     if (x<y) return x;
6     else      return y;
7   }
8
9   int main()
10  {
11    int a1 = 0,  a2 = 42,  a3;
12
13    a3 = MAX(a1,a2);
14    a3 = min(a1,a2);
15
16    return 0;
17  }
```

Another reason for using preprocessor macro functions could be the support of functions that can be applied to arguments of different data types, as long as the operations used within the function are supported for these data types. In the example above the macro function MAX can be used for nearly all native C data types, while the function min is only defined for the data type `int`. If a C++ compiler can be used then the best solution for maintenance, debugging, and flexibility is to use *templates*. The min function in the example is now defined as a templatized function:

```
1   template<class T>
2   inline const& T min(const T& x,  const T& y)
3   {
4     if (x<y) return x;
5     else      return y;
6   }
```

This template will work for different data types as long as both arguments x and y have the same type.

11.3.3 Debug the Preprocessor Output

If a macro cannot be avoided and needs to be debugged, then look directly at the output of the preprocessor. The compiler usually invokes the preprocessor whose output never becomes visible. However, most compilers support the −E flag to invoke the preprocessor, print the output, and then stop. Let us take the MAX macro again as an example:

```
File main.c:
1  #define MAX(x,y)  ((x)>(y)?(x):(y))
```

```
2
3   int main()
4   {
5       int a1 = 0, a2 = 42, a3;
6
7       a3 = MAX(a1,a2);
8   }
```

Now make the preprocessor output visible:

```
> gcc -E main.c > main.post.c
```

This is the output from the preprocessor[1]:

```
    File main.post.c:
1   # 1 "main.c"
2   # 1 "<built-in>"
3   # 1 "<command line>"
4   # 1 "main.c"
5
6
7   int main()
8   {
9       int a1 = 0, a2 = 42, a3;
10
11      a3 = ((a1)>(a2)?(a1):(a2));
12  }
```

Line 11 contains the expanded MAX macro, which is what we want to debug.

Please note the compiler directives in line 1-4 starting with # <line number> <filename>. They instruct the compiler (and thus also the debugger) to map the current source file (file main.post.c) back to a different source file. When you compile file main.post.c and debug it, then the debugger will display file main.c and not main.post.c. If you do not want this, then remove lines 1-4 and compile again.

Note that the generated preprocessor output can be very lengthy because include files are expanded at all levels. A single statement such as #include <iostream> may expand into thousands of lines[2].

11.3.4 Consider Using More Powerful Preprocessors

Though many macros can be replaced by other code constructs that are better suited for debugging, preprocessor macros still have their advantages. For example, when writing code that needs to run on different platforms, when optimizing code for speed by moving tasks from run time to build time, or when guarding special debug

---

[1] The actual output can vary with the compiler that is used.

[2] Approximately 30000 lines using the GCC 3.3.5 compiler and Suse 9 as operating system.

code. In some of these cases it is recommended to use a more powerful macro pre-processor such as m4 (see also Appendix B.9.2) rather than the preprocessors of a development environment. The first reason is that m4 is a much more powerful pre-processor than most preprocessors that are integrated in the compiler packages. The second reason related to debugging is that the m4 preprocessor is invoked *before* the resulting source code is compiled. Therefore, you can directly debug the resulting C/C++ source code, there is no hidden macro expansion that obscures debugging. The following code example illustrates how the m4 preprocessor should be used in the design flow:

```
File matrix.m4cpp:
1   include(forloop.m4)
2   define('identity_matrix',
3        'int id$1[$1][$1] = {forloop('ii',0,eval($1-1),'
4        forloop('jj',0,eval($1-1),'eval(jj==ii),')')}')dnl
5
6   int main (int argc, char* argv[])
7   {
8        int count = 0;
9        identity_matrix(5);
10       ...
```

The code is a blend of C/C++ code and m4-macros. The macro identity_matrix is defining and initializing an identity matrix of variable dimension. It is used with an argument of 5 in this example. m4 preprocesses file matrix.m4cpp and writes the output to a file where the macros are expanded:

```
> m4 matrix.m4cpp > matrix.cpp
> cat -n matrix.cpp
1
2   int main()
3   {
4     int count = 0;
5     int identity_matrix5[5][5] = {
6        1,0,0,0,0,
7        0,1,0,0,0,
8        0,0,1,0,0,
9        0,0,0,1,0,
10       0,0,0,0,1,};
11      ...
```

The resulting file matrix.cpp is then compiled and debugged. The key point here is that the debugger will refer to matrix.cpp, which is plain C code. If the program using the macro does not show the desired behaviour then debug the macro in two steps. First, compare files matrix.m4cpp and matrix.cpp to check if the macro created the expected C code. Next, use the debugger to check if this C code works as expected. When you have found the bug, manually modify the C code until it works correctly and then tweak the macro such that it creates the desired C code.

11.4 Providing Additional Debugging Functions

When developing or debugging complex programs you will occasionally find that there is a set of information from the program state or the data being processed that needs to be displayed over and over again. Often enough it requires the developer to spend some effort to collect the required pieces of information in the debugger or to filter out the information needed. To speed up this process it is a good idea to provide special *debugging functions*. They can either be an integral part of the code or they can be linked additionally into the executable. These debugging functions have the sole purpose of extracting or filtering the information required for debugging. Routines that check data integrity and consistency are other application examples. This includes analysis routines, e.g. showing data distribution in a hash table.

11.4.1 Displaying User-Defined Data Types

Unlike native C/C++ data types, user-defined data types cannot be passed directly to I/O routines in C/C++, such as `printf` or `cout`. The user has to define the appropriate display or streaming methods. For complex data types, these methods should be configurable. For example, to show more or less details (verbosity level) or where to print the output (`stdout`, `stderr` or user-provided `FILE` pointer). These customized I/O methods can also be called interactively in a debugger.

Example: imagine a C++ class `People` that stores a list of person related data (name, address, phone number, date of birth). Debug function `People_debug_print(People* obj, int level)` is now called from inside the debugger. Argument `level` selects printing either just the bare statistics (`level=0`), just the name for each person (`level=1`), or all available data (`level=2`):

```
(gdb) call People_debug_print(my_close_friends,0)
3 persons

(gdb) call People_debug_print(my_close_friends,1)
3 persons
 Meggy Meyers
 Paul Smith
 Martha Miller

(gdb) call People_debug_print(my_close_friends,2)
3 persons
 Meggy Meyers
  addr: 112 Flynn Ave / 12345 LittleTown
  phone: 123-7654-321
  DOB: 1967-02-24
 Paul Smith
  addr: 496 Thompson Lane / 12345 LittleTown
  ...
```

Here are some recommendations regarding such debug functions:

- Consistency over many classes: In a complex program with many classes, it will pay off to use a consistent naming schema and implement these debug functions for all classes. For example, give all classes a method `debugprint(int verbosity)` that prints information about the class object to stdout; parameter `verbosity=0` prints a brief summary, `verbosity=1` prints the most useful information, `verbosity=2` prints everything.
- Inlining: if possible, do not inline debug functions because the debugger may not able to call an inlined function.
- Trigger by environment variable: a typical debug feature is to invoke the debug function(s) from the program if a certain environment variable is set.
- Debug versus efficiency: adding debug function will make the final executable larger. If this overhead is not acceptable for the final production version, then guard the body or even the entire definition of a debug function with a compiler directive such as `#ifdef ENABLE_DEBUG_CODE`.
- Linking: debug functions are typically not used by the program code itself so the linker may skip the debug function altogether. There are several ways to avoid this problem; two easy ones are to write the debug function into a source file that is already linked into the executable or to use a linker flag[3] to enforce linking.

11.4.2 Self-Checking Code

Consider making your program self-checking, by adding assertions and analysis functions. In contrast to the display functions described before, an analysis function also checks data or control state information. This is crucial when it is difficult to maintain the consistency of complex data. Calling the analysis function from the debugger comes in handy when you track down if and when the internal contents of an object get corrupted. A detailed discussion of self-checking code and assertions can be found in [Zeller09].

Design the analysis function so that it returns 1 and creates no output if the internal state is correct. Next, add `assert(analysis_fn(my_object))` assertion statements at appropriate places. The program will abort on its own the first time that the analysis function fails. This will be a valuable check when running regression tests.

Use good judgement where and when to call the analysis function. There will be a trade-off between better chances for debugging (call analysis function more frequently) and less runtime overhead (call less frequently). You should add `#ifdef` guards around the analysis functions and assertions, such that the self-checking code can be turned off.

---

[3] For example, flag `-u <debug-function>` for the GCC compiler.

11.4.3 Debug Helpers for Operators

C++ supports mapping certain operators to user-defined code. It is sometimes not possible to call a specific operator from the debugger. To bypass this limitation, create a global function that internally calls the operator. You can now call this function from the debugger. Here an example:

```
class myClass
{
  ...
  double operator() (int factor) const;
  ...
};

double
myClass_op_parenth (const myClass &c, int factor)
{
  return c(factor);
}
```

You can now call `myClass_op_parenth(my_object,5)` from the debugger to verify the behavior of operator `my_object(5)`.

11.5 Prepare for Post-Processing

The most efficient way to debug is usually to interactively debug the program with a small test case. However, this is sometimes not possible, for example because a crash happens only sporadically or because the test case is not accessible due to confidentiality issues.

This will force you to debug in *post-processing* mode, meaning you have to find out what happened *after* the program has completely ended. Debugging in post-processing mode can be virtually impossible or at least very inefficient in case there is very little data left over from the actual bug or crash. There may be a core file that reveals the call stack, values of certain variables and the memory content at the time when the program crashed. However, there may be very little data about what happened *before* the crash. The only thing left may be a few lines of output in the command shell and whatever the program user remembered.

11.5.1 Generate Log Files

The airline industry is facing a similar dilemma. If an airplane crashes then there is a very strong demand to find out exactly why it crashed and to make sure that this problem (bug) will not occur again. Among other things, the industry tackles this task by adding *black boxes* to airplanes that record the most important activity and status information of the airplane. Data recording happens all the time but only the last 1/2 hour or so is actually stored. This data is usually very important during analysis of the plane crash.

The pendant to a black box in a software program is a log file. It is up to the programmer to create the log file and to define what kind of information should go in there. There is always a tradeoff between runtime/disk space overhead on one side and ease of debugging on the other side.

If the size of the log file is not restricted, then it may eventually fill up the entire disk and thus create a bug on its own. This can be addressed by restricting the size, for example saving only the last 1000 lines or 100 KBytes of data. A simple, robust scheme is to use two log files and toggle between both whenever the current one reaches the defined limit.

Make sure to flush output buffers frequently, otherwise the last few lines of output (which tend to be the most important ones) may be lost when the program runs into a fatal signal. Here an example:

```
...
FILE* log_file;
...
void calibrate(...)
{
    ...
    if(log_file) {
        fprintf(log_file, "Calibrating phalanx %s\n", ...);
        fflush(log_file); /* important or lines may be lost */
    }
    ...
```

Lessons learned:

- Use comments to document what is least obvious from the source code. Describe the intention *what* a piece of code is supposed to do or *why* is was written in a specific way.
- Use a consistent naming convention for constants, classes, members and variables. Chose names carefully.
- Avoid preprocessor macros. There are good alternatives: enums, constants, inlined functions, or templates.
- Add debugging functions that can be called from the debugger. These are functions that do a decent printout of user-defined data types or check the integrity of the database.
- Prepare for post-processing debug: create an optional log file, do not forget to call fflush() frequently, and make the code self-checking.

Chapter 12
How Static Checking Can Help

In this chapter, we present a set of tools called static checkers. Static checkers analyze the source code of a program without actually running the program. Ideally, these tools are run as part of the regular software build process and look for the specific bugs that can be detected with a static analysis of the source code. Typical checks are syntax errors, incorrect use of memory, and unreachable code. Below, we give a more detailed list of errors detected by static analysis, as part of the discussion of the various available tools.

We typically do not apply static checkers as part of a debug session, since practical experience has shown that the probability of finding the cause of one particular bug with a static checker is rather low. However, software that contains many static checker violations or compiler warnings is likely to contain a number of bugs. These bugs may emerge later in the software maintenance cycle, for instance, when the compiler is updated to a newer, stricter version, or when the software is ported to a new CPU platform, or when the software is reused in a new way. Therefore, some software teams have the sensible rule that the source code base must pass one or more static checker tools with close to zero errors. Violations and warnings should be removed at regular intervals, either by cleaning up the code, or by defensive coding practices that avoid the use of advanced features or error-prone coding styles.

The first section starts with the C/C++ compiler as the most basic static code checker. In the following sections we introduce checkers that are more sophisticated, and show what advantages they offer and what extra effort is necessary to use them properly.

12.1 Using Compilers as Debugging Tools

Over the years, C and C++ compilers have become sophisticated enough to not only report syntax errors, but also to acquire static code checking features. A modern compiler will emit, among others, these warnings:

- Missing `case` in a switch statement for enumerated types
- Unused functions, function parameters, or labels
- Taking the address of a `register` variable
- Integer division by zero
- Dead code (i.e. unreachable code)
- Missing function declarations and `return` statements
- Incorrect use of memory: unused or uninitialized variables
- Future incompatibilities with the C++ standard
- Incompatibilities with 64-bit CPUs

A widely used and very successful programming rule for a software project is to enable all warnings in a compiler, and to fix the software during regular development or special cleanup projects so that warnings (almost) never occur.

First, we show how to enable compiler warnings. The mechanism is usually the same: the compile command accepts compile flags on the command line to suppress all warnings, enable all warnings, or to treat all warnings as errors. In addition, there are usually flags to enable/disable certain types of warnings. You should refer to the compiler manual for a list of these warning-related flags. Table 12.1 lists the most common flags related to displaying warnings for three widely used compilers.

Table 12.1 Compile flags for warning messages

	GCC	Sun CC	Visual C++
enable all warnings	`-Wall`	`+w`	`-Wall`
suppress all warnings	`-w`	`-w`	`-w`
convert warnings to errors	`-Werror`	`-xwe`	`-WX`

12.1.1 Do not Assume Warnings to be Harmless

As a first example of the type of problems reported with a compiler warning, the following program has two problems:

```
1   /* testinit.c */
2   int main() {
3       int v[16];
4       int i, j, k;
5       j = i;
6       v[i] = 42;
7       return 0;
8   }
```

The first problem in this program is that the variable k is not used. The second, and more serious problem, is that the variable i is not initialized to a value before being used as an array index.

When the `testinit.c` example is compiled with the GCC compiler using the default settings, the result is no warning. But using the `-Wall` flag will produce these warnings:

```
testinit.c:4: warning: unused variable 'k'
```

When the `testinit.c` example is compiled with the Sun compiler, the result is the following warning, independent of whether +w is used:

```
testinit.c", line 5: Warning: The variable i has not yet
been assigned a value.
```

Microsoft Visual C++, for versions 7.0, 8.0, and 9.0, finds the problem with the variable `i`, using the default settings. It finds both problems when using the flag `-Wall`:

```
testinit.c(4): warning C4101: 'k' : unreferenced local variable
h:\src\testinit.c(5): warning C4700: local variable 'i' used
without having been initialized
```

We recommend not to ignore compiler warnings. If a warning indicates a real or even potential bug, then you should fix the bug. If a warning is harmless, or cannot be fixed, then put a comment in the code to explain this.

Here is another example that illustrates that the same type of warning may be harmless or indicates a serious bug. In our example, we have two pointers, P and Q to `some_class` objects. The code has to check if both P and Q point to the same object. Unfortunately, there is a typo in the source code, the intended comparison == in line 8 was accidentally written as an assignment =:

```
1   /* myfile.cpp */
2   some_class* P = ...
3   some_class* Q;
4   if ( Q=find_pointer(...) )
5     // do something with Q
6   if (P=Q)          <------ typo, should have been P==Q
7     // they are equal, do something special
8   ...
9   ... further processing of P, Q ...
```

The GCC compiler produces these warning with flag `-Wall`:

```
> g++ -Wall myfile.cpp
myfile.cpp:4: warning: suggest parentheses around
                       assignment used as truth value
myfile.cpp:6: warning: suggest parentheses around
                       assignment used as truth value
```

Note that you get no warning at all if flag `-Wall` is not specified – a good reason for always having the maximum warning level enabled.

The warning in line 4 is harmless; the statement first assigns Q and then checks whether it is a NULL pointer or not. This is what the programmer had in mind, so there is no real bug. However, the statement in line 6 is a real bug: the statement does not do what the programmer intended. Instead of comparing both pointers, P is first overwritten with the value of Q, and then compared with a NULL pointer, so the if-statement matches under a completely different condition. Worse, P has been accidentally changed; this may cause further side effects later on.

Both if-statements look equally suspect to the compiler, trigger the exact same warning, and have to be reviewed. The recommendation is to modify the statement in line 4 such that the intention becomes clear to the compiler. The bug in line 6 should be fixed:

```
4   if ( 0 != (Q=find_pointer(...)))
5     ...
6   if (P==Q)
```

We illustrated with the above example that warnings should not be classified as harmless. We also demonstrated that a short investment of time to sweep the software for warnings pays off, because it reduces the need for debugging sessions later on.

12.1.2 Use Multiple Compilers to Check the Code

As we can see from the `testinit.c` example in Section 12.1.1, not every compiler warns about every possible problem. Therefore, it is good practice not to exclusively develop with a single compiler, but to write the C or C++ code in such a style that it is compatible and warning-free with several compilers, or even better, works on multiple platforms.

12.2 Using `lint`

One of the first and best-known static checkers for the C language is `lint`. `lint` appeared in 1979 as part of the UNIX operating system. `lint` is limited to the C language and does not support C++. We will not discuss `lint` in detail here because compilers such as GCC incorporate most of the checks built into `lint`. Please refer to Appendix B.6.2 for more information.

Splint (Secure Programming Lint) is a static checker based on the original UNIX `lint`, with extension for additional checks and for source code annotations. Please refer to Appendix B.6.3 for more information.

12.3 Using Static Analysis Tools

Appendix B.6 lists a set of tools that utilize static code analysis techniques. The following are the most important ones (at the time when this book was written) that perform rule checking for C/C++ code:

- *Coverity Prevent* is a commercial static analysis tool doing rule checking in C/C++ code. See Appendix B.6.1.
- *PC-lint* (also known as *FlexeLint* on non-Windows platforms) is a commercial static analysis tool for checking C and C++ code. See Appendix B.6.7.
- *QA C++* is a commercial static analysis tool checking (among other languages) C and C++, focused on rule checking. See Appendix B.6.8.
- *Codecheck* is a commercial static analysis tool to check C and C++ code for rule violations. See Appendix B.6.9.
- The Enterprise (team development) version of Visual C++ 8.0 supports an `/analyze` code analysis option that is integrated into the Visual Studio. See Appendix B.6.4.
- Parasoft *C++test* is a static analysis tool that offers rule checking and automatic creation of test harnesses. See Appendix B.6.12.

All these tools have similar features and use models, so we will explain them with a Coverity example. The type of bugs found with Coverity and the way to use this tool is representative for other static checker tools.

12.3.1 Familiarize Yourself with a Static Checker

Static checker tools work by parsing the source code of a C or C++ program, and then doing a static code analysis by running rule checks on the code. The program is never executed, and no test cases or input data need to be provided.

The first class of problems detected by a static checker is memory errors: uninitialized variables, memory and file handle leaks, buffer overruns and corruptions, null pointer access, use after `free/delete` and duplicate calls to `free/delete`. There is some overlap of functionality for this type of problem with the dynamic memory checkers such as Valgrind or Purify discussed in Chapter 4. The advantage of a static checker is that it is not necessary to construct a test case so that the problematic code is reached during execution and stimulated with input values. The disadvantage is that for some problems such as memory leaks, a static code checker does not have enough information to decide whether a piece of code is correct or not.

Further software problems detected by Coverity are dead code, unnecessary code such as duplicate null checks, and incorrect API use, such as STL usage errors and incorrect error handling.

To run Coverity, it must be integrated into the build system of your application. Since there is not one "true" version of the C/C++ language, Coverity needs to determine your particular compiler version, compile flags, system headers, etc. before the tool can decide if your source code is correct C++ or not.

Coverity has been integrated into the Linux `make` build command, Visual Studio, Eclipse, and other IDEs. Please refer to Appendix B.6.1 for links to Coverity documentation. The product documentation lists currently supported build systems, and gives details and examples on how to run Coverity as part of your build system.

In order to demonstrate the value provided by Coverity, we give the following example to show the detection of dead code. Dead code is source code that can never be reached during the program's execution. Dead code is quite common in large software projects. Sometimes, execution is no longer intended because it is a leftover from an older state of the software, and no one remembers what the code was supposed to do. In this case, you should remove the dead code, or comment it out.

In most cases, dead code is due to incorrect conditional expressions. The program below gives an example of two nested `if ()` expressions, where the expressions overlap such that the body of the second `if ()` is never executed.

```
 1  /* testdead.cc */
 2  int main() {
 3          int v[16];
 4          int i;
 5
 6          for(i=0; i<16; i++) {
 7                  if(i > 8) {
 8                          v[i] = i;
 9                          if(i <= 8) {
10                                  v[i] = -i;
11                          }
12                  }
13          }
14          return 0;
15  }
```

In the above example, when the first `if ()` expression i > 8 holds, then the second `if()` expression i <= 8 will never be true, and thus the code inside the second `if()` can never be reached. Here the report generated by Coverity:

```
6          for(i=0; i<16; i++) {

Event between: After this line, the value of "i" is between 9 and 15
Event new_values: Conditional "i > 8"
Also see events: [dead_error_line][dead_error_condition][new_values]

7          if(i > 8) {
8                  v[i] = i;

Event dead_error_condition: On this path, the condition "i <= 8"
could not be true
Also see events: [dead_error_line][between][new_values][new_values]

9                  if(i <= 8) {

Event dead_error_line: Cannot reach this line of code
Also see events: [dead_error_condition][between][new_values][new_values]
```

```
10                      v[i] = -i;
```

Note how it is reported that the code inside the `if` statement cannot be reached, and how the precise analysis of the conditional expressions makes it easy to understand the cause of the dead code.

12.3.2 Reduce Static Checker Errors to (Almost) Zero

You can expect the following typical distribution of warnings and errors when using first using a static checker on a large application:

- 40% false positive reports of correct code
- 40% multiple occurrence of same problem
- 10% minor or cosmetic problems
- 10% serious bugs, very hard to find by other methods

As you can see from the distribution of errors above, a lot of effort needs to go into the initial analysis of reported issues. While the report generated by the static checker differentiates between error types, it is good practice to fix or suppress all errors. In some cases, the checker generates a *false positive*: code that is correct but flagged as an error. Most static checkers have a mechanism to suppress false positives, either by an annotation in the code, or by blacklisting the function containing the error in a file. For Coverity, refer to the documentation for the exact format of blacklist items.

In practice, the removal of false positives and multiple reports of the same problems is time-consuming but simple work. Once you have sorted through a large number of trivial-to-fix errors, a small number of serious bugs will surface. You should take care that these problems are not accidentally suppressed. You should also not change code just to make the error message go away. Instead, you may need to do a code review to determine what the code was supposed to do, before making any changes.

We recommend planning for a cleanup with a static checker so that the reported errors are reduced to zero, or to at most a small number of documented cases where it is decided to "not touch the code." Once this baseline of almost no Coverity errors is established, new errors will only occur when code changes are made. For large software projects, the ratio of new lines of code by total lines of code is very small. Therefore, it is not necessary to make the static checker part of the daily edit-compile-run development cycle. It is sufficient to run Coverity during nightly software builds, and to schedule regular Coverity cleanup sessions.

12.3.3 Rerun All Test Cases After a Code Cleanup

After making a code change based on a static checker error report, two tasks are necessary: rerunning the checker to check that the reported error has gone away, and no new errors have been created. More importantly, it is also necessary to execute all dynamic test cases to make sure that the program still works as desired.

12.4 Beyond Static Analysis

Other applications of static source code analysis are:

- Portability: check code for portability issues such as big versus little endian, use of internal (non-standard) header files, 32- versus 64-bit. Example: *Codecheck*, Appendix B.6.9.
- Reverse engineering: create documentation how classes are structured, which other classes are using them, dependencies between software modules, and so on. Example: *Understand C++*, Appendix B.6.14.
- Code statistics: create statistics to evaluate the overall quality of the software. Typical applications are finding duplicated sections of code or interface analysis. Example: *Axivion Bauhaus Suite*, Appendix B.6.10.
- Security: use rule checkers specific for Web applications to check buffer overruns and SQL queries. Examples: *Klocwork*, Appendix B.6.5; *Fortify*, Appendix B.6.6.

Lessons learned:

- Do not ignore compiler warnings, even if they appear to be harmless.
- Use multiple compilers to check the code.
- Familiarize yourself with a static checker.
- Reduce static checker errors to (almost) zero.
- Rerun all test cases after a code cleanup.
- Doing regular sweeps of the source code will pay off in the long term.

Chapter 13
Summary

If you have read this book cover-to-cover, and if we, the authors, have done a good job at explaining various problems and solutions, then you are now equipped with an array of debugging techniques. You know when and how to use the essential software tools in this area: static checker, linker, source code debugger, memory debugger, and profiler. And, most importantly, you know that the most powerful tools are not to be found in the computer; they are your common sense and your analytical skills.

Here are some more things we would like you to take away.

- Debugging is a multi-faceted problem that, in general, neither starts nor ends with a source code debugger.
- Debugging is an important skill for a software developer. It is a prerequisite to mastering large-scale software engineering projects.
- Debugging won't go away. Increasing complexity of hardware and software, increasing re-use (having to deal with buggy software written by other people) and increasing parallelism will rather intensify the problem.
- Consider coming back to this book after some time. New undertakings may change your point of view or expose you to new challenges.

This book does not contain an exhaustive collection of all relevant debugging techniques. If you feel that we missed something essential then please send an email to `authors@debugging-guide.com`. The same holds true if you have spotted one of the many "bugs" that, most likely, managed to sneak into this book. Before doing so, please check the errata under

```
http://www.debugging-guide.com
```

Good luck with your bug hunting!

Appendix A
Debugger Commands

Table A.1 What every self-respecting debugger can do

command name	GDB	Visual Studio
run program	run [args]	F5 **Start Debugging**
start program	start [args]	F10 **Step over**
pause	Ctrl-C	Ctrl-Alt-Break **Break All**
continue running	cont	F5 **Continue**
step-over	next	F10 **Step over**
step-into	step	F11 **Step into**
step-out	finish	Shift + F11 **Step out**
breakpoint	break *file:lineno*	right-click **Breakpoint/Insert Breakpoint**
tracepoint	watch *file:lineno*	right-click **Breakpoint/Insert Tracepoint**
watchpoint	watch *expr*	**Debug/New Bkpt/New Data Breakpoint**
stack trace	bt, where	**Call Stack**
print expression	print *expr*	**Immediate Window**
display expression	display *expr*	**Watch** window
set variable	set var *var=expr*	**Variables** window
set environment variable	set env *var[=val]*	**Properties/Debugging/Environment**
show machine code	disassemble	right-click **Go to Disassembly**
step-over, machine code	nexti	F10 **Step over**
step-into, machine code	stepi	F11 **Step into**

Table A.2 Additional debugger commands used in this book

command name	GDB	Visual Studio
conditional breakpoint	`condition` *bnum*	right-click **Breakpoint/Condition**
event breakpoint	`handle, signal`	-
exception breakpoint	`catch, throw`	**Debug/Exceptions...**
function breakpoint	`break function`	**Debug/New Bkpt/Break at Function**
temporary breakpoint	`tbreak`	F9 **Debug/Toggle Breakpoint**
list all breakpoints	`info breakpoints`	**Breakpoints** window
attach command to bkpt	`commands` *bnum*	right-click **Breakpoint/When Hit**
print in command	`printf`	right-click **Breakpoint/When Hit**
find functions	`info functions` *expr*	**Debug/New Bkpt/Break at Function**
call function	`call` *expr*	**Immediate Window**
change function return value	`return` *expr*	-
print type	`whatis` *arg*	right-click **Go To Declaration**
print type description	`ptype` *arg*	right-click **Go To Definition**
print memory contents	`x` *arg*	**Immediate Window**
select stack frame	`frame` *arg*	**Call Stack** right-click **Switch to Frame**
print frame description	`info frame`	**Call Stack**

Appendix B
Access to Tools

This appendix contains a listing on where to find tools, documentation, further reading, and other material related to debugging. Since some of the information is subject to frequent updates and changes, we expect to revise this appendix in future editions of this book. In addition, we will publish an up-to-date version of this *Access to Tools* appendix in electronic form on our website:

```
http://www.debugging-guide.com
```

B.1 IDEs, Compilers, Build Tools

B.1.1 Microsoft Visual Studio

Visual Studio is the Microsoft IDE. This is a functional, well integrated environment, containing compilers for C++, Java, Visual Basic, as well as source code viewers, and several debugging tools. At the time of writing this book a restricted version of the compiler and IDE called Visual C++ 2008 Express Edition was available for free download. Please check the current license agreement for restrictions of use. All examples in this book were tested with Visual C++ 2005 SP1 (VC++ 8.0) and Visual C++ 2008 (VC++ 9.0). For Visual Studio, the documentation is called the *MSDN Library for Visual Studio*, and is available as part of the software installation.

You can find information about Visual C++, the Microsoft C++ compiler, by going to the central Microsoft website and then following a path through *Developer tools* and *Visual C++*:

```
http://www.microsoft.com
```

B.1.2 Eclipse

Eclipse is an Open Source IDE, with support for Java, C++, and other languages. It runs on Linux and Windows, and is extensible with Plugins. CDT is the C/C++ IDE for Eclipse.

```
http://www.eclipse.org
http://www.eclipse.org/cdt
http://en.wikipedia.org/wiki/Java_eclipse
```

B.1.3 GCC

GCC (The GNU Compiler Collection) is a high-quality compiler, with front ends for C++, C, Java, and Fortran. GCC is available for almost any CPU, due to being Open Source, and very modular and portable. GCC is part of most Linux installations, and also part of Cygwin on Windows (see Appendix B.3.1) We used GCC versions 3.2.3 and 4.2 for the examples in this book. GCC software, documentation, and source code can be found here:

```
http://gcc.gnu.org
```

B.1.4 GNU Make

GNU Make, or `gmake`, is an application for building software. It is part of Linux and Cygwin. Documentation for GNU Make can be found here:

```
http://www.gnu.org/software/make
```

B.2 Debuggers

B.2.1 dbx

dbx is a source code debugger for C and C++ developed originaly as part of Berkeley UNIX, and is available on Solaris and BSD Unix. More information is available here:

```
http://www.oracle.com/technetwork/server-storage/solarisstudio
http://en.wikipedia.org/wiki/Dbx_debugger
```

B.2.2 DDD

DDD is a graphical debugger frontend for GDB and dbx. More information is available here:

```
http://www.gnu.org/software/ddd
http://en.wikipedia.org/wiki/Ddd
```

B.2.3 GDB

GDB is the source code debugger of the GNU project. The GDB manual is available as a book [Stallmann02] and as a web document. More information is available here:

```
http://sourceware.org/gdb
http://en.wikipedia.org/wiki/Gdb
```

B.2.4 ARM Development Studio 5

ARM Development Studio 5 (DS-5) is a set of software development tools for the ARM CPUs, including compiler, assembler, linker, and debugger. The debugger supports Multi-core CPUs, tracing, profiling, emulation of the CPU, and attaching to an embedded system board. DS-5 is based on the Eclipse IDE. More information is available here:

```
http://www.arm.com/products/tools/software-tools
```

B.2.5 TotalView Debugger

The TotalView Debugger is a commercial C/C++ debugger. It is STL aware, has good data visualization capabilities and has special support for debugging parallel programs using threads, MPI, and OpenMP. More information, documentation, demo versions, and pricing for TotalView can be found at:

```
http://www.roguewave.com
```

B.2.6 Lauterbach TRACE32

Lauterbach TRACE32 is a source code debugger for embedded systems. TRACE32 supports the ARM, MIPS, PowerPC, and x86 CPUs, as well as various DSPs. More information can be found here:

```
http://www.lauterbach.com
```

B.3 Environments

B.3.1 Cygwin

Cygwin is a Linux-like development environment for the Windows operating system. Cygwin provides the user with a `bash` shell, editors such as `vi` and `xemacs`, and most commands familiar to users of UNIX and Linux. You can optionally install the GCC compiler, `gmake`, and the debugging tools GDB and `gprof`. Unfortunately, Valgrind is not part of Cygwin. You can find more information, documentation, and download instructions at:

```
http://www.cygwin.com
```

B.3.2 VMware

VMware Workstation is a software package that provides virtual machines on a host workstation. It allows the creation of multiple separate Windows and Linux workstation installations, all of which can run on a single host machine. VMware is typically used when a program needs to be tested with many compiler or OS versions, or when a particular debugging tool is only available on one platform.

VMware contains a useful checkpointing feature, where one or more known stable states of a virtual machine can be saved and restored. This is very useful for obtaining a clean and reproducible debugging environment. For example, use checkpointing if your software alters or destroys a machine installation, or when a working debugging environment needs to be shielded from software maintenance changes. More information, documentation, demo versions, and pricing for VMware can be found at:

```
http://www.vmware.com
```

B.4 Memory Debuggers

B.4.1 Purify

Purify is a commercial memory debugging tool, available on Linux, Windows, and Solaris. Purify works by instrumenting the object code of a program during the link phase. No source code is required, and no special compiler flags or a recompilation of the object files are needed. More information is available here:

```
http://en.wikipedia.org/wiki/IBM_Rational_Purify
http://www.ibm.com/software/awdtools/purify
```

B.4.2 Valgrind

Valgrind is Open Source software. It currently is available on Linux for x86 and PowerPC processors. The use model of Valgrind is simple. Valgrind *interprets* the object code, so it does not need to modify object files or executable, and therefore does not require special compiler flags, recompiling, or relinking the program. The valgrind command is simply added at the shell command line, in front of the program to be executed. A further advantage of Valgrind is that no program source code is required, so Valgrind can be used to analyze black-box software modules from third parties where the source code is confidential and unavailable.

Valgrind comes as a collection of tools for the following purposes:

- Memcheck: a memory checker
- Callgrind: a runtime profiler
- Cachegrind: a cache profiler
- Helgrind: find race conditions
- Massif: a memory profiler

Documentation and download instructions for Valgrind are available here:

```
http://valgrind.org
```

B.4.3 KCachegrind

KCachegrind is the graphical front-end for the Valgrind/Callgrind profiling feature. KCachegrind is Open Source software. KCachegrind visualizes traces generated by profiling, including a tree map and a call graph visualization. Documentation and download instructions for KCachegrind are available here:

```
http://sourceforge.net/projects/kcachegrind
```

B.4.4 Insure++

Insure++ is a commercial tool for detecting runtime memory errors. Insure++ uses source code instrumentation: it modifies the source on the fly just before it is given to the compiler. This use model requires recompilation of the source files. There is some provision to support object code libraries where source code is not available. More information is available here:

```
http://www.parasoft.com
```

B.4.5 BoundsChecker

BoundsChecker is a commercial memory checking tool for Visual C++ on Windows. BoundChecker has two modes: *ActiveCheck*, which monitors calls to the operating system and memory management routines, and FinalCheck, which adds object code insertion to detect buffer overflows and uninitialized memory reads. More information is available here:

```
http://en.wikipedia.org/wiki/BoundsChecker
http://www.microfocus.com/products/devpartner
```

B.5 Profilers

B.5.1 gprof

`gprof` is an Open Source profiling tool that is usually shipped as part of the GCC compiler. It may be necessary to select `gprof` as an additional option or package when downloading and installing the GCC compiler. The documentation for the `gprof` profiler can be found at:

```
http://sourceware.org/binutils
```

B.5.2 Quantify

Quantify is a very powerful commercial profiling tool sold by IBM as part of their IBM Rational family of software quality tools. Quantify is part of the Rational PurifyPlus tool suite. Information about Quantify can be found by going to the IBM website and searching for Software and Quality Products.

```
http://www.ibm.com/software/awdtools/purifyplus/
```

B.5.3 Intel VTune

Intel VTune is a performance analysis tool for the x86 and x64 processors. It is available on Windows and Linux. More information, documentation, demo versions, and pricing can be found at:

```
http://www.intel.com
```

B.5.4 AQtime

AQtime is a commercial tool sold by AutomatedQA. It is a runtime and memory profiler that works on Windows with the Microsoft, Borland, Intel, Compaq, and GNU compilers. AQtime is integrated into Microsoft Visual Studio and Borland Developer Studio. More information can be found at:

```
http://www.automatedqa.com/products/aqtime
```

B.5.5 mpatrol

`mpatrol` is an Open Source software memory debugger which also has memory profiling abilities. It is a library that is linked into the executable and intercepts calls to `malloc()`, `free()`, and similar functions. The use model is similar to `gprof`. Information can be found at:

```
http://sourceforge.net/projects/mpatrol
```

B.6 Static Checkers

B.6.1 Coverity

Coverity Static Analysis is a commercial static code checker sold by Coverity, Inc., and is based on bug-finding technology developed at the Computer Systems Laboratory at Stanford University, USA. More information, documentation, download instructions, and pricing are available at:

```
http://www.coverity.com
```

B.6.2 Lint

lint appeared in 1979 as part of the UNIX operating system. lint has become a synonym for code checking of various computer languages, even though the original tool works only on the C language. lint is part of some OS distributions such as Solaris and Linux. The man lint command will print information on usage and options. The man page can also be found here:

```
http://en.wikipedia.org/wiki/Lint_(software)
http://www.unix.com/man-page/FreeBSD/1/lint
```

A manual can be found at:

```
http://www.thinkage.ca/english/gcos/expl/lint/manu/manu.html
```

B.6.3 Splint

Splint (Secure Programming Lint) is a static checker. It is based on the original UNIX lint, with extension for additional checks and for source code annotations. Splint is also available as a Cygwin package. Documentation, source code, and binaries are available at:

```
http://www.splint.org
```

B.6.4 /analyze option in Visual Studio Enterprise Versions

The more expensive Enterprise (team development) version of Visual Studio supports an /analyze static code analysis option that is integrated into the Visual Studio IDE.

B.6.5 Klocwork

Klocwork Insight is a commercial static analysis tool addressing Web security, software architecture, and general code defects. Information, documentation, pricing, and trial software are available at:

```
http://www.klocwork.com
```

B.6.6 Fortify

The *HP Fortify Static Code Analyzer (SCA)* is a commercial static analysis tool. More information is available at

```
http://www.fortify.com
```

B.6.7 PC-lint/FlexeLint

PC-lint (also known as *FlexeLint* on non-Windows platforms) is a commercial static analysis tool for checking C and C++ code. The software is sold by Gimpel Software. For further information, see:

```
http://www.gimpel.com
```

B.6.8 QA C++

QA C++ is a commercial static analysis tool to check (among other languages) C and C++ code for rule violations. It is sold by Programming Research. For further information, see:

```
http://www.programmingresearch.com
```

B.6.9 Codecheck

Codecheck is a commercial static analysis tool focused on checking C and C++ code for rule violations. It is sold by Abraxas software. For further information, see:

```
http://www.abraxas-software.com
```

B.6.10 Axivion Bauhaus Suite

The *Axivion Bauhaus Suite* is a commercial static analysis tool for doing architectural analysis of source code. Features are clone detection (source code that got duplicated and slightly modified) and interface analysis (how different modules communicate with each other). It is sold by Axivion GmbH. For more information, see:

```
http://www.axivion.com
```

B.6.11 C++ SoftBench CodeAdvisor

CodeAdvisor is a commercial static analysis tool checking C/C++ code for rule violations. It is part of the *SoftBench* tool suite from HP. For more information, go to the HP website and search for "Code Advisor":

```
http://www.hp.com
```

B.6.12 Parasoft C++test

Parasoft C/C++test is a commercial tool sold by Parasoft for C/C++. It is a static analysis tool and offers rule checking and also automatic creation of test harnesses. For more information see:

```
http://www.parasoft.com
```

B.6.13 LDRA tool suite

The *LDRA tool suite* is a commercial static analysis tool doing rule checking and other code analysis. See the following link for more information:

```
http://www.ldra.com
```

B.6.14 Understand C++

Understand is a code analysis tool based on static analysis. It's focus is to reverse engineer and document source code. It is sold by Scientific Toolworks Inc. See the following link for more details:

```
http://www.scitools.com
```

B.7 Tools for Parallel Programming

B.7.1 Posix Threads

Posix Threads is a standard for threads on Linux and Solaris. There is also a Windows implementation. For more information, see [Butenhof97] and also:

```
http://en.wikipedia.org/wiki/Posix_threads
https://computing.llnl.gov/tutorials/pthreads
```

B.7.2 OpenMP

The OpenMP Application Program Interface (API) supports shared-memory parallel programming in C, C++, and Fortran, on Linux, Windows, Solaris, and MacOS platforms. For more information, see [Chandra00], [Chapman07], [Eigenmann01], and also:

```
http://www.openmp.org
http://en.wikipedia.org/wiki/Openmp
```

B.7.3 Intel TBB

Intel TBB (Threading Building Blocks) is a C++ template-based class library that provides an abstraction layer around raw OS threads. TBB has a runtime library with memory allocators that are thread-safe and avoid *cache conflicts*. Available for x86 (Pentium 4 and later) and compatible processors on Linux, Windows, and MacOS. There is also an Open Source version of TBB. For more information, see [Reinders07] and also:

```
http://www.intel.com
http://threadingbuildingblocks.org
http://en.wikipedia.org/wiki/TBB
```

B.7.4 MPI

MPI (Message Passing Interface) is a message-passing interface to program large clusters of computers. MPI is language independent, there is implementations for C, C++, Fortran, Java, Perl, and Python. For more information, see:

```
http://www-unix.mcs.anl.gov/mpi
http://www.mpi-forum.org
http://en.wikipedia.org/wiki/Message_Passing_Interface
```

B.8 MapReduce

Google MapReduce is a framework for parallel computations spread over widely separated clusters with unreliable nodes. For more information, see:

```
http://code.google.com/edu/parallel/mapreduce-tutorial.html
http://en.wikipedia.org/wiki/MapReduce
```

B.8.1 Intel Parallel Studio

Intel Parallel Studio is a development suite consisting of compiler, analysis tools, and profilers. Intel Parallel Advisor is a tool to detect deadlocks and data races. The tool maps potential errors to the memory reference and to the source-code line. Results are grouped into different severity levels such as comments, warnings, and errors. Intel Parallel Amplifier is a tool to measure and visualize the parallel execution of threads. It is compatible with OpenMP and TBB.

Intel Parallel Studio is available on Linux and Windows. More information, documentation, demo versions, and pricing can be found at:

```
http://www.intel.com
```

B.9 Miscellaneous Tools

B.9.1 GNU Binutils

The GNU binutils are a collection of binary tools available on UNIX, Linux, and Cygwin. Useful commands for debugging are: `nm` to list symbols from object files, `objdump` to display object file information, `strings` to list the printable strings in a binary file, and `strip` to remove symbols from an object file. More information can be found here:

```
http://www.gnu.org/software/binutils
```

B.9.2 m4

The GNU M4 macro processor is Open Source software. For documentation and downloading sources see:

```
http://www.gnu.org/software/m4
```

B.9.3 `ps`

`ps` is a UNIX, Linux, and Cygwin utility that shows the current status of processes running on a host. It can be instructed by command line arguments to provide different types of information. Note that command line args vary on different operating systems; use `man ps` to get more information.

B.9.4 `strace`/`truss`

The Linux utility `strace` (`truss` on Solaris) logs all accesses to the operating system, such as memory allocation, file I/O, system calls, and launching sub-processes. Use `man strace` on Linux or `man truss` on Solaris to get more information.

B.9.5 `top`

`top` is a UNIX, Linux, and Cygwin utility that shows in a simple graphical form which processes are running on a host and gives details on memory usage, CPU time consumed so far, priority, etc. It also gives a summary of the status of the host, e.g. total memory usage and overall CPU time usage in terms of user/kernel/idle time. The utility is very useful to get a first glance on what is happening on the host. Use `man top` to get more information.

B.9.6 VNC

VNC is software to view and remote-control a computer's desktop across a network. More information, documentation, and software to download can be found here:

```
http://www.realvnc.com
http://www.tightvnc.com
```

B.9.7 WebEx

WebEx makes software for remote meetings, allowing users to view and share applications on a remote desktop. For more information, see:

```
http://www.webex.com
http://en.wikipedia.org/wiki/Webex
```

Appendix C
Source Code

C.1 testmalloc.c

This example is used in Chapter 5 to check if `free()`/`delete` return deallocated memory to the operating system.

```
1   /* testmalloc.c Copyright 2007 Groetker, Holtmann, Keding, Wloka */
2   #include <stdio.h>
3   #include <stdlib.h>
4   #ifdef _MSC_VER
5   #define sleep(x) _sleep(1000*(x))
6   #endif
7
8   #define blocksize 1024
9
10  /* make the program wait, to inspect process for memory use */
11  void wait_for_input(const char *prefix, int is_interactive) {
12      char c;
13      if(is_interactive) {
14          printf("%s hit return to continue\n", prefix); fflush(stdout);
15          c = getchar();
16      }
17      else
18      {   sleep(1); }
19  }
20
21  /* program entry point */
22  int main(int argc, char **argv) {
23      const char *usage = "usage: testmalloc i[interactive]|n n iter\n";
24      int n, i, j, iterations, is_interactive = 0;
25      int **myarray;
26
27      if(argc != 4) {
28          fprintf(stderr, usage);
29          return 1;
30      }
31
32      if(argv[1][0] == 'i')
33          is_interactive = 1;
34
35      n = atoi(argv[2]);
36      iterations = atoi(argv[3]);
37      if(n <= 0 || iterations < 0) {
38          fprintf(stderr, usage);
39      return 2;
```

```
40        }
41
42        for(i=0; i<iterations; i++) {
43      wait_for_input("before malloc: ", is_interactive);
44  #ifdef USE_NEW
45              myarray = new int*[n];
46  #else
47              myarray = (int **) malloc(n * (sizeof(int *)));
48  #endif
49            for(j=0; j<n; j++) {
50  #ifdef USE_NEW
51                  myarray[j] = new int[blocksize];
52  #else
53                  myarray[j] = (int *) malloc(blocksize * sizeof(int));
54  #endif
55            }
56            wait_for_input("after malloc:  ", is_interactive);
57            for(j=0; j<n; j++) {
58  #ifdef USE_NEW
59                  delete [] myarray[j];
60  #else
61                  free(myarray[j]);
62  #endif
63            }
64
65  #ifdef USE_NEW
66            delete [] myarray;
67  #else
68            free(myarray);
69  #endif
70        }
71        return 0;
72  }
```

C.2 genindex.c

This example is used in Chapter 5 to demonstrate on how to measure memory consumption over data structures

```
1   /* genindex.cc Copyright 2007 Groetker, Holtmann, Keding, Wloka */
2   #include <stdio.h>
3   #include <string>
4   #include <list>
5   #include <vector>
6   #include <map>
7   using namespace std;
8
9   /* make the program wait, to inspect process for memory use */
10  void wait_for_input(const char *prefix) {
11      char c;
12      fprintf(stderr, "%s hit return to continue\n", prefix);
13      fflush(stderr);
14      c = getchar();
15  }
16  // word index data structure: word as key, list of integers
17  // each integer stores the line number where the word occurs
18  typedef map<string,list<int>,less<string> > WordIndexType;
19
20  // wrapper class, stores one index per text file
21  class FileIndexType
22  {
23  public:
```

```
24        FileIndexType();
25        ~FileIndexType();
26        int scan_file(char *fname);
27        int add_to_index(string &key, int l);
28        void print_index();
29        int verify_index();
30        void clear();
31        void clear_lines();
32        int print_memory_stats();
33  protected:
34        string filename;
35        int filesize;
36        WordIndexType wordindex;
37        vector<string> lines;
38  };
39
40  // constructor
41  FileIndexType::FileIndexType()
42  {}
43
44  // destructor
45  FileIndexType::~FileIndexType() {
46        clear();
47  }
48
49  // clear the index
50  void FileIndexType::clear() {
51        filename.clear();
52        filesize = 0;
53        wordindex.clear();
54        clear_lines();
55  }
56
57  // clear the lines buffer
58  void FileIndexType::clear_lines() {
59        lines.clear();
60  }
61
62  // generate a report of memory usage
63  int FileIndexType::print_memory_stats() {
64        unsigned i;
65        int mem_filename = sizeof(string) + filename.size();
66        int mem_wordindex = 0;
67        int mem_lines = 0;
68        int mem_total = 0;
69
70  // compute size of wordindex data structure
71  // Note: very rough approximation, measures the payload, not
72  // the internal search structure of map.
73        WordIndexType::const_iterator it;
74        list<int>::const_iterator wt;
75        for(it = wordindex.begin(); it != wordindex.end(); it++) {
76            mem_wordindex += it->first.size();      // add size of word key
77            for(wt = it->second.begin(); wt != it->second.end(); wt++)
78  // double-linked list element size is at least 2 pointers plus content
79                mem_wordindex += sizeof(int) + 2 * sizeof(void*);
80        }
81
82  // compute size of lines data structure payload
83        for (i=0; i < lines.size(); i++)
84            mem_lines += lines[i].size();
85
86        mem_total = mem_filename + mem_wordindex + mem_lines;
87
88        fprintf(stderr, "-- memory size for index of '%s' file size=%d\n",
89                filename.c_str(), filesize);
90        fprintf(stderr, "--   filename=%d wordindex=%d lines=%d total=%d\n",
```

```
91                   mem_filename, mem_wordindex, mem_lines, mem_total);
92      fflush(stderr);
93      return mem_total;
94  }
95
96  // add a (word, line) pair to the index
97  int FileIndexType::add_to_index(string &key, int l) {
98      if(key.size() == 0)
99          return 0;
100     wordindex[key].push_back(l);
101     return 0;
102  }
103
104  // open file, break text into words, add words to index, close file
105  int FileIndexType::scan_file(char *fname) {
106     filename = fname;
107     filesize = 0;
108     FILE *fp = 0;
109     int c = 0;
110     string newword = "";
111     int current_line = 1;   /* start counting lines at value 1 */
112     string buffer;
113
114     if(NULL == (fp = fopen(filename.c_str(), "r"))) {
115         fprintf(stderr, "-- error: cannot read file '%s'\n",
116                 filename.c_str());
117         return 1;
118     }
119     while(1) {   // very simple tokenizer to break text into words
120         c = getc(fp);
121
122         if(c == EOF || c == '\n') {
123             add_to_index(newword, current_line);
124             newword = "";
125             current_line++;
126             lines.push_back(buffer);
127  #ifdef FIX_LINES
128             buffer = "";
129  #endif
130             if(c == EOF)
131                 break;
132         }
133         else if(c == ' ' || c == '\t' || c == '\r') {
134             add_to_index(newword, current_line);
135             newword = "";
136             if(c != '\r')
137                 buffer = buffer + (char) c;
138         }
139         else {
140             newword = newword + (char) c;
141             buffer = buffer + (char) c;
142         }
143         filesize++;
144     }
145     fclose(fp);
146     return 0;
147  }
148
149  // output of the program: a word index
150  void FileIndexType::print_index() {
151     WordIndexType::const_iterator it;
152     list<int>::const_iterator wt;
153     printf("index of file '%s'\n", filename.c_str());
154     for(it = wordindex.begin(); it != wordindex.end(); it++) {
155         printf("'%s'", it->first.c_str());
156         for(wt = it->second.begin(); wt != it->second.end(); wt++)
157             printf(" %d", (*wt));
```

```
158              printf("\n");
159          }
160        fflush(stdout);
161  }
162
163  // verification code: cross-check generated index
164  int FileIndexType::verify_index() {
165        int result = 0;
166        WordIndexType::const_iterator it;
167        list<int>::const_iterator wt;
168        string w;
169        int i;
170        for(it = wordindex.begin(); it != wordindex.end(); it++)
171        {
172            w = it->first;
173            for(wt = it->second.begin(); wt != it->second.end(); wt++) {
174                i = (*wt);
175                if(string::npos == lines[i-1].find(w))
176                    return 1;
177            }
178        }
179        return result;
180  }
181
182  /* program entry point */
183  int main(int argc, char **argv) {
184        const char *usage = "-- usage: genindex filename [filename...]\n";
185        if(argc < 2) {
186            fprintf(stderr, usage);
187                return 1;
188        }
189        vector<FileIndexType> fileindex(argc-1);
190        int result = 0;
191        int total = 0;
192        int i;
193
194  // for each file, compute an index
195        for(i = 0; i<argc-1; i++) {
196            result = fileindex[i].scan_file(argv[i+1]);
197            if(result)
198                return result;  // something went wrong with file read
199            result = fileindex[i].verify_index();
200            if(result) {
201                fprintf(stderr, "-- error: index verification failed.\n");
202                return result;
203            }
204  #ifdef CLEAR_INDEX
205            fileindex[i].print_index();
206            fileindex[i].clear();
207            total += fileindex[i].print_memory_stats();
208  #endif
209  #ifdef PAUSE_INDEX
210            wait_for_input("-- done generating index: ");
211  #endif
212        }
213
214  #ifndef CLEAR_INDEX
215  // for each file, output index
216        for(i=0; i<argc-1; i++) {
217            fileindex[i].print_index();
218            total += fileindex[i].print_memory_stats();
219        }
220  #endif
221        fprintf(stderr, "-- memory size, all data structures: %d bytes\n",
222                total);
223        return result;
224  }
```

213

C.3 isort.c

This example is used in Chapter 6 for general profiling.

```
1    /* isort.c Copyright 2007 Groetker, Holtmann, Keding, Wloka */
2    #include <stdio.h>
3    #include <stdlib.h>
4
5    typedef double Stype;
6
7    /* Print an array of the given size on stdout. */
8    void print_array(const char* prefix, const Stype *array, int size) {
9        int i;
10       printf("%s:", prefix);
11       for(i=0; i<size; i++)
12           printf(" %f", array[i]);
13       printf("\n"); fflush(stdout);
14   }
15
16   /* swap 2 elements */
17   void swap(Stype *a, int i, int j) {
18       Stype tmp;
19       tmp = a[i];
20       a[i] = a[j];
21       a[j] = tmp;
22   }
23
24   /* check if 'a' is less than 'b' */
25   int less(Stype a, Stype b) {
26       return (a < b) ? 1 : 0;
27   }
28
29   /* insert a[0] into pre-sorted array a[1]...a[n-1] */
30   void insert_value(Stype *a, int n) {
31       int i;
32       for(i=1; i<n; i++)
33           if(less(a[i], a[i-1]))
34               swap(a, i, i-1);
35   #ifdef ISORT_FAST  /* compile with -DISORT_FAST to speed up */
36           else return;
37   #endif
38   }
39
40   /* toplevel routine for isort */
41   void isort(Stype *a, int n) {
42       if(n <= 1)
43           return;
44       isort(a+1, n-1);
45       insert_value(a,n);
46   }
47
48   /* partition array a, so that all values smaller than pivot a[n-1]
49    are placed in a[0]..a[result-1], the pivot is in a[result],
50    and the values larger than the pivot are in a[result+1]..a[n-1]
51   */
52   int partition(Stype *a, int n) {
53       int i, result = 0;
54       for(i = 0; i<n-1; i++)
55           if(less(a[i], a[n-1])) {
56               swap(a, result, i);
57               result++;
58           }
59       swap(a, result, n-1);
60   #ifdef DEBUG
61       print_array("partition:", a, n);
62       printf("pivot at: %d\n", result);
```

```
63  #endif
64      return result;
65  }
66
67  /* toplevel routine for quicksort */
68  void quicksort(Stype *a, int n) {
69      int i;
70      if(n <= 1)
71          return;
72      i = partition(a, n);
73      quicksort(a, i);
74      quicksort(a+i+1, n-(i+1));
75  }
76
77  /* program entry point */
78  int main(int argc, char **argv) {
79      const char *usage = "usage: isort i|q n iter, n>0, iter>0\n";
80      int n, i, j, iterations, use_isort = 1;
81      Stype *input, *result;
82
83      if(argc != 4) {
84          fprintf(stderr, usage);
85          return 1;
86      }
87
88      if(argv[1][0] == 'q')
89          use_isort = 0;
90
91      n = atoi(argv[2]);
92      iterations = atoi(argv[3]);
93      if(n <= 0 || iterations <= 0) {
94          fprintf(stderr, usage);
95          return 2;
96      }
97
98      input = (Stype *) malloc(n * sizeof(Stype));
99      result = (Stype *) malloc(n * sizeof(Stype));
100     if(input == 0 || result == 0) {
101         fprintf(stderr, "out of memory\n");
102      return 3;
103     }
104
105     srand48(1); /* always generate the same random sequence */
106     for(i=0; i<n; i++)
107         input[i] = drand48();
108
109     for(j=0; j<iterations; j++) {
110         for(i=0; i<n; i++)
111             result[i] = input[i];
112         if(use_isort)
113             isort(result, n);
114         else
115             quicksort(result, n);
116     }
117 #ifdef DEBUG
118     print_array("input", input, n);
119     print_array("result", result, n);
120 #endif
121     free(input);
122     free(result);
123     return 0;
124 }
```

C.4 filebug.c

This example is used in Chapter 6 for profiling I/O problems.

```
1   /* filebug.c Copyright 2007 Groetker, Holtmann, Keding, Wloka */
2   #include <stdio.h>
3   #include <stdlib.h>
4
5   /* program entry point */
6   int main(int argc, char **argv) {
7       int i, n, use_flush = 1;
8       const char *usage = "usage: filebug f[ast]|s[low] file n\n";
9       char *filename;
10      FILE *fp;
11      char c;
12
13      if(argc != 4) {
14          fprintf(stderr, usage);
15          return 1;
16      }
17
18      if(argv[1][0] == 'f')
19          use_flush = 0;
20
21      filename = argv[2];
22
23      n = atoi(argv[3]);
24      if(n < 0) {
25          fprintf(stderr, usage);
26          return 2;
27      }
28
29      if(!(fp = fopen(filename, "w"))) {
30          fprintf(stderr, "can not open file '%s' for write\n", filename);
31          return 3;
32      }
33
34   /* write n characters to file, to observe effect of fflush() */
35      for(i=0; i<n; i++) {
36          c = 'a' + (i % 26);
37          fputc(c, fp);
38          if(use_flush)
39              fflush(fp);
40      }
41      fclose(fp);
42      return 0;
43  }
```

References

[Agans02] D.J. Agans, *Debugging: The Nine Indispensable Rules for Finding Even the Most Elusive Software and Hardware Problems.* American Management Association, 2002

[Ball98] S. Ball, *Debugging Embedded Microprocessor Systems.* Newnes, 1998

[Barr06] M. Barr, A. Massa, *Programming Embedded Systems.* O'Reilly, 2nd Edition, 2006

[Brown88] M.H. Brown, *Algorithm Animation.* The MIT Press, 1988

[Butenhof97] D.R. Butenhof, *Programming with POSIX Threads.* Addison-Wesley, 1997

[Chandra00] R. Chandra, R. Menon, L. Dagum, D. Kohr, D. Maydan, J. McDonald, *Parallel Programming in OpenMP.* Morgan Kaufmann, 2000

[Chapman07] B. Chapman, G. Jost, R. van der Pas, *Using OpenMP: Portable Shared Memory Parallel Programming.* The MIT Press, 2007

[Cormen01] T.H. Cormen, C.E. Leiserson, R.L. Rivest, C. Stein, *Introduction to Algorithms.* The MIT Press, 2nd Edition, 2001

[Eigenmann01] R. Eigenmann, M. Voss (Editors), *OpenMP Shared Memory Parallel Programming.* International Workshop on OpenMP Applications and Tools, WOMPAT 2001. (Lecture Notes in Computer Science). Springer, 2001

[Ford02] A.R. Ford, T.J. Teorey, *Practical Debugging in C++.* Prentice Hall, 2002

[Fritzson93] P.A. Fritzson (Editor), *Automated and Algorithmic Debugging.* First International Workshop, Aadebug '93 Linkoping, Sweden, May 3–5, 1993: Proceedings (Lecture Notes in Computer Science). Springer, 1993

[Kaspersky05] K. Kaspersky, *Hacker Debugging Uncovered.* A-List Publishing, 2005

[Lencevicius00] R. Lencevicius, *Advanced Debugging Methods.* Springer, 2000

[Levine00] J. Levine, *Linkers & Loaders.* Morgan Kaufmann, 2000

[Luecke06] G.R. Luecke, J. Coyle, J. Hoekstra, M. Kraeva, Y. Li, O. Taborskaia, Y. Wang, *A Survey of Systems for Detecting Serial Run-Time Errors.* Concurr. Comput. : Pract. Exper. 18(15): 1885–1907, Dec. 2006

[Metzger03] R.C. Metzger, *Debugging by Thinking: A Multidisciplinary Approach.* Digital Press, 2003

[Meyers04] G.J. Meyers, C. Sandler, T. Badgett, T.M. Thomas, *The Art of Software Testing.* John Wiley & Sons, 2004

[Pappas00] C.H. Pappas, W.H. Murray, *Debugging C++.* Osborne Publishing, 2000

[Reinders07] J. Reinders, *Intel Threading Building Blocks: Outfitting C++ for Multi-core Processor Parallelism.* O'Reilly Media, 2007

[Rosenberg96] J.B. Rosenberg, *How Debuggers Work: Algorithms, Data Structures, and Architecture.* Wiley, 1996

[Sedgewick01] R. Sedgewick, *Bundle of Algorithms in C++, Parts 1–5: Fundamentals, Data Structures, Sorting, Searching, and Graph Algorithms.* Addison-Wesley Professional, 3rd Edition, 2001

[Silberschatz04] A. Silberschatz, G. Gagne, P.B. Galvin, *Operating System Concepts.* John Wiley & Sons Inc, 2004

[Stitt92] M. Stitt, *Debugging: Creative Techniques and Tools for Software Repair.* John Wiley & Sons Inc, 1992

[Stallmann02] R.M. Stallmann, R.H. Pesch, S. Shebs, *Debugging With GDB: The Gnu Source-Level Debugger.* Free Software Foundation, 2002

[Tanenbaum01] Andrew S. Tanenbaum, *Modern Operating Systems.* Prentice Hall PTR, 2001

[Telles01] M.A. Telles, Y. Hsieh, *The Science of Debugging.* Coriolis Group Books, 2001

[Zeller09] A. Zeller, *Why Programs Fail: A Guide to Systematic Debugging.* Morgan Kaufmann, Second Edition, 2009

Index